UNCLE SAM'S STEPCHILDREN

Uncle Sam's Stepchildren

THE REFORMATION OF UNITED STATES
INDIAN POLICY, 1865-1887

LORING BENSON PRIEST

A BISON BOOK

UNIVERSITY OF NEBRASKA PRESS · LINCOLN

PREFACE

AMERICAN INDIANS ALTHOUGH NEVER TOTALING OVER A MILLION, have always aroused an interest out of proportion to their numbers. Volume after volume discusses the habits and history of each of the numerous tribes. Lengthy accounts of the struggle for supremacy between the red man and white fill library shelves and are devoured by eager readers. Yet in the millions of words written about the race, very little has been said regarding the efforts of the United States government to establish a policy for dealing with peaceful Indians. Only strange tribal customs, bloodshed, robbery and hate have been considered sufficiently exciting to merit attention. There is great need, therefore, to relate an equally important part of the story, which while treating of more peaceful activities contains the same elements of novelty and intrigue that make previous accounts so stimulating.

Abundant primary materials are available to the student who wishes to understand the origin of contemporary Indian policies. Indian Office records for the period are excellently preserved and indexed. The Carl Schurz Papers in the Library of Congress reveal much concerning government policy from 1877 to 1881 when Schurz was Secretary of the Interior. The recently-acquired Dawes Papers include invaluable material on the formulation of the Dawes Severalty Act (1881-1887). Correspondence of the Board of Indian Commissioners, miraculously uncovered in a remote corner of the Indian Office Library, supplies detailed information concerning Board activities especially in its most important early years (1869-1874). Clipping collections in the New York Public Library and a two-volume scrap book kept by the Board offer unusual facilities for studying newspaper opinion. The activities of leading Indian organizations may be followed closely in the annual reports and pamphlets of each group. Innumerable books, pamphlets and arti-

Preface

cles, in which contemporaries examined the "Indian question," may be found; while the case of the opponents of reform is exhaustively presented in the *Council Fire* (1878-1887). When added to the mass of material in congressional debates, Senate and House records, court decisions, presidential messages, official statutes and treaties, and the annual reports of Indian officials, such documents provide opportunities for research seldom encountered by those seeking knowledge of the past.

Based upon a thorough examination of these sources, the following volume is published in hope of supplying the need for a comprehensive study of the agitation which led to drastic changes in American Indian policy between the close of the Civil War and passage of the Dawes Severalty Act of February, 1887. This Act still served as a guide to United States Indian officials when the author began examination of its origins as a research project at Harvard University in 1931. Yet before the task of gathering material had been completed in 1934, the New Deal administration of Franklin D. Roosevelt had wiped the measure from the statute books after bitter attacks which made analysis of the reasons for its adoption even more desirable. The following account in many respects repeats the debates of today. Because of current disagreements, particular effort has been made to fulfill the historian's obligation to discuss controversial issues impartially. Extensive footnotes have been included for those who wish to obtain more detailed information than is possible in the confines of a single volume. On the ground that more specific knowledge may be gained by employing footnotes on particular subjects than by referring to a long list of books and articles, any separate bibliography has been considered unnecessary. While it is hoped that this volume will be of use to the specialists in Indian affairs, however, its primary purpose is to offer an account of Uncle Sam's stepchildren which will provide new and interesting information for the many Americans less professionally concerned with the red man and his problems.

Sincere thanks are due to many individuals who helped make this a better book than it otherwise would have been. Valuable assistance in the search for material was provided by staff members of America's three great storehouses of learning—the Harvard Library, the Library of Congress, and the New York Public Library—and by Mr. Brent Morgan of the Indian Office Library. The Dawes Papers were opened to the author through the kindness of the Senator's daughter, Miss Anna L. Dawes. But the largest share of credit for the merits this study of Uncle Sam's stepchildren may possess belongs to Professor Frederick Merk of Harvard University, under whose direction it was begun and without whose advice and encouragement it never would have been completed.

LORING B. PRIEST

New Brunswick,
New Jersey

ERRATA

Pp. 25, 63, and 303: *For* Theodore A. Bland *read* Thomas A. Bland
P. 139, 1. 3: *For* a thousand *read* a hundred

CONTENTS

Preface   v

I

FOUR UNSUCCESSFUL EFFORTS AT REFORM

1. Concentration   3
2. The Transfer Problem   15
3. Church Nomination of Indian Officials   28
4. The Board of Indian Commissioners   42

II

THE RISE OF INTEREST IN INDIAN REFORM

5. The Period of Individual Effort, 1865-1880   57
6. The Turn of the Tide 1880   66
7. Indian Organizations and Sectional Opinion   81

III

DESTRUCTION OF THE OLD INDIAN SYSTEM

8. The Treaty System and Tribal Autonomy   95
9. The Annuity System and Congressional Economy   106
10. The Reservation System   121
11. The Problem of Indian Education   132
12. The Last Stand of Supporters of the Old Indian System   155

Contents

IV

FORMULATION OF THE NEW INDIAN POLICY

13. Precedents for Reform 167

14. The Failure of Early Severalty Plans 177

15. Severalty Debates of the Eighties 188

16. Indian Citizenship 198

17. The Development of Indian Land Policies 217

18. The Decision to Use Force 233

19. The Dawes Act and Indian Reform 248

Notes 253

Index 303

I. *Four Unsuccessful Efforts at Reform*

1. CONCENTRATION

Few people in the history of the world have suffered so long or so severely as the American Indian. The unhappy red man, who now depends upon the sympathy of others for his existence, is the descendant of men who once ruled a continent. Possessors of an apparently inexhaustible supply of the earth's riches, the Indian's fifteenth century ancestors roamed the Western hemisphere with no premonition of impending disaster. But in Europe, awakening from the lethargy of Middle Age indolence, men of another race laid plans to comb the seven seas in quest of the riches of distant lands. Once white explorers discovered the continent which blocked their passage to the Far East, the days of Indian freedom were numbered.

The problems of United States Indian administrators did not originate with the establishment of American independence; inevitable counterparts of inter-racial contact, most of the difficulties had been faced by a long succession of Spanish, French and English colonists. Experience could not have molded people with more variable tastes and traditions than the Indian and the settler. The white man's concept of individual ownership was as alien to the red man as the Indian's communal practices were to Europeans. As few members of either race were willing to surrender customs which had become habitual, a heritage of hatred and strife was bequeathed to later generations. Only when Indian resistance was exhausted after several centuries were efforts made to effect a peaceful settlement of inter-racial difficulties.

European settlers met the Indian problem in diverse ways. Spanish padres and conquistadores, passionately desiring Indian friendship as a means of conversion and conquest, often adopted the customs of red men instead of insisting upon their own. Inter-marriage, regarded with horror by most other Europeans, became so common in Spanish colonies that distinctions between settlers and natives soon were indistinguishable. Such a method of harmonizing inter-racial relationships was intolerable to both

3

the French and English. The French and Indians were drawn together, however, by hatred of English settlers and a mutual interest in exploration and trade. With the more numerous colonists from the British Isles, who established permanent residences and frankly proclaimed their intention to tame the Indian, red men found very little in common. Victory for France or Spain in the contest for the northernmost parts of the American continent might have prevented the misfortunes of later years; victory for the English made inevitable a relentless clash between Indian and white ideals.

Refusing to change their habits at the command of English colonists, the great majority of Indians from Maine to Georgia had to expel their British neighbors or move to other hunting grounds. Some tribes endeavored to force settlers to abandon their homes. But since such efforts invariably ended with annihilation of the guilty Indians, few red men attempted to emulate the Pequots or King Philip in their hopeless contests against the settler and his rifle. Instead, a steady stream of Indians migrated to the west and joined fellow red men on land not yet coveted by white invaders. Tension between the races was never completely relieved; and as colonists began to move inland, the Indian problem again became serious. Dissatisfaction over the failure of imperial officials to solve Indian troubles was a major factor in criticism of the mother country. Reservation of western land for Indian occupancy, restrictions on intercourse with the tribes, and drastic levies for frontier defense caused many colonists to feel that separation from England would offer many advantages. With the success of the Revolution, the settlers themselves were in complete control of American Indian policy for the first time.

The achievement of American independence produced no improvement in the relations between Indians and whites. Red men were carefully excluded from the privileges of citizenship; and the wave of expansion which swept the young nation again brought them into conflict with frontier settlers. The resulting struggle revealed for a second time the inability of Indians to resist the superior number and equipment of their rivals. Recently acquired territory west of the Mississippi provided a new home for dis-

4

possessed red men, but as the country continued to grow and as available land became more barren, satisfactory locations were increasingly difficult to find. Indians, who had been able to supply their own needs for centuries, required more and more assistance from the government. Whites had long been able to avoid responsibility for Indian welfare. At last, however, a fundamental readjustment of established policies was imperative. Mistreated for years by their hostile half-brothers, Uncle Sam's stepchildren had sunk so low by 1865 that even their stubborn foster father heeded their plea for justice. Belatedly, and only at the last possible moment, Americans seriously endeavored to find what might be done to compensate for three centuries of abuse.

The Indian Problem of 1865

Determination of the proper method of handling the Indians perplexed United States officials from the time the government was organized. The constitution recognized the importance of the problem and President Washington was particularly zealous in his efforts to deal justly with all tribes. But despite the frequent embarrassment caused by Indian problems in the early years of the country, United States administrators always had a solution at hand. With extensive undeveloped areas in the West, particularly after the Louisiana Purchase of 1803, each difficulty was met by moving the offending tribe to the west. Red men often strongly resisted a change of location, as Andrew Jackson learned well in the case of the Georgia Cherokees, but it was only when the wisdom of settling Western lands with Indians began to be questioned following the gold rush of 1849 that the Indian problem really became serious. Even then the country was too preoccupied with the slavery issue to worry much about the Indians. It was not until the Civil War had ended and over seven million acres of Western land were being sold annually that the nation recognized that a permanent solution of Indian problems could not be much longer postponed. Once government reserves were rapidly being depleted, Indians either must be permitted to remain where they were or must be moved again at once before the last places available for settlement were exhausted.[1]

Faced with the necessity of determining whether to carry out further removals or establish Indians permanently in their existing homes, government officials did not hesitate in reaching a decision. Too many tribes occupied land needed by Western railroads or coveted by settlers to make acceptance of the *status quo* expedient. Such Indians must be located upon land less essential to the country's expansion. With railroad lines proceeding rapidly in the northern, southern and central portions of the West, congressional investigation showed that but two areas remained as possible centers for Indian settlement—the public lands to the north of Nebraska and to the south of Kansas. Here, the administration of President Grant decided, all Indians must be gathered. The policy guiding the government's effort to confine Indian settlement within these areas was known as concentration and arose from a sincere but futile desire to solve Indian problems forever.

For several years after the Civil War, the policy of concentration was extremely popular. Settlers who wished the removal of neighboring Indians enthusiastically welcomed the scheme, and there were few at the moment to object to the post-war treaties which provided for locating tribes either in the Indian Territory to the south of Kansas or in the newly-established Sioux reservation to the north.[2] Senate ratification of these agreements during the late sixties provided legislative support for the policy, which was applied successfully in removals of the Osage, Kaw, Otoe and Pawnee tribes from Kansas and Nebraska to the Indian Territory. But while many people agreed when Secretary of the Interior Delano declared that the fate of the Indian depended upon successful completion of the concentration program,[3] several groups of opponents resisted from the first and became stronger with each succeeding year.

Early Opposition to Concentration

The first important factor responsible for the growing unpopularity of concentration was the local rivalry of Western communities. Indians could not be moved from the vicinity of one group of whites without being settled near another; and the latter was likely to object to removal just as loudly as the neighbors of a tribe demanded it. Thus the first significant opposition to concentration appeared during debates upon a resolution offered by Senator Thayer of Nebraska, which provided that all removals must be sanctioned by Congress. This proposal, actuated by a desire to be consulted if any Indians were to be moved in the direction of Nebraska, was strenuously opposed by all congressmen who wished to speed concentration. Senator Pomeroy of Kansas and Delegate Burleigh of Dakota Territory, representing constituents surrounded by Indians, declared that the resolution was a plot to prevent all removals of Indians from their existing locations.[4] Just such local controversies were ultimately to defeat concentration, for although Pomeroy and Burleigh supported consolidation and were able to table the Thayer resolution by a 42-41 vote in the House, there was doubt whether changing local interests would not lead them to oppose concentration at some later date. In fact, less than a decade later the positions of Kansas and Nebraska were reversed in debates over the removal of the Sioux Indians of northern Nebraska to the Indian Territory. Kansas, with the area of Indian reservations within her borders reduced from 4,064,460 to 223,991 acres, was able to resist further removals in 1877. Nebraska, satisfied with the *status quo* in 1867, was anxious by the time of the Sioux wars to have her neighboring Indians removed as far as possible.[5] Forced to encounter such shifting local desires, administrators found concentration policies easier to formulate than to carry to conclusion.

In resisting further removals, prospective Indian neighbors had strong support from a second group: railroad men already in possession of open routes opposed any readjustment of tribal settlement. Senators from Michigan, Wisconsin, and Minnesota, for example, strongly opposed the establishment of a great reservation north of Nebraska as a threat to the construction of western railroads from their states.[6] A proposed removal, hailed by the supporters of one route, was almost certain to be condemned as a sectional plot by the friends of another, as no section of the

7

West seemed to lack plans for its development by some group of capitalists.

Opposition to concentration was not confined to selfish interests. Many sincere friends of the Indians believed that the racial segregation resulting from concentration would be unwise. Bishop Whipple of the Episcopal church of Minnesota, noted for his championship of the Indians, resolutely opposed concentration on the ground that the policy would offer facilities for extensive Indian combinations and place peaceful tribes where they must be overawed by the violent.[7] Indians needed to be prepared for contact with whites rather than encouraged to persist in outmoded customs by segregation. Although Senator Henderson of Missouri advocated concentration because tribes "ought to be mixed up with the whites as far as possible," [8] most legislators realized that the policy would discourage inter-racial relationships. A realistic concern for Indian interest seemed to demand that red men be fitted for future responsibilities rather than removed from them. Thus many friends of the Indians did not hesitate to join less altruistic interests in opposing concentration. This union was necessary to defeat the policy, for it was only after several years of persistent criticism that the government was forced to abandon all plans for further removals.

The Rise of Congressional Opposition to Concentration

The gradual increase of opposition to concentration is best revealed by the shifting attitude evident in congressional legislation. Early resistance to consolidating the tribes was confined almost entirely to a small group of Eastern senators.[9] So many Indians lived in Western states in the early seventies that every legislator from the frontier hesitated to oppose removal. But a measure for moving Eastern Indians across the Mississippi was all that was necessary to arouse frontiersmen to the danger of allowing unlimited removals.

The first successful opposition to concentration was the temporary defeat of a proposal to remove wandering Winnebagoes from Wisconsin to the Western plains. A measure authorizing this action passed the Senate by 22-18 in the spring of 1872 over the opposition of Westerners who insisted with some logic that Eastern champions of the Indian should civilize their own tribes rather than push for removal.[10] Abandonment of the same proposal the following year offered evidence of the growing opposition to concentration, for while a request by the Senate Appropriations Committee for additional funds to finance the venture at first passed by a majority of one, it was dropped from the Indian Appropriation Bill two days later by a 27-19 vote.[11] Ultimate inclusion of the item in the Miscellaneous Appropriation Bill, which successfully passed near the end of the session, could not obscure the significance of this opposition to removal. Thereafter enemies of concentration moved from one victory to another.

The next proposal to arouse enemies of removal was the contemplated transfer of the Sioux Indians from their reservation north of Nebraska to the Indian Territory. The plan, although overwhelmingly rejected by the Indians, inevitably attracted the attention of Congress early in 1877. At first, Senate leaders were able to prevent attack by declaring that since the Indians were certain to reject concentration proposals, any measure prohibiting removal would be an unnecessary and dangerous tampering with treaties already concluded.[12] Members of the House from states surrounding the Indian Territory were not so easily satisfied. Angry at the Senate's failure to approve an amendment prohibiting the removal of any Sioux without an act of Congress, Representative Mills of Texas refused to support a bill for ratification of Sioux treaties until such a prohibition was included.[13] His success, despite the determined opposition of Senator Paddock and Representative Crounse of Nebraska, was the first indication that an area opposed to receiving Indians might defeat a section equally anxious to be rid of theirs. The victorious revolt of senators and representatives from states surrounding the Indian Territory resulted from the formation of a powerful group that could be counted upon to oppose all schemes for concentration. Other parts of the West might favor the removal of their Indians, but Missouri, Kansas, Texas, and Arkansas were sure to offer opposition.

9

Uncle Sam's Stepchildren

Two years after the prohibition of Sioux removal, the advocates of consolidation won their final congressional victory. Yet unusual conditions were responsible for the sanction given to the settlement of the Nez Percé Indians of Oregon in the Indian Territory. Before the problem was presented to Congress, the members of the tribe were prisoners of war, whose return to their home was strenuously opposed. The decision to force the Indians to accept land in the Territory was not surprising as a result. Indeed, the combined opposition of New England and Western senators was the significant feature of the debate.[14] With a union in prospect between Eastern friends of the Indian and a group of Westerners, some of whom now frankly admitted a desire to open the Indian Territory to white settlement,[15] all less complicated proposals seemed doomed to defeat. A proposition to send the Apaches of Arizona to the Territory provided a test before another year had passed.

The prohibition of Apache removal in 1878 marked the complete success of the movement against concentration. While much of the previous opposition to consolidation had been a result of the disastrous effect upon Indian health produced by changes of latitude, the Apache question presented the issue without that obstructive factor. Yet the Senate left no doubt of its stand by defeating the proposal by a vote of 32-8.[16] The issue had actually been determined in the House, where slight deviations from a strict party vote were responsible for the prohibition. A united Republican front would have authorized concentration as five Democrats supported removal. But although only the Kansas representatives deserted the cause, their three votes were sufficient to defeat removal to Indian Territory by a 98-94 vote.[17] Strong appeals to party ties had proved insufficient to maintain the loyalty of Western congressmen when an issue involving a readjustment in the number of neighboring Indians was at stake. Thus concentration was defeated in a debate in which leading parts were taken by three Kansas Republicans and a Colorado Democrat, all four of whom energetically opposed the stand of their party because of local interests.[18] Only fear that their victory might be jeopardized caused the victors to oppose pressing their advantage further, Senator Ingalls of Kansas abandoning an attempt to extend the prohibition of Apache removal to all tribes only upon the request of friends of the measure in the House.[19]

After the defeat of Apache removal, concentration was never again seriously considered by Congress. If circumstances had demanded a measure prohibiting all removals to Indian Territory, it undoubtedly would have succeeded. Such a bill was reported favorably during 1880 by the House Indian Committee and only the failure of the House to sanction an investigating committee in 1886 checked adoption of an amendment prohibiting removals to the Territory.[20] But congressional opposition would not have been so successful if a series of disasters in administering the policy had not aroused the wrath of Eastern friends of the Indians.

Last Days of the Concentration Policy

While the early opposition to concentration centered in an idealistic group of Eastern senators, the burden of the struggle was carried by Westerners after 1872. Voters east of the Mississippi were not sufficiently interested in the Indian problem to force their representatives to militancy. As a result, the majority of Eastern legislators did not resist official requests. Such indifference became impossible after 1879, however, for publicity given the failure of three removal efforts roused an Eastern opposition as strong as that in the states surrounding Indian Territory.

The incidents responsible for arousing Eastern resistance to the policy of concentration were the disastrous events accompanying the removal of the Poncas, Nez Percé, and the Northern Cheyenne to Indian Territory. Many Poncas, forced to leave their Nebraska reservation despite years of friendship with the whites, succumbed during their journey to the Territory. Inadequate preparations and unhealthy surroundings reduced the tribe still further the following year. Yet these hardships would have passed unnoticed outside of official reports, if the effort of a few members of the tribe to go back to their former homes had not forced the government to insist upon their return to the Territory. The incident not only aroused support for the Indians who had escaped but by attracting attention to the wrongs of the whole tribe became a powerful force for general reform. The Nez Percé and Northern Cheyenne difficulties which occurred during the same period, only intensified public indignation. The former tribe suffered greatly after being sent to Indian Territory as punishment for resisting settlement on a northern reservation. The sensational flight of the Indians from pursuing troops, the civilized bearing and noble appeals of their chief, Joseph, and the government's repudiation of General Miles's promise that they might return home if they surrendered won sympathy which served the cause of all Indians. The Cheyenne were less peaceful Indians, but the slaughter of men, women and children which followed their escape from an insufficiently guarded fort, where they had been placed as punishment for attempting to return to their northern homelands, led to charges that they had been purposely encouraged to flee to their death. Any one of the incidents would have aroused the East. The three, occurring almost simultaneously, ended all possibility that the East would support any system involving Indian removal.[21]

The reaction of Easterners to the unfortunate Indian removals of 1878 and 1879 was immediate and powerful. The Board of Indian Commissioners, a group of Eastern philanthropists who advised the Interior Department regarding its administration of Indian affairs following 1869, had insisted from the first that tribal consent must be obtained for removals even though such a requirement would seriously jeopardize the policy. When Representative Scales of North Carolina proposed negotiations for removing a large number of Indian tribes at the very time of the disastrous removals, Board members led the battle against his proposal.[22] They were joined by numerous groups of Indian friends who had been moved to action by stories of Indian suffering. Church groups in particular gave the Board energetic support and powerful Indian organizations were founded which made resistance to concentration a major item in their programs.[23] As a result, congressional opposition to concentration was decisively aided and the policy was ultimately relinquished as a possible solution of the Indian problem.

In spite of the growing unpopularity of removals, government

12

administrators abandoned the policy of concentration slowly. Both Miss Annie Abel and Miss Elsie Rushmore, who have written able accounts of Indian relations during these years, err in stating that interest in concentration ceased abruptly when Grant left the presidency in 1877.[24] Instead, a belief that economical use of land was essential to Indian advancement led officials to urge a consolidation of holdings for many years thereafter. Carl Schurz, erstwhile German liberal who had fled to the United States and won a national reputation as Civil War soldier and political reformer, supported concentration enthusiastically when he first came into contact with the Indian problem following his appointment as Secretary of the Interior upon Grant's retirement. He finally opposed the policy in his 1880 report, it is true, but his successor reverted to the older position and declared that Indian affairs could be managed to better advantage if all tribes west of the Mississippi were gathered upon four or five reservations.[25] Even though such concentration seemed a remote possibility in 1882, the savings which might be effected by reducing the number of agencies led Congress to appropriate $10,000 "to enable the Secretary of the Interior to defray the cost of removing Indians and property in consolidating agencies." [26] Unless exceptional circumstances warranted, actual removal of Indians was opposed. But this concession was made out of respect for public opinion rather than because of personal conviction, as both Commissioner Atkins and President Cleveland made clear as late as 1885 in expressing regret that consolidation was impossible.[27] The defeat of concentration was due to the combined opposition of Eastern philanthropists and Western settlers rather than to any change of opinion among government officials. Yet popular disapproval of the policy had become so strong by 1887 that the possibility of successful concentration was just as remote as if the government had shared the public's dislike.

The defeat of concentration was of tremendous importance to all Americans interested in Indian advancement. With government officials offering reasonable certainty of the permanence of tribal locations, reform could at last be pressed without fear of disruption by periodical removals. No longer was there danger of progress being resisted by a united mass of red men. But while abandonment of plans for consolidation greatly simplified many Indian problems, further difficulties remained. Several other policies were proposed or tried and found unsatisfactory before one was adopted which gave promise of a successful solution.

2. THE TRANSFER PROBLEM

AT THE SAME TIME UNITED STATES ADMINISTRATORS WERE ENdeavoring to concentrate Indians upon a few selected reservations, the advisability of transferring authority over the Indians from the Department of Interior to the War Department was also being earnestly discussed. Since 1849 problems of Indian administration had been handled by a Bureau of the Interior Department. The Army, never fully reconciled to civilian control, thus found occasion in the confused situation following the Civil War to demand restoration of the power it had originally possessed. As the Interior Department was not willing to surrender its control without a struggle, a debate concerning the relative aptitude of soldiers and civilians for Indian administration was inevitable, and from 1867 to 1879 the question of whether a change in control would be wise dominated every consideration of the Indian problem.

While the transfer of the Indian bureau to the War Department would probably not have caused any fundamental change in general policy, the concern of the American public over the issue was warranted. Since the spirit governing inter-racial relationships as well as methods of enforcement would have been very different under Army domination, one was justified in believing that the future of the American Indian was vitally involved in the outcome of the debate. The Army never succeeded in securing control of the tribes from Congress, but frequently the change was prevented by only a few votes and for over a decade steady pressure by friends of the Indians was required to ward off a change which they regarded as a threat to the welfare of the race.

The contest between the Departments sprang from problems which arose during the Civil War. Lured into hostility by Confederate agents or capitalizing upon the government's embarrassment to press for concessions, many tribes fought actively against the North.[1] The Interior Department had no objection to granting the Army jurisdiction over *warring* tribes in accordance with previous practice.[2] The problem was to decide when and where

15

such control began, what constituted hostility, and who should have the final decision in questionable cases. With numerous tribes wavering between peace and war, disputes resulting from the separate administration of peaceful and warlike Indians inevitably led the Army to demand full authority. The diary of Secretary of Navy Welles reveals that Lincoln's cabinet frequently discussed this request.[3] The President's advisers were too evenly divided upon the issue to recommend action, however, and the transfer question became a major problem of post-war Indian relations.

Leadership in the transfer debate naturally was assumed by the two parties which would be most intimately affected by any readjustment of administrative methods. The Army, in particular, devoted every effort to securing the change. Habitually contemptuous in their attitude toward civilian administrators, military officers saw nothing but inefficiency in the conduct of Indian affairs by the Interior Department. General Sherman, who headed the Army following Grant's election to the presidency, told his brother that three generals could settle current Indian difficulties in an hour.[4] His attitude was typical of the views of his subordinates from fellow generals to privates. But although most military men felt that Indians would profit from Army control, they were more interested in stressing civilian mistakes than in proving Army efficiency. The case of the War Department in these years was that of the transfer advocate who told an English public as late as 1891 that while the soldier on the frontier was "almost the only class of Federal official . . . free from the taint of political corruption" the civil official was "the incarnation of everything . . . scandalous in administration."[5] Army men were obviously convinced that the best chance of securing control of Indian policy lay in constant criticism of their rivals rather than in elaborate efforts to prove their own competency.

In replying to Army criticism, members of the Interior Department also stressed attack instead of defense. Although Army control of Indian affairs before 1849 was severely criticized, later examples of inefficiency were the most popular targets. Thus a brief and unsuccessful military control over a few unruly tribes during the first months of Grant's administration was frequently cited as an example of Army incapacity.[6] Delegate Maginnis of Montana, it is true, claimed that the difficulties which caused Congress to dismiss all officers in the Indian service were due to the lack of full control;[7] but whether or not this was the case, champions of the Interior Department did not allow Congress to forget that the presence of Army officers had failed to improve Indian affairs. Supporters of civilian administration often blamed the Army for all the mistakes of American Indian policy. While some agents accused the military of interference, others condemned officers for refusing to co-operate.[8] No greater self-control was exercised by defenders of the Interior Department than by its enemies. So excited did opponents of the Army become that an inspector accused General Sherman of encouraging insubordination at an agency to aid the campaign for transfer, and a Commissioner of Indian Affairs stated in an official report, "The first lesson to be given the Indian is that of self-support by labor with his own hands—the last lesson which a man in uniform teaches." [9] Only six out of fifty-one agents believed Army administration advisable in 1875, and two of these held that only the necessity for order would justify the immorality which civilian supporters held to be inseparable from Army rule.[10] With such charges flying between the hostile camps, senators and representatives were quick to join the battle over an issue whose final solution was their responsibility.

The Transfer Issue in Congress

The branch of Congress which supported the cause of the Army was the House of Representatives. Indignant because the Senate was able to regulate Indian affairs through its power of treaty ratification, members of the House seized every opportunity to influence Indian relations following the Civil War. The interest of representatives in transfer was only one phase of the struggle of the House to gain the right to discuss Indian treaties, but it was a stand which encouraged the Army to fight for power and forced the transfer problem into the political arena. The first serious conflict over the matter arose on January 31, 1867 when

17

the House voted for transfer by 76-73 despite the report of a joint congressional committee opposing the change.[11] Several senators expressed interest in the proposal during a long debate which featured appeals for force by Western members. By a vote of 24-13, however, the majority refused to surrender to the House, which replied by rejecting a counter proposal for investigation in hope that conditions would soon be so favorable to their cause that no concessions would be necessary.[12] Despite this optimistic outlook, nearly two years passed before House leaders were able to present another transfer measure to the Senate. The decisive factor in delaying such proposals was the attitude of the Peace Commission appointed in 1867 to deal with warring tribes. In their report of January 7, 1868, the members of the Commission, including such well known soldiers as Generals Sherman, Augur, and Terry, declared that transfer would mean war.[13] The publication of such an outspoken statement by a commission including military leaders threatened to discredit the cause of transfer permanently. But the dispute was not to be settled so easily, as a renewal of Indian hostilities in the summer of 1868 led all but one of the Commissioners to announce on the following ninth of October that circumstances had forced a change of opinion.[14] With transfer officially recommended by the Peace Commission, the House left no doubt concerning its position by passing a transfer bill by a vote of 116-33 as soon as organization for the 1868-1869 session had been completed.[15]

Developments during 1869 seriously checked the possibility of transfer despite the overwhelming support of the House. Late in 1868 the measure backed by the representatives was referred to the Senate Indian Committee over the objection of senators who urged that it should be sent to the Committee on Military Affairs.[16] As a similar bill had been killed by the Indian Committee only a year earlier, the Senate's refusal to let the favorable Committee on Military Affairs consider the proposal ended all hope of effecting transfer by a special enactment. Attempts were made in both House and Senate to add an amendment providing for transfer to the Indian Appropriation Bill. This method failed, however, as many congressmen who would have backed the change as a separate bill voted against legislation by amendment.[17] Great hope was entertained that action might be forthcoming in the following Congress. Instead, the inauguration of Grant on the fourth of March, 1869 initiated a period during which the transfer issue was less prominent because of the President's interest in trying peaceful methods. For several years afterward, pressure for transfer was reduced out of respect for the President's desire to avoid even a pretense of force.

But while President Grant opposed Army control, interest in transfer was too strong to be suppressed completely during his administration. Representative Garfield, who was himself to become president, always believed that transfer would have been authorized in 1873 if Colonel Baker had not aroused opposition by massacring a band of peaceful Piegans just as congressional debate was reaching its height.[18] In any case, Indian atrocities which occurred constantly despite the vigilance of civilian administrators often threatened to cause a sudden adoption of military control. When the Sioux protested against invasion of the Black Hills by inaugurating the bloodiest Indian outbreak since the Civil War as Grant's second term drew to a close in 1876, transfer again became a dominant political issue.

The champion of transfer in 1876 was again the House of Representatives, although it was now a Democratic body hoping to embarrass a Republican administration instead of a Republican House jealous of a Senate controlled by the same party. With the important elections of 1876 approaching, Democratic representatives eagerly seized the opportunity presented by clashes with the Sioux to criticize the Interior Department and passed a transfer bill on the twenty-first of April with but few party deviations.[19] The opinion of senators on the issue was known to be closely divided. Fortunately for the opponents of transfer, Senate leaders were able to force the decisive vote in the unpopular form of an amendment to the Indian appropriation bill. Yet even after this success the desertion of three Western Republicans just failed to carry the amended bill.[20] As it was, close party votes in the House kept the issue on the floor long enough to allow Democrats to place the defeat squarely upon the shoulders of Republican senators and to announce to the country that efficient prosecution of the Sioux war made temporary surrender by the House imperative.[21] For that reason alone the battle was postponed until after election.

Although Democrats threatened to press relentlessly for transfer in 1876, the subject was not seriously discussed again until the House succeeded in adding a transfer amendment to the Army Appropriation Bill on May 27, 1878.[22] The Senate, still determined to resist the change, countered by urging appointment of a joint congressional investigating committee of four senators and three representatives. Although the proposal was clearly intended to forestall action, House Democrats decided to yield after securing an additional committee member to balance party representation.[23] Appointment of the committee, however, merely shifted the dispute to a different arena. Testimony only repeated familiar arguments, as both sides had already exhausted their cases. The prejudices motivating a large majority of the witnesses were reflected in the committee's report. In spite of the need to reach an agreement free from partisan bias, the members could not agree.[24] The separate reports offered by each party emphasized that the investigation had only been a waste of time as far as specific accomplishments were concerned. Yet the failure to reach any decision was itself of significance. Opponents of transfer had secured a vastly important delay. After 1878 decreasing danger of war and extensive reforms undertaken in the Interior Department rapidly weakened the cause of transfer.

The collapse of the transfer issue was evident as early as February 8, 1879, when the House defeated several measures providing for the change. Although representatives had voted for transfer only the previous May, they now refused even to grant the Army control of warlike Indians.[25] An attempt to allow such administrative changes to be made at presidential discretion won still less support,[26] for Democrats still willing to vote for transfer would not consent to place responsibility for action in the hands of a Republican president. A similar proposal, although sponsored by a member of the Republican majority and reported favorably by the Committee on Indian Affairs, was dropped in the Senate.[27]

The Transfer Problem

When members of the House attempted to add transfer amendments to the Indian appropriation bills of 1880 and 1881 both efforts were declared out of order.[28] The decline of interest in transfer was so great that although Representative Hooker of Mississippi begged the House to vote against the 1881 bill as a means of protest he was able to muster only a dozen votes. But the final stand of the advocates of transfer did not occur until Representative Throckmorton of Texas failed to force the appointment of military inspectors upon the Indian Bureau in 1884. The measure was at first considered so conservative that even the energetic opposition of such able parliamentarians as Representatives Keifer, Reed, and Cannon was unable to prevent the House from upholding a decision declaring the measure in order by a vote of 114-14. But although the representatives adopted the proposal by 69-54 and 91-67, Senate opposition led House conferees to admit that the proposal should be abandoned.[29] Whether or not the hope of electing a Democratic president who would control the Indian Bureau caused Throckmorton to proclaim the inadvisability of the measure he had desired as an opening wedge for transfer, his confession marked the end of a powerful movement.

Because of the sudden disappearance of transfer as a political issue several significant phases of the dispute have been overlooked by students of American Indian policy. In the first place, an analysis of votes on transfer measures reveals the surprising extent to which the Indian became a tool of partisan schemes. Only a complete disregard for Indian welfare enabled the transfer proposal, championed by Republicans in the late sixties, to become a rallying point for Democrats a few years later. Yet House Republicans who voted for transfer by 105-12 in 1868 opposed transfer by 102-9 ten years later, while Democrats who had opposed the change by 21-11 supported it by 121-13 in 1878. Of six representatives and five senators who voted on transfer measures throughout this period, but a single representative and a single senator were consistent.[30] With most congressmen failing to consider the problem on its merits, military control was prevented only by the resistance of a large number of Republican senators to political pressure in the early days and by the refusal of such

Democrats as Cox of New York and Wilshire of Arkansas to follow their leaders during the final crisis. Even such men could not have withstood pressure for transfer during 1878, however, if they had not been ably supported by Secretary of the Interior Schurz.

The importance of Carl Schurz's rôle in the final victory of the Interior Department is another factor in the transfer dispute which has never been sufficiently recognized. A sensational reformation of the Indian Bureau which took place under the Secretary's supervision was an indispensable part of the fight against military control. Republican leaders could not have effectively defended the Department if a successful attack had not been made against corrupt administration. Yet Schurz aided the opponents of transfer in still other ways. Whenever civilian administration of Indian affairs seemed most in danger, the Secretary was to be found in the middle of the battle. In one notable instance when General Sheridan stated that Indian affairs were too complex to be reformed by civilian administrators, Schurz not only objected to the implication in a personal letter but publicly demanded either an apology or specification of charges.[31] As Sheridan was only able to repeat his unsupported conviction as to Schurz's helplessness in his rejoinder, military criticism was so discredited that even a general sent the Secretary a confidential letter hailing his victory.[32]

The final impression resulting from a study of the transfer debate is the amazing selfishness of the forces demanding an end of civilian rule. The self-seeking of Army officers who desired to secure control of the Indians was often quite moderate when compared with statements made on the floor of Congress. Unwilling to stress only the need of whites and Indians for protection, transfer advocates jockeyed for political profit. Thus Representative Boone of Kentucky insisted that some transfer measure should be passed because it was the duty of Democratic congressmen to strip the President of as much patronage as possible; while Representative Lane of Oregon was so grasping as to urge that the money saved from such a reduction of patronage should be spent for developing the Columbia River! [33] Although there was much to be condemned in contemporary Indian administration, both Re-

The Transfer Problem

publican and Democratic supporters of transfer were too intent upon their own ends to present reasonable arguments. A more sincere discussion was engaged in by the public, whose attitude played a decisive part in determining how the problem should be settled.

Public Opinion and the Transfer Issue

The reaction of the public to the arguments of transfer debaters was far from steady. Although the exposure of fraud or the defeat of some cherished plan frequently caused Indian friends to support military rule, subsequent reports of Army cruelty were sure to result in a return to one's original opposition. No lasting solution of the problem could be expected as long as Americans failed to reach any settled conclusion regarding the advisability of transfer. Yet many of the best known individuals and organs of public opinion reached no final decision for many years. The Nation, which welcomed the possibility of transfer in 1868 but was somewhat less certain about its advantages in 1870, did not openly oppose the change until moved by admiration for Secretary Schurz in 1879.[34] William Welsh, the Philadelphia philanthropist generally recognized as the leading champion of the Indian, on the other hand, urged transfer in 1876 because of disappointment over the failure of efforts to reform the Indian Bureau.[35] Many other friends of the Indians, including such noted reformers as Edward Everett Hale and Secretary Herbert Welsh of the Indian Rights Association, recommended similar action as they lost faith in civilian administrators.[36] Personal opinions shifted so frequently that neither the opponents nor advocates of transfer ever had a group of any size upon whose support they could depend.

Although individual views regarding the advisability of transfer were unstable, public opinion upon the subject displayed sectional contrasts. A study of congressional votes reveals that all but a few Western legislators desired transfer. Frontier opinion, as a matter of fact, was even more firmly in favor of the change than the stand of congressmen from beyond the Mississippi would lead one to believe. A move to censure Senator Pomeroy of Kansas for opposing transfer in the late sixties was typical of pressure existing in all Western states throughout the period.[37] When Representative Crounse of Nebraska supported transfer in 1876, for example, he announced that he was surrendering personal convictions to satisfy his constituents.[38] Westerners suffered too severely from Indian outbreaks to admit that any scruples should be permitted to check efficient control. As Army rule seemed to offer undeniable advantages, legislators resisting the change faced certain defeat. In the East, on the other hand, a majority opposed military rule. Prominent individuals occasionally advocated transfer, but most Easterners feared the change. Since they were sufficiently removed from contact with the Indians to take a less prejudiced position than frontiersmen, citizens from states east of the Mississippi supported the Indian Bureau. Protestant churches, assisting the Interior Department in Indian administration praised the Interior Department with particular enthusiasm.[39] But participation in the existing set-up was not essential to stir sympathy with civilian administrators. Even leaders of the Catholic Church, which was poorly treated by the Indian Bureau, refused to back the Army despite the promise of better conditions.[40] Both Protestant and Catholic believed that Army control would prove disastrous. Their energetic opposition to a change was of considerable value in preventing the evils they feared. Had transfer at any time won general support in the East, union with Western forces would have insured its success.

Recognition of the important part which public opinion would play in determining whether control over the Indians should be transferred to the Army was responsible for the publication of a large amount of literature on both sides of the problem. Many soldiers quickly dropped sword for pen in 1881 when a prize was offered for the best essay by a military man on the American Indian and the United States Army. Captain Edward Butler won the contest with a treatise defending United States Indian relations from the founding of the government and urging institution of a system of forceful education by an Army which would reluctantly accept the duty of improving upon a weak civilian administration. The successful manuscript not only appeared with its closest competitors in the *Journal of the Military Service Institution of the United States*, but was also published in book form.[41] More numerous and more effective, however, were attacks against the Army, of which *Our Indian Wards* by George W. Manypenny was the outstanding example. Possessing special authority because of his previous experience as Commissioner of Indian Affairs, Manypenny offered a detailed study in which every massacre, every cent spent in war, every personal prejudice expressed by officers, was fully considered. The bitterness of the author's tone, the mass of his evidence and the fixity of his purpose combined to make an argument that was both powerful and impressive. Any reader who accepted the facts, such as a typical statement that official records for 1877 showed 11,941 convictions for gambling in an Army of but 25,000 men, was not likely to regard the possibility of transfer with equanimity.[42] The only publication rivaling *Our Indian Wards* in this respect was the *Council Fire*, a monthly magazine which voiced intense opposition to transfer from its founding in 1878. Edited by Alfred B. Meacham and Theodore A. Bland, who were undoubtedly correct in feeling that a gratuitous distribution of the early numbers among congressmen was influential in securing the final defeat of transfer in that year,[43] the magazine continued to condemn the Army. A series of articles written by Bland and characteristically entitled "Abolish the Army," revealed the excesses to which criticism of the military might be carried.[44] But as long as such attacks were included in the mass of literature discussing transfer, ignorance of the problem could not be excused.

Public interest in the transfer problem was further demonstrated by the number of schemes proposed to end the quarrel by compromise. Most popular were plans for creation of a separate Indian Department. "An Indian Department, independent of all others, is to be instituted, very different in many points from the old Indian Bureau," the Catholic missionary, de Smet, wrote in 1868.[45] Although this information was false, the plan was frequently recommended during the next decade by such prominent men as Chairman Brunot of the Board of Indian Commissioners and the anthropologist, Lewis H. Morgan.[46] There was reason to agree with a correspondent of Secretary Schurz who believed that the Secretary of the Interior had "too many pans on the fire for any one Chef to handle"[47]; but creation of a separate department would have been foolish in view of the desire of the same reformers to render such a department unnecessary by treating the Indians like whites. Suggestions advanced in Congress for dividing authority by granting the Army jurisdiction over special tribes or employing military agents under civilian direction were even more impractical,[48] as a contest over jurisdiction had originally been responsible for the dispute. Any arrangement other than full Army or full civilian control was sure to prove unsatisfactory.

While there has been some disagreement over the reason why transfer was never sanctioned, the primary factor was a sincere conviction on the part of a large majority of the public that the Army was not fitted to direct Indian affairs. There was too much earnest discussion of the merits and defects of transfer by both Congress and the public to warrant Professor Paxson's belief that transfer was defeated by "inertia."[49] Many people, who were genuinely concerned over corruption in the Indian Bureau, held that Army control would only make conditions worse. Little in the history of relations between the Army and the tribes inspired confidence in the discretion of military officers. They were, of course, generals who angered the West by demanding justice for the tribes. "General Kautz is relieved and so is Arizona," a local paper wrote of one such offender.[50] The majority of military men, however, believed that "to have peace it is necessary to fight for it."[51] They made heroes of aggressive fighters like Custer and considered any criticism of Army actions treasonable. Thus while Lieutenant Whitman was court-martialed for criticizing officers involved in the Camp Grant massacre of 1872 and General Sherman criticized General Sully's captious report upon the Piegan massacre as "an unofficer-like and wrong act,"[52] officers responsible for mistreating Indians escaped prosecution. Army men, whether at Indian schools such as Hampton and Carlisle or in the field, showed an inability to consider the Indian's point of view and a tendency to resort to force rather than reason. Military control might have been advisable if discipline had been the only end. But as long as civilization was an aim, Army connections could only prove a handicap to an administrator. The work of such men as Generals Crook, Howard, and Miles was frequently embarrassed by their military affiliations, and even a humble post chaplain was forced to confine praise of the work of Secretary Colyer of the Board of Indian Commissioners to a few platitudes for fear that further remarks might be misconstrued.[53] Under such conditions, the decision of students of Indian affairs that a reformation of existing agencies would be preferable to a change of jurisdiction was not surprising.

The final defeat of transfer was fortunate for all concerned. Progress in Indian relations had been postponed for ten years, as reformers devoted their energies to preventing Army control. Once transfer was defeated, however, even its most ardent advocates joined in seeking more fundamental reforms. In 1880, for example, Senators Coke of Texas, Beck of Kentucky, and Burnside of Rhode Island all declared that they supported a proposal for allotting land to Indians because the hope of transfer had passed.[54] The possibility that a makeshift change might be substituted for real reform had come to an end. Although the Indian Bureau was not ideal, reformers could at least be certain of the difficulties to be met now that there was no longer any danger reforms would be interrupted by a sudden shift of jurisdiction. Whatever mistakes were made, responsibility could at last be fixed. Just as the defeat of concentration had aided the cause of reform by eliminating uncertainty as to the locale of the Indian problem, so the defeat of transfer sped Indian advancement by securing continued administration by the civilian branch of the government. But although the defeat of transfer removed another obstacle from the path of reform, difficulties of an entirely different nature impeded progress.

3. CHURCH NOMINATION
OF INDIAN OFFICIALS

ONE WAY IN WHICH MANY AMERICANS REVEAL THEIR IGNORANCE regarding the history of United States Indian policy is by their failure to realize that the churches of the country once participated in the selection of Indian agents for nearly ten years. A people, strongly hostile to any union between church and state, are generally unaware that the aversion was temporarily overcome at one time by a desire to secure more honest Indian officials. Even the few who realize that church nomination of Indian agents was an outstanding feature of President Grant's peace policy have failed to examine the operation of the plan with sufficient care. Statements regarding the improvements achieved by the churches fail to point out that the failures of the policy were more significant than its successes. The story of America's experiment with the denominational control of Indian appointments needs to be studied more thoroughly, not only to promote a better understanding of United States Indian policy, but also to serve as a warning against the pitfalls of state-church relationships in a country composed of people of greatly varied religious affiliations.

Church nomination of Indian agents was instituted with a firm belief in its ability to improve Indian relations. Enthusiasm regarding the policy so completely obscured its fundamental difficulties that almost every friend of the tribes believed that the change would soon solve all problems of administration. In truth, as long as the worth of contemporary Indian policies was not questioned, there was every reason to believe that appointment of honest agents was the only requisite for success. For such a task, the churches were well qualified. Their failure to produce any noticeable reforms, therefore, had the value of proving that the defects of United States Indian policy were matters of far greater significance than mere administrative incompetency.

The inauguration of church appointments following the Civil

Church Nomination of Indian Officials

War resulted from the disreputable character of many contemporary Indian officials. The United States had long experienced difficulty in securing honest agents. Posts in the Indian service were located so far from civilization and offered so little compensation that good men could be secured only when moved by a peculiar zeal for self-sacrifice. As the stress of war requirements revealed the corruption and inefficiency of officials with increased clarity, continuance of existing methods became intolerable. Several years before the churches were invited to join in the selection of agents religious co-operation was urged. Certain senators recommended inclusion of a church representative on the 1867 Peace Commission as a means of satisfying the nation's sense of justice,[1] but only the Quakers actively sought permission to participate in the reformation of Indian policy. It was the enthusiasm of Quaker leaders for Indian work, in fact, which led President Grant to place several agencies under their direction in 1869.[2] The success of this experiment, plus the refusal of Congress to permit the appointment of Army officers as Indian agents,[3] resulted in extension of the policy in 1870. With the distribution of responsibility for satisfactory administration of Indian agencies among leading United States denominations, the new policy was under way.

American churches did not welcome the opportunity to appoint Indian agents with much pleasure. Just as the Friends had hesitated to accept the right of nomination in 1869 without a clear understanding of the problems involved,[4] so other churches studied the question carefully before accepting any responsibility. William Welsh, a Philadelphia merchant who was to render outstanding service as a friend of the Indians, had to "drag" the Episcopal Church into the work because its members were reluctant to aid a government that seemed powerless to educate or civilize.[5] In several other cases, denominations moved slowly because of opposition to participation in political matters. But the chief cause for delay was the failure of the government to provide adequate security. "If General Grant were going to be President for the next 20 years or so, our leading men would be willing I think . . . to enter upon the work," wrote a Baptist representative.[6] Such a guarantee of stability was naturally impossible. But although the government refused to pledge continuation of the policy for even four years, most churches finally decided to risk sudden removal of their privileges. Since their interest was determined by the degree of confidence in the government which each possessed, however, such uncertainty was disastrous. Church participation would have been much more effective if the government had been able or willing to promise a reasonable amount of co-operation.

Yet inadequate government support was not the only problem of the churches. If officials had been able to give unlimited assistance, American churches still would have had difficulty in raising funds for Indian work. The average layman was not interested in the Indian problem. For many years money had been sent abroad to convert the heathen while local needs remained unnoticed. Even when the problem was pointed out, the churches did not feel at liberty to curtail the meager funds of foreign enterprises which depended upon their support.[7] As a result, churches anxious for the prestige of selecting an Indian agent were often unable to supply missionaries. Lutheran officials, for example, were forced to announce that they had neither the men nor the means to support the effort of agents with religious assistants.[8] Occasional efforts were made to stimulate interest in Indian work, but only in a few cases did churches succeed in either satisfying the government's desire for active support or increasing the contributions of their members.[9]

The failure of the churches to arouse interest in the Indian problem was especially unfortunate, because Indian work presented difficulties which would have tried the patience of even the most enthusiastic groups. The inability of the Methodists to recommend more than one of 145 candidates examined during 1874 was typical of a problem facing every church.[10] Candidates inevitably seemed to lack either honesty or ability, if they were not deficient in both respects. Although the Reformed Church displayed an unusual sense of responsibility by nominating all its candidates from other sects,[11] pressure within each organization forced most to place church interests before those of the Indians.[12] Even churches which took unusual care in making selections so soon learned the possibility of misjudgment that they hurried to remove appointees who proved unacceptable to the government. "If any of our men are not entirely satisfactory to the Department," a Friend wrote the Commissioner of Indian Affairs in 1875, "I think we can effect a change, and no one will know where the information of incompetency comes from." [13] His attitude was typical. Churches were willing to offer recommendations, but appointment problems were too complex to make them desirous of assuming responsibility for errors.

Equally difficult problems were encountered in the field, where even churches undertaking Indian work with a desire to do their best achieved little success in converting the Indians. The Catholic Church alone seemed able to appeal to the tribes through the personality of its workers and the splendor of its ceremonials.[14] Although Protestant sects strove to adapt their doctrines to tribal needs, Indian ignorance presented too great an obstacle to the success of creeds depending upon individual interpretation of the Bible and appeals to the intellect. Protestant churches could hope for victory only if granted exclusive rights on a reservation, and the request for exclusive rights involved denominations in disputes which threatened the welfare of all.

The Failure of Inter-Church Co-operation

Because of the difficulties of Indian administration and the lack of interest displayed by laymen, church officials needed to work in close agreement if denominational participation in the selection of agents was to solve Indian problems. Successful reform required a mutual respect for the rights of fellow workers. But instead of seizing the opportunity to co-operate for Indian welfare, the denominations immediately began to quarrel among themselves. Thus all hope of success was dissipated and church nomination of Indian appointees failed miserably amid the clamor of disputing churchmen.

Hardly had the original assignment of agencies been announced in 1870 than disputes arose. The most vociferous objectors were churches which had been omitted from the list. Practically every sect excluded, no matter how insignificant the number of its adherents, complained that its failure to receive an agency was regarded as a wrong which must be righted. Mormons, of course, knew that nothing could be expected from the government despite their excellent work among Utah Indians,[15] and a Jew wrote that it was "in controversy with the teachings of the Hebrew Religion to make Proselytes or to engage missionaries for such a purpose." [16] Otherwise there seemed a universal desire to be recognized as "one of the Christian families of the land."[17] For a time Indian officials welcomed requests for inclusion and assigned available agencies to new churches. The flood of applications soon aroused such severe opposition, however, that the Christian Disciples received an agency in 1880 only after pressure had been exerted by President Hayes and Senator Garfield! [18] Indian administrators were willing to provide opportunities for churches anxious to contribute to Indian advancement; but it is not surprising that they resented the tone of letters like that of the Lutheran representative who wrote:

We ask & believe that you will & can give us an Agency now, as well as in the future. If their is no vacancy at present, it would not take long to make one. We are not asking you to do any more for us than you have done for other churches. You have assigned Agencies to others without their sending special Missionaries to the tribe and can do so in our case if you desire. On the authority of the Lutheran Church we insist on an Agency being assigned to us.[19]

But inter-denominational rivalry was not confined to churches omitted from the original list. Those which were included caused the Indian Bureau even greater difficulty by peremptory demands for additional assignments or shifts of location. Not a single church seemed satisfied with the government's plan of distribution. Officials endeavored in each case to select the church which had done missionary work among a particular tribe; but certain claims had to be ignored to accommodate churches new to Indian work and in instances where more than one church was active a choice had to be made in which a decision favoring either side was certain to provoke complaints. Thus attempts of Congregationalists to protect their missions among the Sioux resulted in a series of crises which were typical of difficulties that constantly disturbed the Bureau. Soon after the authority to nominate was first distributed, Congregational representatives condemned assignment of a Sioux agency to the Episcopal Church as an indication of bad faith and a move toward church establishment.[20] Six years later, facing the prospect of transfer of the Santee Sioux agency from the Quakers to their Episcopal rivals, the church objected to the prospective missionary of whom the son of the Indian Commissioner had written, "There are several Indian maidens here who remember him with pleasure and he is quite noted for his remarkable luck at draw poker." [21] The most embarrassing problem was raised in 1880, however, when the Congregationalists insisted that no church should be allowed to expel the missionaries of another for any reason whatever.[22] Such a principle was entirely unacceptable to small churches, which depended upon exclusive privileges for successful Indian work; and although the more powerful denominations desired freedom, it could only increase the possibility of disputes. Yet between freedom and exclusion, there could be but one choice. Church quarrels over Indian affairs might be reduced by restricting spheres of influence, but Indian officials were no more willing than a large majority of their countrymen to abandon entirely the principle of religious freedom.

Even if the country had been willing to scrap religious freedom in dealing with Indians, quarrels over the appointment of agents would not have been ended by assigning full authority within each reservation to a particular denomination. Indian work frequently aroused such bad feeling that members of a single church fought bitterly among themselves. Bishop Hare of the Episcopal Church and Samuel D. Hinman, a leading Episcopal missionary, were the principal figures in a bitter dispute which divided high and low church adherents and ultimately became so personal that a libel suit resulted in 1884.[23] A Methodist agent from Oregon complained to the Indian Bureau that the local conference of his church was endeavoring to secure his dismissal for refusal to create unnecessary positions for its placemen.[24] Even a peace-loving Quaker warned President Grant not only to avoid appointing

Hicksite Friends but also to make sure that all selected from the Orthodox branch were true converts! [25] With such antagonisms dividing individual churches, rivalry between Catholics and Protestants was naturally intense.

Although abundant documentary material exists dealing with the Catholic-Protestant dispute, there are few variations in detail. Wherever the two groups met, difficulties arose. While Catholic and Protestant missionaries had worked for years among the Indians without serious conflict, friendship ceased once the government offered to aid their work. Catholic opposition to the policy was not surprising, as the Church contributed over half the funds spent on Indian missions and yet received but seven of ninety-four agencies under the original distribution.[26] Government officials soon frankly admitted that Catholic claims had been incompletely recognized. Yet attempts to rectify the error by assigning additional agencies only served to arouse the Protestants. Complaints concerning such readjustments were numerous and the Methodists, who had surrendered one Oregon agency to accommodate superior Catholic claims, warned that they would cease all co-operation with the government if further concessions were asked.[27] Since this attitude was general, the Catholic Church realized that successful Indian work would be possible only if its missionaries were allowed to enter any reservation. Catholic leaders consequently demanded a free field for missionary activity; and it was this fact which caused powerful Protestant churches to hesitate before supporting the demand. Congregationalists precipitated the issue of freedom in 1880 largely because they wished to enter a Catholic reservation! While the interest of Catholics in religious freedom was likewise governed by circumstances rather than conviction, the confession of the Church's leading representative that exclusion would be desirable if employed to defend churches originally in the field [28] should not obscure the fact that for several years Catholics alone advocated religious freedom for Indian workers.

Catholics had many reasons to denounce government Indian policy following 1871. Although officials had no intention of using denominational appointments to test the potentialities of a state church as some excitable Catholics claimed, Catholic writers were justified in charging the government with hostility. The scanty reference to the work of the Church in official reports was alone sufficient to prove the existence of an anti-Catholic bias. Even more disturbing was the scarcity of Catholics in responsible Indian positions, the full extent of which was revealed when the Church discovered that only fourteen of 220 posts in Indian schools had been held by Catholics under President Cleveland, and but three under Harrison! The administration of Indian affairs was clearly dominated by Protestants whose churches were constantly urging positive action against Catholic Indian interests. Conditions might have been worse if the chief purpose of Catholic Indian policy since the seventies had not been to prevent actions detrimental to the interests of the Church.[29]

While Catholics could expect little sympathy from government officials, they realized at once that better treatment could be obtained by presenting administrators with such a clear statement of their position that decisions against the Church could be attacked as prejudiced. To accomplish this end the Catholic Bureau of Indian Missions was established in Washington in 1874 under the direction of General Ewing and Father Brouillet. By keeping the wishes of the Church before the government, and by making appeals in only the most justifiable cases, the Bureau was able to prevent further steps being taken to injure important Catholic interests. Both men were frequently handicapped, however, by the unreasonable criticism of Protestant administration common among fellow Catholics. Official interest in securing fair treatment was hardly encouraged when Archbishop Blanchet of Oregon asked Commissioner Parker how the government could expect a true civilization to be given to the Indians by sects, not Christian but infidel.[30] Fortunately the Catholic Bureau opposed excessive claims, and when Father Tomazin aroused national attention by encouraging Catholic Indians on the White Earth reservation to resist the Indian Office in 1882, the Bureau joined the government in condemning his action.[31] As most government officials were disposed to treat the Catholics fairly, systematic presentation of the arguments of the Church confined action on Protestant demands within bounds which were reasonably just to both parties.

The Attitude of Government Officials
Toward Church Appointments

Loss of the right of nomination did not reduce the power of the Indian Bureau as much as might be expected. Not only did Indian officials insist upon retaining the right to reject appointments, but through mediation of inter-church quarrels they played almost as important a part in determining official policies as they had before. Whenever disputes arose, the churches involved appealed to the Bureau for an official decision. Such announcements always stressed a resolution that Indians should not suffer because of religious disputes. When Protestant churches complained of Catholic interference with reservation schools, therefore, removal of all parties endeavoring to prevent attendance was authorized. But it was only when such interference threatened the peace and order of a reservation that government officials moved to exclude a denomination. Otherwise churches which held that the right to nominate an agent implied the right to exclude all other sects were regularly opposed.[32]

While most Americans were extremely·critical of all collaboration between the government and churches in the conduct of Indian affairs, the collapse of the system of denominational appointments was primarily due to political opposition. As averse as the public was to having its taxes used to further religious work among the Indians, the loss of political patronage resulting from church selection of officials exercised greater influence in repressing the practice. Loyalty to President Grant delayed attacks on the system for several years, but once the presidential election of 1876 approached politicians felt free to express their contempt for the policy. With members of both parties insisting that all possible sources of patronage should be opened, church nomination of Indian agents was not spared. Hostilities began early in March when the Senate rejected Quaker appointments to Nebraska agencies on the ground that the nominees were not residents of that state. If nominations could be confined to the state of service, legislators hoped local politicians might dictate the choice of men whom reformers would regard as incompetent. Although the Board of Indian Commissioners complained that its usefulness would be destroyed if agents were chosen on sectional grounds,[33] the churches never regained their former freedom of selection, and President Hayes's administration witnessed a steady decline in the frequency with which churches were consulted regarding Indian affairs.

The process by which denominational appointments were abandoned is difficult to trace because the absence of an agreement between the Indian Bureau and the churches enabled administrators to modify the policy gradually. With the exact relationship between the factions undefined, Indian officials were able to impair the right of nomination from time to time without being open to charges of bad faith. There was not a single rule which the churches could cite in resisting the establishment of more rigid requirements or in challenging the constant insistence of officials that emergency appointments were necessary. By proceeding cautiously, the government was able to wreck the policy before any violent opposition was aroused.

The aversion which outside interference inevitably inspired among Indian administrators was a fundamental weakness of the attempt to improve Indian relations by securing church co-operation with governmental agencies. Officials of the Indian Bureau naturally resented the efforts of churchmen to dictate the details of Indian policy, while increasing evidence of the incompetence of religious appointees caused administrators to demand restoration of the privilege of selecting their own subordinates. Once criticism of the churches could no longer be condemned as opposition to President Grant, officials were free to express their opinion of church control. Few prominent administrators revealed their attitude outside of private correspondence, but confidential statements disclose that the pretensions of the churches were regarded with almost universal contempt. Thus when the Unitarian Church asked why a candidate had been rejected, Commissioner Hayt frankly wrote Secretary of the Interior Schurz that the nominee had been turned down merely because he was a minister! [34] Both the Secretary and President-elect Garfield agreed with this policy, for they soon joined in seeking an Indian Commissioner who would be "sufficiently poised to be able to hear all the extravagant sentimentalism of the Churches without losing his head." [35] For men of such decided opinions, officials in charge of Indian affairs tolerated church nominations unusually long. Being trained politicians, however, they realized that delay and evasion provided the best means of ending the policy with a minimum amount of criticism.

The remarkable ability with which government officials concealed their opposition to church appointments successfully postponed complaints for several years. Criticism was forestalled not only by insisting that political appointments were necessary in emergencies, but by such a simple process as deferring replies to embarrassing letters. In one instance, a letter of November 14, 1878, telling President Hayes of the Department's mistreatment of the churches, was not received by the Secretary of the Interior until February 5, 1879, nor by the Commissioner of Indian Affairs until July 15. [36] Still worse was a letter to Commissioner Hayt from a representative of the Friends dated April 20, 1878, but appearing in the 1880 office file labeled "old when rec^d." Only the Commissioner's resignation in January of that year apparently rescued the letter from oblivion. [37] Yet such methods could not delude the churches indefinitely. By 1880, the rejection of one nomination after another left no doubt that church influence had ceased. Most churches, once their impotence was realized, preferred to surrender the right of nomination rather than battle the Indian Bureau. [38] While the immediate reaction was one of hostility, the loss of power had been so gradual that the feeling of injustice soon passed. Only two years later the churches jointly presented a plan for redistributing the agencies in hope that a display of fairness might cause the government to re-adopt the plan of denominational control. [39] But though mutual defeat had at last led the churches to reconcile differences, a return to the system was out of the question. The government had had enough experience with denominational appointments to realize that religious assistance was of much greater value when unofficial.

The government was only occasionally criticized for abolishing the system of denominational appointments, as the churches had won few friends despite their ten years of work. Army criticism, in particular, induced many citizens to question the value of the policy. Few points in the case for transfer scored more heavily than assaults upon the inefficiency of religiously-appointed agents. While General Pope was satisfied to point out the loss of business ability occasioned by the appointment of moral agents, Colonel Dodge went so far as to deny that any gain in character had resulted.[40] With this harsh judgment large numbers of citizens showed every sign of agreeing. Many strangely worded letters received by the Indian Bureau expressed the belief of humble citizens that honesty and church membership were seldom joined.[41] So little had been done by churches to improve Indian relations that all but a few close friends of Grant's policy welcomed the end of church influence.

Significance of the Failure of Church Nominations

Americans who hailed abandonment of the system of denominational appointments were wise, for the churches had exercised power long enough to reveal that they were poorly qualified to cope successfully with Indian problems. Too many religiously-minded agents believed Bishop Hare was correct in condemning discussions of the red man's future as dangerous because they diverted one's attention from "present duty." [42] Conversion was more important than civilization in the opinion of most church appointees. However admirable in theory, such lack of concern for material matters was a poor basis for administering Indian affairs. Real success was achieved only where missionaries opened schools in practical education and did not refuse to labor in the fields. Unfortunately such work was seldom attempted, as the average church-appointed agent was more interested in "Sunday religion" than the "kind which lasts seven days a week." [43] Few contributions to progress could be expected from men who approached Indian problems from the point of view of the Washington agent who considered return of a borrowed umbrella proof of the great merit of Christian training.[44] Yet as late as 1887 Dr. Harrison of the Indian Rights Association discovered that many teachers in prominent Indian institutions were more interested in conversion than instruction.[45] As long as such an attitude colored the views of Indian workers, racial advancement was impossible. The gradual abandonment of denominational appointments following 1876, therefore, was an important step in the direction of more intelligent Indian administration.

While an exaggerated conception of the significance of spiritual values reduced the effectiveness of the work of American churches among the Indians, their efforts also suffered from the aversion of their members to political action. Churches, afraid to support even the best of public causes, provided little assistance in fighting corruption. Their annual resolutions, the product of compromises between the friends and foes of political action, were too indefinite to be useful. Their conferences with the Board of Indian Commissioners, intended to provide an opportunity for a clearer understanding of administrative difficulties, degenerated into mere "experience" meetings at which delegates vied in relating their success instead of discussing their problems in any systematic manner. As long as churches had to bargain with opponents of political action, they contributed little to the cause of Indian reform.[46]

Even if the churches had been able to act politically, they were poorly fitted to manage the affairs of a reservation. Power and a rare practicality were just as necessary as sincerity to successful direction of Indian affairs. Unable to supply either, churchmen soon found that it was easier to develop a theory of how to civilize Indians than to execute it. Quakers, in particular, entered Indian work with enlightened plans only to discover the inadequacy of peaceful methods.[47] John D. Miles, for many years Cheyenne-Arapahoe agent, was more successful than other Quaker representatives because he frequently sacrificed his principles to necessity.[48] As much as reformers might regret the fact, the first requisite for successful Indian administration was force. Since such authority was possessed by the government and not the churches, Indian

40

affairs could never be efficiently conducted as long as the churches played a leading part.

While the withdrawal of American churches from participation in Indian administration was wise, the policy did contribute to Indian advancement. If the type of Indian agent had alone been improved, as all but a few prejudiced observers concede, church nomination of Indian officials would have marked a turning point.[49] But the greatest service of the policy was in revealing that the evils of the Indian system were more serious than even the sincerest Indian friends hitherto had imagined. With the failure of the churches to effect fundamental reforms, the need for a complete overhauling of the old system could no longer be disputed.

4. THE BOARD OF INDIAN
COMMISSIONERS

During the same period that United States officials were testing the possibilities of church appointments to the Indian service, an experiment of very similar purpose was inaugurated with equally disappointing results. The Board of Indian Commissioners, composed of nine philanthropists serving as unpaid advisers to the Indian Bureau, was appointed in 1869 to stimulate closer co-operation between Indian administrators and the public. Such a group, it was hoped, not only would study Indian problems and recommend improvements, but also would stimulate popular interest in the Indians. The new body, discontinued only when Franklin D. Roosevelt revised American Indian policies in 1934, fulfilled both these purposes for a time. But the history of the Board of Indian Commissioners from its origin to 1887 was unfortunately that of a group with tremendous potentialities for good, few of which were realized because of the uncompromising opposition of other government agencies.

Appointment of the Board was the result of careful forethought. As early at 1862, the Episcopal Church had proposed that a commission of citizens should be appointed to devise a better Indian policy.[1] The suggestion was naturally ignored during the war; but President Grant had hardly assumed office in 1869 before a similar plan was recommended by a group of Philadelphia citizens.[2] Congress was quite ready to undertake such an experiment, for Indian affairs were in a crisis which made the possibility of outside assistance especially welcome. Faced with the necessity of providing for the administration of an unallotted two million dollar fund because of the refusal of the House of Representatives to vote specific appropriations promised in treaties concluded following the Civil War, Congress saw a possible solution in the proposal for a board of commissioners. The Indian Appropriation Bill of 1869, therefore, included $25,000 for the establishment of a group

The Board of Indian Commissioners

of nine men to report on the expenditure of the fund and to consult with the Interior Department regarding Indian problems in general.[3] No further details were provided at the time, because the Board was regarded either as an emergency organization or as a body whose proper function should be determined only after experiment. Consequently, there was at the start no careful definition of the Board's relation to established administrative agencies, and the failure of Congress to clarify this matter continued to be a source of trouble from that time until the Board's death sixty-five years later.

The main cause of the disputes which periodically arose between the Board of Indian Commissioners and government officials was the provision of the original bill stating that the group should "exercise joint control with the Interior Department." When Senator Fessenden was asked which agency was intended to have final authority under this arrangement, he could only reply that the decision would rest with the President, who would "order probably under the advice of the Interior Department."[4] Such an administrative makeshift was clearly too indefinite to operate successfully, but congressmen undoubtedly hoped that the problem might be averted. The necessity for defining the power of the Board more exactly was avoided again the next year when the remainder of the original fund was re-appropriated in 1870 without any further authorization.[5] While some legislators claimed that failure to provide new money for the Board had the effect of forcing dissolution once the money was exhausted, the commissioners continued to operate under the act of 1869. A more exact description of the proper position of the Board, however, could not be postponed much longer. Although the Senate tried to evade any decision on the problem in the 1871 Indian Appropriation Bill by providing for continuance of the Board with the "powers and duties heretofore provided," the House refused to sanction its extension until a clause was added stating that the Secretary of the Interior should have power "to sustain, set aside, or modify the action of said board."[6] Acceptance of this proposal by the Senate clearly indicated that Congress would refuse to support the Board against the Department. But even if Congress had

43

upheld the Board, it could not have prevented quarrels which arose over differences incapable of settlement by congressional fiat.

The Battle for Power

Antagonism between the Board of Indian Commissioners and officials of the Interior Department was inevitable. As there was no reason for the Board's existence if proposed reforms could be rejected by the government, the commissioners refused to accept an inferior position. Permanent administrators, on the other hand, could not tolerate subordination to a temporary group of unpaid theorists and retain their self-respect. Indian Commissioner Parker, who once had advised President Grant to establish a board of civilians to conduct Indian relations, can not have regarded his suggestion favorably after reading, "In the several interviews which have been had with the President, the commissioners have received assurances that he will harmonize with them in all matters they may deem essential for the practical benefit of the Indians. The real Commissioner of Indian Affairs, General Parker, is consequently, of slight importance, as he is subordinate to the Board of Commissioners and religious communities." [7] In the course of events, either the Board or Indian administrators must be reduced to impotence. The ensuing struggle for power, as a result, lacked nothing in excitement and color.

The opposing interests of the Department and Board led to immediate conflict. The latter had been organized less than a month when its first chairman, William Welsh of Philadelphia, resigned because officials refused to allow the Board full supervision over all Indian expenditures.[8] As the remaining commissioners were unwilling to demand such power until the Board's requirements and the opportunities for future action had been more carefully studied, they refused to back their chairman. Unacquainted with Grant and thus far utterly ignorant of Indian affairs from personal experience, the other Board members were satisfied to depend for a time upon Secretary Cox's assurance that the powers of the Board would be adjusted to meet its needs.[9] But the promise that a reasonable amount of authority would ultimately be granted was never fulfilled, for every change which followed decreased rather than strengthened the influence of the Board.

In spite of the inability of the Board of Indian Commissioners to secure sufficient power to direct American Indian policy effectively, its early years were not without a victory. A successful campaign against Commissioner of Indian Affairs Parker served notice during 1871 that the Board's influence upon Indian affairs should not be regarded too lightly. The hostility of the Commissioner had been suspected from the first. "Mr. Sargent of the Committee of Appropriation in the House seems to think that the Executive strangled the Commission therefore it should be buried. Can you find out Dr Parkers real sentiments. I may be wrong in suspecting that he did not advocate the continuance of the Commission," [10] William Welsh stated in a letter sent to Secretary Colyer of the Board in February of 1870. As there seemed little doubt that Welsh's doubts were justified, Chairman Brunot warned Colyer to be cautious in dealing with Parker, and when information regarding corrupt contracts was uncovered he secretly encouraged Welsh to attack the Bureau. [11] Although Board members officially attempted to improve relations by commending the Department's "co-operation" in the concluding section of their 1870 report, one of their number privately explained that the praise was "soft soap" stuck on the end "like the last joint in the monkey's tail." [12] The commissioners had reason to rejoice, therefore, when Welsh's exposures made Parker feel resignation preferable to continuance in office. [13] But while the Commissioner's downfall was a victory for the Board, the members still faced so many other problems that additional evidence against Parker was not publicized for fear of wasting ammunition on a man who was already defeated. [14]

Parker's disgrace only increased the difficulties of the Board with a more dangerous opponent—Secretary of the Interior Delano. Although neither Board nor Secretary expressed their true sentiments publicly, private correspondence reveals that little love was lost between them. Thus when President Grant contemplated appointing Delano as Secretary of the Treasury and choosing

Brunot to fill the Interior vacancy, a member of the Board wrote that if the President was disposed to do a foolish thing to accomplish an excellent one he would rejoice in the latter and express no opinion regarding the former.[15] Such bitter antagonism soon arose between Delano and the Commissioners that Brunot advised Colyer to turn to the Master for a full supply of the patience necessary in dealing with an ill-tempered and changeable Secretary of the Interior.[16] Delano's success in forcing Colyer's resignation during a test of strength which arose in January, 1872 as a result of this hostility indicated that the Board did not seriously threaten the supremacy of the Department.[17] When less than three months later Delano asked money to survey all reservations except a group in Washington considered of especial importance by the Board,[18] the dependence of the commissioners upon the Secretary's good will could no longer be disputed.

The Board's Indian work was seriously handicapped by its lack of authority in both field work and administration. Policies considered essential by the commissioners, if not defeated at the start on the ground of impracticality, were easily thwarted by unfavorable officials. Because of repeated inability to enforce their demands Board members soon learned to make no promises, since even the most ignorant Indians quickly realized the impotence of men who frankly confessed that they had "full authority to devise a plan" but "no authority to change" conditions.[19] But while the commissioners constantly complained that they could accomplish nothing as long as the government failed to carry out Board pledges,[20] no further power was granted. Even in the matter of the letting of contracts and inspection of accounts, where the Board's powers were more specifically stated, similar difficulties were encountered. Although the Board was required to examine over 3,000 accounts and 300 contracts annually, Congress decided in 1872 that payments might be made without the Commissioners' approval! [21] Realizing that this action made their efforts purposeless, Board members asked relief from the responsibility only to be ordered to continue the work by Attorney General Harlan. Hence the commissioners spent much time in reaching decisions which were seldom respected. When payment was withheld on only

46

The Board of Indian Commissioners

$5,697.00 (2%) of rejected accounts totaling $426,909.96 in 1873, the Board's usefulness seemed at an end.[22] With Interior Department officials successfully exercising control over every aspect of Indian affairs, the commissioners themselves admitted defeat.

The failure of the Board to secure respect for its decisions led its six most prominent members to resign early in 1874. The refusal of these men to specify the reason for their action produced considerable confusion concerning their motives.[23] But whether their inability to prevent the use of force against Indian tribes or the insistence of the Department upon paying rejected accounts was the major reason, the move ended any possibility that a truly independent Board might be established. Although the vacancies were immediately filled, the Board was never allowed to regain its early power. Thereafter men were appointed only if they would submit to departmental control. When congressional opposition threatened the Board's existence a few years later, consequently, the Board was so completely dominated by regular officials that the Interior Department was now among its most energetic defenders.

Congressional Opposition

While the opposition of the Interior Department seriously reduced the effectiveness of the Board of Indian Commissioners, congressional animosity jeopardized its very existence. Operating expenses could be secured only if a majority of the legislators were friendly. Board members could not submit to every whim of congressmen, however, without removing all reason for their continuance. As long as the Board presumed to play a part in the formulation of Indian policy, it was obliged to resist unwise legislation. Yet, except in rare instances, there was no need of pressing objections. The Board's guide in such matters was the excellent advice which Brunot offered Secretary Cree in writing:

You had better not meddle with Dyers bill. It looks in the face to be a cheat, but it is the business of the Committee and we must presume in all such matters that they understand their business—or at least that they think they do—and we must be careful not to offer masked opinions on any matters about which we have not pretty

47

conclusive *knowledge*. The Langford bill is probably another job. Whilst it is well enough to know of and note them, nevertheless most of the Bills of all sorts which are referred to the Committee will get no further & in any case they rarely report favorably without having a fair understanding of the subject. . . . Even if we can show beyond doubt that a private (or sometimes even a public Act) is wrong, better let it take its course than volunteer, until we see that interference is necessary to prevent its final passage. You will thus waste no labor, excite no needless enmity, and when you do interfere will get some credit for it if properly done.[24]

But although the Board seldom interfered with congressional procedure under this policy, dissension could not be entirely avoided. Congressmen might welcome the Board as a curb on the Interior Department; they were less enthusiastic when their own acts were criticized.

Congressional attacks on the Board of Indian Commissioners, like criticisms of the Indian Bureau by advocates of transfer, were first Republican and then Democratic in origin. As long as the Board checked the activities of the Interior Department, most Republicans considered it an unwise restraint upon freedom of action, while Democrats applauded it as a valuable bulwark against Republican corruption.[25] When subservient members were appointed in 1874, however, such arguments lost their force. Conditions had shifted so completely by 1875, in fact, that abolition of the Board was recommended by only five Republican representatives and opposed by but one Democrat! [26] Republicans were able to forestall further criticism for a few years, saving the Board appropriation in 1877 by a vote of 47-38.[27] But the Democrats, satisfied to concentrate upon the transfer issue as long as there was hope of success, attacked the Board again as another means of embarrassing their opponents, once a shift of Indian administration to the War Department appeared impossible following 1879. As the Democrats controlled both branches of Congress from 1879 to 1881, the life of the Board hung in the balance for several years.

Although proposals to abolish the Board of Indian Commissioners were partisan, desertions from party ranks in April, 1880 revealed that the issue was becoming sectional. The House voted for abolition by 113-65 on the seventeenth, it is true, but four Democrats opposed the move and only sixteen out of seventy-seven Republicans supported it. The Board was saved by the Senate eleven days later, as the hostility of five Western Republicans which caused them to desert their party's stand against abolition was more than balanced by the refusal of fourteen Democrats from east of the Mississippi River to join sixteen party colleagues who voted for abolition. Sectional feeling influenced the outcome in both branches. While every Democratic senator and representative from states west of the Mississippi wished to dismiss the commissioners, not a single Democrat from the East opposed the Board in the Senate. As for the Republicans, all opponents of the commissioners in the Senate and six of the sixteen in the House were frontiersmen.[28] By 1880 the Board had become so popular in the East and so unpopular in the West that certain representatives were willing to desert their party on the issue of the Board's continuance. Several factors account for the sectional attitude revealed in such votes. Westerners not only resented the appointment of Easterners to direct Indian affairs, but strongly objected to the practice of letting Indian contracts under Board auspices in Eastern centers.[29] Easterners, on the other hand, were as firmly convinced that the Board provided a necessary restraint on Western greed. This opinion proved decisive, as Democratic senators from the East saved the Board by their loyalty. Yet their argument, like that which later caused House Democrats to cease their attacks in 1882, instead of being a direct defense of the Board was a plea for preservation of an agency which would check Republican secretaries of the interior.[30] Both friend and foe considered the Board more important in its sectional and partisan aspects than as an agency for aiding the Indians.

Important as the support of Eastern Democrats proved in preserving the life of the Board, the battle against congressional criticism would have failed but for aid received from Interior Department officials. Secretary Schurz, who had become convinced of the Board's value following personal investigation in 1877, contributed to its continuance by denouncing the hostile attitude of his predecessors.[31] The Secretary's championship of the Board, it is true, failed to prevent the House Appropriation Committee from recommending the Board's abolition in 1881 as Representative Hawley had predicted,[32] but his defense of the organization was effectively employed in the debate. If Schurz had not abandoned the Department's customary opposition to the Board, civilian assistance in administering Indian affairs must certainly have ceased.

While the Board was fortunate to survive congressional attacks, victory was achieved only after its power for good had been destroyed. In 1880 the Senate successfully tricked the House into sanctioning a Board appropriation by burying the item in the Sundry Civil Appropriation Bill where it passed unnoticed by the chairman of the House Indian Committee. Repeal of the statute authorizing the Board was prevented the following year, however, only when the Senate agreed that no funds should be provided for its operation! This preposterous situation was rectified in 1882 when House Democrats supported the Board as a means of restricting the freedom of Republican secretaries of the interior, but appropriations were never to reach their former level.[33] Congressional opposition to the commissioners was abandoned only after the Board had been reduced to impotence by lack of authority and funds. Since the commissioners could accomplish little in winning the public support essential to successful Indian reform without adequate appropriations, other agencies arose to perform the task. As an agency for the promotion of Indian welfare, the Board of Indian Commissioners was now powerless.

The Board and Public Opinion

The declining influence of the Board of Indian Commissioners produced a corresponding decrease in the confidence with which the public regarded its members. Little criticism of the commissioners was heard during the first years, for they enjoyed the prestige of reformers without yet having had time to arouse opposition. Realizing the necessity of retaining popular support if they were to benefit the Indian, Board members carefully avoided antagonizing any interest. Caution was most necessary in cases involving nomination of Indian agents by the churches. The religious convictions of individual members, while often clear in private correspondence, were not allowed to affect the policy of the Board. Chairman Brunot, who placed Indian interests above church considerations on every occasion despite his personal hostility to Catholic claims, urged fellow members to be equally impartial.[34] Such prudence prevented the commissioners from taking sides on many important issues, but it did enable the Board to retain the friendship of groups which must otherwise have been alienated.

Public distrust of the Board assumed serious proportions only after the resignation of the original Board members in 1874. The dramatic nature of this action inevitably awakened suspicions concerning the independence of the new commissioners, which were not alleviated when Clinton B. Fisk, secretary-treasurer of the railroad running through Indian Territory, was chosen chairman of the new Board. This move alone was sufficient to convince many citizens that the new appointees were little more than tools of the Interior Department. When the first report of these men reversed the stand of their predecessors against territorial government for Indian Territory, all doubts regarding their independence were confirmed and no commissioners thereafter were able to secure even a small share of the support which the first Board had once enjoyed.[35]

The decline of faith in the Board was not the result of indifference toward the Indian problem. Interest in the tribes was increasing at the very time the Board's popularity began to diminish. Friends of the Indians criticized the commissioners as harshly as any other group. No compliment was intended when the Congregational missionary, A. L. Riggs, declared that passage of the Santee Sioux Bill of 1877 gave the commissioners "some reason for existence."[36] The New York *Herald*, while praising the decision of the House to continue the Board in 1882, confessed that the group had done little to meet public expectations.[37] All who sincerely sought an explanation for the Board's failure soon realized that its members had neither the time nor the means to popularize reform measures, that only men who were free from government dictation and able to devote their full energies to reform could be expected to make more than minor contributions to the cause of Indian advancement.

The efficiency of the Board of Indian Commissioners was not enhanced by the many personal feuds which marked its activities. John D. Lang, who claimed to have been in Indian work for over a quarter of a century, almost at once resented the prominence of Chairman Brunot and complained of his own "humble & peculiar position among wiser men." [38] His colleagues of the early days showed equal touchiness by refusing to invite General Howard and former Secretary of the Board Colyer to the 1874 meeting of the Board and churches, although their presence could only have embarrassed men who feared open discussion. [39] Personal relationships grew even more acrimonious when Chairman Fisk became the target of complaints following the appointment of the new commissioners in 1874. So restless were fellow members under Fisk's rule that one of the ablest wrote Secretary Schurz that resignation from an "offensive association" was necessary to preserve "an unblemished reputation," and another retired soon afterward charging that the Board was a Methodist "kitchen cabinet" with Fisk the "head center." [40] Popular respect might have been retained if Board members had united in championing reform; but with the commissioners more interested in airing personal grudges than in fighting for the Indian, there was no chance to secure the public support necessary for effective operation.

Yet even if there had been no personal animosities and public support had been overwhelming, the Board's work must have proved disappointing. Lasting reforms could never have been attained by a group organized for the purpose of inspection. Indian policy needed more than a mere overhauling; and if but for that reason alone, any agency resting on government support and limited by the necessity of demanding annual appropriations was certain to prove unsatisfactory. Independent action was essential. Just as in the case of church participation in Indian appointments, the failure of the commissioners was of more significance than their accomplishments. Only after the Board had demonstrated its inability to effect vital improvements did organizations appear which successfully roused the people to action.

While the Indian policies introduced between 1865 and 1880 were uniformly unsuccessful, the prospect for reform was definitely brighter because they had been attempted. Concentration, transfer, church nominations, and civilian advice had either failed to improve Indian relations or been rejected as unwise by 1880, but the collapse of each removed a serious obstacle to an intelligent consideration of future policy. Unrewarding as each experiment had proved, more people were interested in Indian affairs in 1880 than at any previous period of American history, and existing policies had been subjected to such devastating criticism that their replacement was now but a matter of time. The history of Indian policy following the Civil War can be fully understood, therefore, only if both the growth of public interest in Indian problems and the progress of attacks upon long-established administrative policies are examined (Parts II and III).

II. *The Rise of Interest in Indian Reform*

5. THE PERIOD OF INDIVIDUAL EFFORT, 1865-1880

While united states indian workers have always been forced to combat indifference toward questions involving the welfare of the red men, the problem of rousing interest was never so serious as during the years immediately following the Civil War. The struggle to free the slaves had so exhausted popular sympathies that there was little opportunity for other reforms to attract attention. The average American of 1865 felt that serious post-war problems must be settled before energy was spent on new reforms. As a result, men attempting to aid American Indians found the public unusually apathetic.[1] Interest in the tribes was stirred only after many workers had toiled for over a decade to convince the country of its responsibility to the "first citizens" of the nation.

In spite of the lack of interest in altruistic ventures which existed following 1865, the labor of Indian reformers would have been much simpler if public indifference had not been aggravated by a remarkable lack of knowledge concerning the red man. The average American of the time either knew nothing of tribal conditions or was badly misinformed. Public opinion was so shaped by propaganda that accurate descriptions of the Indians were widely condemned as sentimental or prejudiced.[2] With ignorance prevailing, the public was easily swayed for years by men whose interests were served by misrepresentation. Only as the more important newspapers appointed special correspondents to cover Indian news and such magazines as *The Republic* and *Harper's* solicited official information before publishing articles did discussions of the Indian question reveal an understanding of the problem;[3] and for some time thereafter public tastes caused the press to feature minor revolts while printing accounts of tribal progress toward civilization in inconspicuous positions. The task of Indian workers was one of education as well as publicity.

The difficulties besetting Indian reformers following 1865 produced a pessimism which only increased their work. Public enthusiasm over the possibilities of Indian advancement could hardly be expected as long as the friends of the race were themselves discouraged. Yet few champions of reform had faith that their efforts would succeed. An author of 1864, who condemned the public for questioning the possibility of successful reform only to confess that he himself was writing without hope, was typical of most fellow reformers of the following decade.[4] Until workers displayed more confidence in the future and were prepared to face the many disappointments of Indian work, little progress was possible.

The task of arousing interest in Indian affairs would have been considerably easier if the Negro and Indian problems had been connected in the popular mind. While the former slaves were generally better qualified to share responsibilities with other Americans, both races faced the problem of adjusting themselves to white society. A common effort to prepare both minority elements for the obligations of civilized life might well have been undertaken. When Congress conferred citizenship on the Negroes in 1866, however, any mention of the Indians was omitted.[5] Many Americans argued that the Indians were included by implication, but the absence of specific reference to the race prevented reformers from treating the Negro and Indian problems as a unit. The campaign for Indian advancement had to be conducted as if nothing had been accomplished for the Negro.

The Leading Indian Reformers

The necessity of pursuing an independent campaign forced Indian reformers to start modestly. Unable to employ either the public opinion or the organizations created by friends of the Negro, champions of the red men turned to building sentiments and organizations of their own. The cause of Indian reform, like all similar movements, was originally sponsored by individuals. A few of the workers entered the campaign fresh from labors for the Negro. Lydia Maria Child added a highly emotional pamphlet hailing the report of the 1867 Peace Commission to her long list of successful publications attacking slavery; Mrs. Stowe, the author of *Uncle Tom's Cabin*, headed the list of twenty-one vice-presidents of the Connecticut Indian Association in the eighties; and John Greenleaf Whittier wrote a few articles.[6] But outside of Wendell Phillips, who took an active part in the movement until his death in 1884, the anti-slavery leaders participating in the new crusade exerted an influence through the magic of their names rather than as authors or organizers.[7] The real work was performed by younger men and women, who finding a new cause for enthusiasm concentrated their efforts upon Indian work alone.

The individual nature of contributions to the Indian cause from 1865 to 1880 makes a complete study of the progress of reform impossible. Fortunately, valuable information exists regarding the work of three prominent reformers, each representative of the Indian movement of this period at different stages of its development. Yet emphasis upon the labors of Father Beeson, Alfred B. Meacham, and Helen Hunt Jackson should not obscure the fact that they were merely the foremost exponents of types of reform employed by numerous other Americans. The Indian cause progressed not only because of the labor of the three individuals whose significance will be discussed, but also because of the toil of many lesser workers whose local efforts, while insignificant in themselves, were extremely effective in the aggregate.

The earliest phases of reform movements are seldom free from fanaticism. The greatest accomplishments of mankind have often resulted from the success of ideas originally advanced by ignorant zealots who, failing to comprehend the difficulties in their path, refused to turn aside. Such a man was Father Beeson, whose misspelled letters scattered through the Indian Bureau files reveal him as the first prominent Indian reformer following the Civil War. From the time he was forced to leave Oregon for sympathizing with local Indians in the 1850's until his final request for government assistance was rejected in 1879, Beeson refused to be discouraged by obstacles. Neither the refusal of government officials to support his work nor the public "appathy" of which he frequently complained caused him to abandon his efforts. Rejection of a proposal for return to Oregon only led him to petition Congress for permission to visit all the Indian tribes so that he might discover a means of avoiding wars. Rebuffed in this request, he hurried to write President Hayes that failure to support his efforts was "a national disgrace." Yet vain as he was, Beeson was also energetic enough to persist not only in his demands upon the government but in his work for the Indian. Basing his efforts on a compassion for all oppressed people, which even the self-seeking purpose of his letters to the government could not obscure, he made a record which established him as the outstanding representative of the 'fanatic fringe' of Indian reform. Later reformers were less eccentric, but they profited from the work of men who had championed the tribes with zeal if not with understanding in days when Indian work demanded great sacrifices.[8]

Agitation for better treatment of the Indian took a more practical course with the efforts of Alfred B. Meacham following 1873. Dismissed as incompetent during his early days in the Indian service,[9] Meacham capitalized upon the good fortune which enabled him to survive an Indian massacre. One of three commissioners appointed to deal with chiefs of the Modoc Indians of California following their war with the United States in 1873, Meacham was left for dead when the tribe attacked the commissioners during peace negotiations.[10] When he finally recovered from his injuries, no man was in a better position to make sensational attacks on the Indians. Instead, Meacham toured the country for almost two years exposing his scars and demanding justice for the race. The spectacle of a victim of Indian revenge condemning white injustice was a dramatic presentation of the need for reform. Many people who would not otherwise have become interested in Indian affairs attended Meacham's lectures, and many others who could not hear him in person read his account of Modoc troubles in books which became models for a just presentation of tribal difficulties. Meacham's greatest contribution to the cause, however, was the establishment of the *Council Fire* in 1878. This magazine, although never sufficiently successful to enable the editor's family to join him in Washington, was an invaluable inspiration to Indian workers for over ten years. Later pages will reveal the great extent of its contribution to the discussion of Indian reforms. Such a beneficial influence already had been exerted through its columns when

60

The Period of Individual Effort, 1865-1880

Meacham died at his desk in 1881 that Secretary Schurz declared him the most faithful and generous friend the Indians had ever had.[11] No better evidence of Meacham's services exists than the bitter comment of Westerners when the reformer successfully prevented the Ute Commission of 1880 from being used as an agency for robbing the Indians. To the Dolores (Col.) News, Meacham was "a coward by nature, a thief by instinct, a hypocrite by choice";[12] to the friends of the Indian, he was a man who had taken advantage of an event which might have embittered his life to work for the welfare of an unfortunate race. His work as editor, author, lecturer, and public servant established him as the leading champion of the Indian from 1875 to 1881. His only superior as a propagandist was the woman who soon after his death became the Harriet Beecher Stowe of the Indian cause.

Mrs. Helen Hunt Jackson was the last and most influential of the individual reformers. An able writer already known for her prose and poetry, she was deeply stirred during the late seventies by accounts of the unjust treatment of American Indians.[13] In tracing the origin of contemporary disputes in government records, she was shocked to find that existing problems were only the outgrowth of many years of abuse. She resolved as a result of her studies to devote her efforts to demanding reform through publication of a history of the most disgraceful episodes. The product, A Century of Dishonor, immediately became the classic of the Indian movement with its publication in 1881. The bias of the author was too obvious to deceive even the dullest reader; but the unqualified tone of indignation, the careful choice of the most despicable events and the omission of any explanation of the white man's case only made the book more effective for the purpose of propaganda.[14] A balanced account of American Indian history would have attracted little attention. Mrs. Jackson's outspoken indictment was widely read and aroused much interest in Indian problems. Even greater in emotional appeal was Mrs. Jackson's novel on the sufferings of California Indians. In A Century of Dishonor, the author had been forced to follow government records; in Ramona, the novel which appeared in 1884, she was free to adapt the material to her purpose. There were few Americans who were not familiar with one or the

61

other. Although publication of letters criticizing Secretary Schurz in *A Century of Dishonor* handicapped the efforts of a sincere friend of the Indian, the books described the sufferings of the race so effectively that ultimate revision of government policies in the red man's interest no longer seemed impossible. They were the last important contributions of an individual to the cause of Indian reform, for Mrs. Jackson had presented the case against the government so completely that later reformers could only repeat what she had said or join with others in seeking ways by which past evils might be rectified. The accomplishments of the next few years were those of organized groups rather than of individuals.

The increase of interest in the Indian between 1865 and 1880 led many people to participate in the work who were unable to devote as much time to the cause as the better known reformers or who were more largely concerned with exerting individual pressure than in arousing others. Many churchmen followed the lead of Bishop Whipple of Montana in combining work for the Indian with public and private appeals for legislative reform. Similar service was rendered by philanthropists, whose most typical representative was William Welsh. Occasional lecturing and presentation of plans also appealed to more humble citizens. Thus an instructor of Williston Seminary in Massachusetts asked the Indian Bureau for information which would enable him to expand upon informal talks which he had been accustomed to give for several years before small audiences as opportunity offered.[15] A similar request from a Wisconsin college professor showed that this desire for accurate material upon the Indian question was shared by some Westerners.[16] But the average citizen writing the Bureau was more apt to tell the government what should be done than to request information. The growing interest in the Indian question, which the individual reformers had aroused, was best reflected in the numerous suggestions for a change of policy received by Indian administrators during the seventies.

Individual Plans for Solving the Indian Problem

Examination of the extraordinary flood of proposals for settling Indian problems which swamped the Indian Bureau from 1870 to 1880 offers convincing evidence of the genius and imagination of a people who never seemed to be at a loss for a new idea. The suggestions were often valueless, but their outstanding characteristic was their remarkable variety. Innumerable citizens plainly agreed with the correspondent who wrote that he could not see why his opinion should not be as good as that of any other person.[17] "Each speaker and writer has a theory of his own, much wiser in his eyes than that of any other," declared the Washington *Daily Chronicle* of the Indian question in 1873, a truth which became only too clear to Indian officials as the number of proposals in their files constantly mounted.[18] While determination of the best manner of dealing with the Indian proved extremely difficult, the government could not complain that suggestions were lacking.

Since dissatisfaction with contemporary policies inspired most of the letters to the government, a large majority of the proposals urged radical changes. There was little agreement, however, regarding the nature of the necessary adjustments. While many reformers condemned the current administration of Indian affairs, recommendations varied from plans for abolition of the Indian Bureau to schemes for improved methods of regulation.[19] Many individuals believed that changes introducing an added amount of self-government on Indian reservations would be of great help in preparing the tribes for future responsibilities. Theodore A. Bland, who succeeded Meacham as editor of the *Council Fire*, even suggested that tribes be allowed to vote annually for or against retaining their existing agent.[20] Although few persons were willing to extend Indian power so rapidly, many equally radical proposals were offered for application within the existing administrative structure.

Interest in the Indians was not the sole inspiration for proposed changes in government policy. Ingenious devices for combining Indian advancement with personal profit showed that many citizens hoped to benefit from their philanthropy. Thus William Manning of Hays City, Kansas, who recommended the establishment of an experimental farm, not only announced that Hays City offered the best location, but expressed a desire to be placed in charge of the plan himself.[21] Similar interest in securing a government post led O. N. Wozencraft of Jacksonville, Florida, to apply several times for permission to undertake private negotiations with the Indians under a conviction that he possessed an extraordinary capacity for pacifying hostile tribes.[22] Although such selfish suggestions were not adopted, a wool salesman successfully convinced the Indian Bureau that Indians should be taught to support themselves by the use of hand looms. In blaming the ultimate failure of this plan upon the hostility of Indian administrators, its originator was undoubtedly correct, for only the Army succeeded in mixing selfishness and philanthropy with equal facility.[23] The persistent plea of Colonel Ihrie and other retired officers who pestered Secretary Schurz for Indian appointments during the latter's term as Secretary of the Interior arose, like the transfer struggle itself, as much from a hope of individual profit as from interest in Indian advancement.[24] Yet the fact that the tribes were considered at all in such schemes was only further evidence of the growing concern over Indian affairs.

When selfish motives did not distort the perspective of correspondents who recommended changes, the results were especially noteworthy. A few of the most striking proposals will give an impression of the remainder. As a means of educating the Indian America's commissioner to the Paris Exposition of 1878 urged Secretary Schurz to offer transportation expenses to all German immigrants who would agree to train two Indian apprentices upon arrival.[25] Equally novel was a proposal to solve the Negro and Indian problems simultaneously by sending ex-slaves to instruct the tribes.[26] Similar ingenuity was revealed in suggestions for preventing inter-racial conflict, of which the most popular urged the use of islands as reservations.[27] If the desirability of isolation was accepted, no one could dispute the wisdom of the Georgia banker who endeavored to sell the government a coastal island by writing:

To put them on a reservation is simply preparing for another war with them. They cant be kept *on* it, & whites cant be kept *off* it. But if they were brought to the East & put on an island on the Atlantic coast, all earthly hope of getting back through the country to their mountains wd be lost, the power of the whites wd impress them, as it can in no other way, & on such an island, in a mild climate, and with abundant game & fish, & fertile lands to cultivate if necessary, they wd be more easily become reconciled to the inevitable, & submit to learn the ways of civilization. Their supplies of all kinds could be furnished them much more cheaply & with fewer opportunities for accusations of fraud against Agents. More liberty could be allowed them than when confined in the forts in Florida, & a very small force, if indeed any at all, wd be needed to watch them.[28]

Even greater advantages might have been gained, however, from another plan which with a little co-operation from Mexico might have gratified expansionists and ended the Indian problem at the same time! In presenting this masterpiece, the author explained:

Look at a map of N. America. You see that only a few miles South of San Diego, Cal is the north line of the Mexican Territory of Lower Cal. I assume that a small sum of money would buy that Territory; and that Uncle Sam will buy it if you ask him. The acquisition of Territory almost anyhow is almost always popular with his boys. The Territory being acquired, a Roman or Chinese or some better kind of wall could be build across the peninsula from Gulf to Ocean, say in the neighborhood of 29° N. Lat., and then all South of the wall, or as much of it as might be deemed proper, could be given to the wards of your Indian Dep't. with a fair prospect of their being allowed to remain in undisturbed possession for a generation or two.[29]

As long as Americans were able to conceive such varied remedies, ultimate discovery of a satisfactory Indian policy did not seem impossible.

Yet the very number of the suggestions offered the government complicated the search for a solution of the Indian problem. Until individual reformers stopped insisting upon promoting projects of their own to the exclusion of the proposals of others, little could be accomplished. The growing interest in Indian affairs could be utilized only when organizations arose to weld the best features of many plans into a unified program. Without the excitement caused by a series of events during 1880, agreement would have been impossible for some time. As it was, in a single year several unusual incidents combined to produce a sudden transition from the period of individual effort to that of effective organization.

6. THE TURN OF THE
TIDE—1880

THE YEAR 1880 WAS A TURNING POINT IN THE HISTORY OF AMERI-
can Indian relations. Public sentiment, long unmoved by the sufferings of the red men, suddenly became alert to the need for tolerance and justice in handling the Indian problem. When the
Modoc Indians attacked the peace commissioners in 1873, only a
few voices were raised in the tribe's defense. Father Beeson, a
majority of the Board of Indian Commissioners, and a few Indian
workers urged leniency, but an overwhelming majority of Americans
demanded relentless punishment. The press, with few exceptions, supported the desire for vengeance and reported the subsequent hanging of the guilty Indians with obvious relish. Only the
New York *Times* pointed out that a United States officer had
treated the Modocs very similarly a few years earlier and advised
that humanity was as necessary as firmness in solving the Indian
problem.[1] Yet when the White River Utes of Colorado killed the
agent and male employees on their reservation in 1880, only local
residents demanded war. The government, it is true, forced reforms upon the Indians during negotiations following the outbreak;
but the fact that the women on the reservation had been ravished
was purposely suppressed.[2] Thus the desire of the public for peace
was fulfilled and a disturbance, which would have caused a cry for
revenge seven years earlier, was settled without further loss of
life.

The revolution in public opinion which enabled peaceful settlement of the Ute outbreak was aroused by three abuses, long characteristic of the United States Indian relations. Fraud, invasion of
Indian land, and disastrous removals had failed to stir public attention for many years, but by 1880 sufficient interest was at last
aroused to cause alarm over such evils. The difficulties of Secretary
of the Interior Schurz with government corruptionists, the threatened invasion of Indian Territory, and the tragic removal of the

The Turn of the Tide—1880

Ponca Indians were only the most recent instances of injustice. They assumed importance in the history of Indian relations because they occurred at a moment when Indian reformers had succeeded in awaking the public to the need for change. Over ten years of effort by individual workers thus bore fruit at last in public pressure for improved treatment of the Indian.

Indian Frauds

The frauds which prompted public resentment during 1880 were merely the latest manifestations of practices which had been prevalent since the Civil War. Many of the scandals for which President Grant's administration was notorious involved the Indian service. Less than a year after the President's inauguration, Indian Commissioner Parker was summoned before the House Appropriation Committee to answer charges that he had neglected to advertise the letting of contracts. While the Committee announced that "no evidence of any pecuniary or personal advantage" was found, it also decided that the Commissioner's record revealed "irregularities, neglect, and incompetency, and, in some instances, a departure from the exact provisions of law." [3] Such a rebuke soon led Parker to resign and the House temporarily turned its attention to studying the frauds perpetrated against the Five Civilized Tribes of Indian Territory by private attorneys.[4] But after the highly-respected economist, Francis A. Walker, resigned as Indian Commissioner in 1873 to accept a Yale professorship, criticism of the government was renewed. The new commissioner, Edward P. Smith, was at first exonerated by a special investigating committee of charges accusing him of concluding a corrupt lumber contract while Chippewa agent, but he decided to surrender his office when the House Committee of Indian Affairs revealed evidence of a lax accounting for Indian funds.[5] His successor, John Q. Smith, managed to survive Grant's second term only because he was not directly connected with the issue of rotten beef and rancid flour to the Red Cloud Sioux in 1875. As it was, an Indian agent was dismissed, four contracting companies were blacklisted and the Commissioner was criticized for carelessness as the result of an investigation forced by the charges of Professor Marsh, a Yale geologist.[6] Yet these continual revelations did not disturb the public. Even knowledge that Secretary of War Belknap had let Indian tradeships to the highest bidders aroused only momentary criticism.[7] Until President-elect Hayes announced the appointment of Carl Schurz as Secretary of the Interior in 1877, no positive action was taken to check the spread of crimes against the American Indians.

In attempting to reform the Indian service, Secretary Schurz undertook an extremely difficult task. Government officials had long been accustomed to disregard misuse of the millions appropriated annually for supplying the Indians. Poorly-paid agents were entrusted with large sums of money and little concern was expressed when they resigned after a short period with full pockets.[8] There was no obligation to be particularly scrupulous, Americans reasoned, in matters involving a race which was fortunate to receive any assistance from the government. Schurz encountered powerful resistance, therefore, whenever he attempted to prevent fraud. When he insisted that all goods delivered to reservations should be weighed, contractors objected that such a practice had not been previously required![9] But even after supplies were carefully weighed, corrupt dealers either reduced the quality of their goods or tampered with the scales.[10] A costly system of inspection alone could prevent diversion of a large proportion of Indian funds into the hands of Indian contractors and agents. Until incorruptible officials paid close attention to all details of the service, there was little possibility that United States Indian administration would be distinguished for its justice.

In spite of the opposition of many subordinates, Secretary Schurz decided to reform the Indian service at once. Replacement of existing officials with men of his own choice was the first requisite. Commissioner John Q. Smith, who lacked the confidence of reformers, consented to resign. More difficulty was encountered in disposing of Chief Clerk Galpin, whose supporters included former Commissioner Walker and President Seelye of Amherst College. Asked early in 1877 whether he would retain his position, Galpin had replied, "If the dam dutch secretary don't give it to some dam dutchman I think I will be able to remain." [11] The "dam dutch secretary," who had had no intention of keeping his disrespectful subordinate before he learned of this comment, sped new investigations which led to the clerk's dismissal. While this action was necessary to obtain harmony, and while Schurz was able to prove that Commissioner J. Q. Smith had contemplated Galpin's removal, ex-Commissioner Walker was prevented from a public protest only through the intervention of former Secretary of the Interior Cox, and President Seelye announced that the Secretary was fond of theatrical attitudes and sensational effects but had none of the stuff out of which reformers were made. [12] Popular as Galpin's dismissal proved with Schurz's friends, there was wisdom in Seelye's warning that the reliability of Galpin's critics should be carefully investigated. Schurz, in common with other secretaries of the interior, received much evidence concerning fraud from private citizens, but in most instances his correspondents were either jealous contractors or individuals who hoped to be rewarded by being appointed to the service. [13] The Secretary could not rely on men of this calibre, one of whom actually regarded his defiance of a presidential order against trespassing as a leading qualification in applying for an Indian inspectorship. [14] If the Indian service was to be improved, men had to be found who would report abuses even though they did not hope to profit from their revelations. The reform program could succeed only if all responsible positions were filled by men of unquestionable integrity.

Since any improvement in Indian relations depended upon selection of an honest Indian commissioner, Schurz was unusually careful in searching for the right man. His first choice was William Welsh, the leading Indian reformer of the day; and although Welsh refused to accept the position, he consented to visit New York to investigate the advisability of appointing Edward A. Hayt, former member of the Board of Indian Commissioners. As Welsh reported that the presidents of two large banks had indorsed Hayt after thorough inquiry, and as he added that corrupt contractors were resisting the appointment, Schurz decided that Hayt would prove satisfactory. [15] Yet despite the care expended upon his selection, the new Commissioner did not even possess the confidence of his former colleagues on the Board. "Mr. Hayt will be an honest Comssr. not more so than his predecessors the Smiths," Secretary Whittlesey of the Board wrote a fellow member on learning of the choice.[16] But if such suspicions reached Schurz, they failed to shake his resolution to give his appointee uncompromising support.

Commissioner Hayt at once encountered serious resistance to his program for reforming the Indian service in spite of the aid of Secretary Schurz. So many officials were dismissed following his appointment that even friends of the Indian were alarmed.[17] But while Hayt admitted that good agents frequently suffered, he refused to retain any agent in whom he did not have the fullest confidence.[18] With one dismissal following another in rapid succession, charges of personal prejudice in removing agents and examining accounts became every day matters.[19] Chief Clerk Leeds, who resigned following disagreements with the Commissioner, informed a Senate Committee that Hayt had proved "a positive obstruction to business" and that efforts to arouse him to his responsibilities had "no more effect than a drop of water on a hot stove." [20] Privately, Leeds supplied Chairman Fisk of the Board of Indian Commissioners with a long list of charges which led that group to attack Hayt and which belied a letter to Secretary Schurz denying participation in efforts to remove the Commissioner.[21] Even when Hayt's enemies secured his indictment for misrepresenting the assets of his Jersey City bank, Secretary Schurz defended his Commissioner because of evidence that opponents of the administration's Indian policy had prior information regarding the suit.[22] Unless definite proof of incompetence was presented, the Secretary was determined to support the man upon whose shoulders he had placed the burden of improving the Indian service.

In spite of their elaborate schemes to force the Commissioner's dismissal, Hayt's opponents would have failed if he had not committed a grave personal blunder. Secretary Schurz resolutely refused to credit the charges against his appointee, announcing that no one who wished to cheat the Indians was in the Interior Department.[23] Yet seven days after he had made this statement, the Secretary requested Hayt's resignation! Enemies of the Commissioner had uncovered evidence that he had authorized his son to purchase a silver mine at a reduced rate in return for the with-drawal of charges against an Arizona agent![24] Informed of this arrangement on January 29, 1880, and receiving no denials from the embarrassed Commissioner, Schurz's only recourse was to dismiss the man in whom he had had the utmost confidence.

The shock of Hayt's removal did much to arouse the country to the need for Indian reform. The failure of such a well-known reformer as Schurz to check corruption attracted national attention. The occasion was heartily seized by enemies of the Secretary as an opportunity for censure. A Choctaw attorney claimed that Schurz had not exposed Hayt's incompetence for fear that the Commissioner might retaliate by revealing information regarding the Secretary's participation in disreputable Saint Louis contracts.[25] Less extreme critics charged Schurz with unreasonable infatuation for a dishonest man, while others reverted to familiar attacks on his German origins.[26] Yet in spite of the abuse which the Secretary suffered, the cause of Indian reform benefited from his difficulties. The Hayt scandal sensationally disclosed the evils of a system under which fraudulent transactions could be easily hidden, and, whether praising or attacking the Secretary, newspapers demanded that increasing caution be taken to avoid further offenses. Schurz did not need to be warned; and he now had the aid of many people in searching for a new commissioner. No less a personage than Senator Edmunds of Vermont wrote that he desired the nomination because he did not want removal to become customary and felt that the appointment of the most prominent candidate would be a mistake![27] Although President Hayes sped the choice of a new commissioner,[28] the Secretary decided to keep a close personal watch over Indian affairs. The illness of the new appointee enabled Schurz to follow the advice of friends who urged him to maintain close ties with the Indian Bureau.[29] He devoted much attention to Indian affairs until his administration ended in 1881, and even tried to play a part in the training of a new commissioner and the selection of his own successor.[30] Schurz's first effort to improve the Indian service came to a disastrous end; but the very gravity of his plight played a large part in rousing the powerful national sympathy for the red man which led to the establishment of better Indian relations during the decade of the eighties.

Trespassing

The second development of 1880 which strengthened the demand for reform was the dramatic effort of settlers to enter the Indian Territory between Kansas and Texas in defiance of the government. No method of robbing Indians angered reformers more than invasion of tribal reservations. Yet frontiersmen settled upon Indian land so frequently that by 1879 there was hardly a reservation which had not been subject to white encroachment.[31] As the country expanded, pressure for land led to increased disregard for tribal rights. Officials often noticed that establishment of Indian titles only added to the desirability of land, many frontiersmen preferring the ruggedest flint hill of the Cherokee or Sioux to the greenest areas open to homesteaders.[32] From every section of the nation, citizens wrote requesting permission to enter Indian reservations. The postmaster of Tiff City, Missouri, declared that it was hard for Americans to be ordered from any portion of the country "by Indians." Twelve Southerners headed by a "late sentor of Lousana" prayed for the privilege of settling in areas set aside for red men. Two women applied for Indian husbands so that they might secure land.[33] As many others realized the futility of consulting the government on such matters and threatened to invade reservations without asking permission once protection from Washington was relaxed, constant vigilance was necessary to prevent pressure on Indian land from getting out of hand.

While the United States often resisted attempts to force admission to reservations, there was occasionally evidence that invasion of Indian land was tolerated if not actually encouraged. Congressmen resented General Pope's implication that Indians could not expect their rights to be protected; and yet at the same time they carefully upheld the rights of citizens who settled on reservations which had not been officially opened. Not only were premature settlers on Osage and Cherokee lands energetically supported; but a law was passed in 1876 which actually provided that because of a grasshopper plague pre-emptors on Indian reservations might leave their lands without hurting their potential claims! When Senator Morrill tried to secure a statute making willful squatters guilty of misdemeanor and liable to fine and imprisonment, Western senators succeeded in tabling the measure by a vote of 20-18.[34] But it was in the case of the Black Hills that the government's inability to prevent settlement was most clearly revealed. News that a government exploring party had discovered gold caused an immediate rush to enter this portion of the Sioux reservation in 1874. After a few futile attempts to halt the invasion, officials decided that the Indians must surrender the area. Efforts to purchase the land failing because the Indians regarded the price offered as too low, war resulted. Once hostilities had begun, the cause of the Indians was entirely deserted, and by 1876 all Indians who opposed the cession had either been driven from the country or forced to sanction a treaty surrendering the Hills in order to secure the renewal of ration issues discontinued during the crisis.[35] Although Indian officials defended the justice of this war at length, President Grant admitted that fear of Army desertions had forced the government to allow the consummation of a robbery.[36] Certainly Senator Paddock's statement that Americans could not be restrained when opportunities were presented for advancing their fortunes was a confession of government weakness.[37] But whether the victory of the Black Hills trespassers was achieved in spite of, or because of, the government, most citizens were convinced that the invasion could have been stopped if the administration had desired. The public now felt certain that whenever popular pressure for expansion became sufficiently strong other reservations would be opened.

The strength of the government's determination to prevent further trespassing was soon to be tested, for frontiersmen had long expressed a desire to settle upon the Indian lands south of Kansas. Although the Indian Bureau had surrendered to pressure in some localities, the future of the reservation system depended upon preservation of the Indian Territory. As much as invasion of Indian rights in other sections of the country might be regretted, the strength of the treaties promising protection and the large number of Indians in the Territory centered the interests of the country and the efforts of the government in that area. Attempts to speed white admission by establishing a territorial government were discussed annually in Congress during the early seventies. Although sponsors of the proposal frequently denied any ulterior purpose, the Indians and their friends insisted that territorial government was intended as an entering wedge for more fundamental changes.[38] Their resistance was successful. By speaking a minute with Grant, Secretary Cree of the Board of Indian Commissioners convinced the President that invasion of the territory should be condemned in his annual message of 1872.[39] Board members welcomed this action as decisive and endeavored to hide their connection with its inclusion.[40] Such discretion proved wise for after the most comprehensive bill for establishing a territorial government was tabled by a vote of 95-43 following a long debate in the House in 1873, the Indian Territory issue did not again become serious until 1879.[41] While Senator Schurz introduced a territorial bill by request in 1874, and the newly-appointed Board of Indian Commissioners reversed the stand of its predecessor against such measures,[42] all efforts to open the Territory by indirection were easily defeated.

Revival of concern over invasion of the Indian Territory in 1879 was due to the activities of men known as the Oklahoma Boomers. When Elias C. Boudinot, a Cherokee citizen, announced in the *Chicago Times* of February 17, 1879, that thirteen million acres of the Territory were available for settlement, C. C. Carpenter, a leader of the Black Hills invasion, at once began to organize groups for immigration. In spite of protests from the Indian Office, these plans progressed; and even President Hayes's proclamation of April 26 against invasion failed to check the movement.[43] Although a show of force temporarily prevented most immigrants from crossing into the Territory, Boomers began to enter in such large numbers under the leadership of Captain David L. Payne in 1880 that the President's proclamation was reissued.[44] Taking advantage of a law which provided expulsion and fines but not imprisonment for intruders, Payne and his followers pressed into the Territory at every opportunity. As Congress refused to amend the laws despite insistent appeals from administrative officers and as the invaders were penniless, courts could only release those who had been expelled to undertake another invasion.[45] Invasions of the Territory occurred so frequently under these circumstances that the affair soon grew into a series of processions to and from the Kansas border. Payne hoped that this persistent defiance of the government would arouse a popular demand for opening the Territory. Instead, his efforts to enter by force aroused a strong feeling that settlement should be allowed only after adequate provision had been made for protecting Indian interests.[46]

The hostility aroused by invasion of the Indian Territory was an important factor in the renewal of interest in Indian problems. Both the Women's National Indian Association and the Indian Rights Association were founded to protest violation of treaties with Indian Territory tribes.[47] The use of force was so generally deplored that murder of trespassers was frequently justified and one Schurz correspondent recommended establishment of a death penalty for all invaders.[48] Criticism of the Boomers was not confined to the East. Professor Buck undoubtedly exaggerates the opposition to territorial invasion when he says that "The Boomers roused the hostility of the whole Middle West"; but Professor Gittinger would seem equally at error in declaring that "On the whole, public opinion in the Middle West ran strongly in favor of the Boomers." [49] Large numbers of Westerners opposed the Boomers not only because of hostility to force, but because many feared that the invaders intended to monopolize the Territory.[50] As even the Boomers themselves finally realized, more could be gained by diplomacy than by coercion. The invaders, while unsuccessful in their immediate aim, contributed to a solution of the Indian problem by stimulating an interest in the question which inspired a thorough reconsideration of the relations of Indians and white men during the eighties. The Kansas City convention of 1888, which resolved to institute efforts to open the Territory "properly respectful of the rights and interests of the Indians," marked a conviction that the welfare of both Indians and whites could be harmonized.[51] Passage of a satisfactory bill for opening the Oklahoma district of the Territory just two days before the end of Cleveland's term in 1889 was a victory for those who had united in the critical days of 1880 to demand justice for the red man.

Uncle Sam's Stepchildren

The Ponca Removal and Its Aftermath

The third incident which encouraged the rise of an effective Indian movement following 1880 was the excitement aroused by complications resulting from the disastrous removal of the Ponca Indians in 1877. The Poncas were a small tribe which had peacefully occupied a reservation in the southeastern corner of Dakota for many years. Their right to the land was undisputed until the area was included by oversight in an 1868 grant to the Sioux. Although the Ponca claim was superior, the Sioux refused to return the land and frequently raided the Poncas's homes and fields. The situation became so serious by 1877 that the government realized peace would be impossible unless the Poncas were moved or the hostile Sioux were forced to surrender their rights. As the government hesitated to risk war by exerting pressure on the Sioux, negotiations were initiated for removal of the Poncas to Indian Territory. This proposal was resisted by the tribe, but its leaders finally agreed to sanction settlement in the Territory if a delegation found suitable land. This condition seemed a sufficient protection of their rights. But when a majority of those who inspected Indian Territory locations continued to oppose removal, the government decided to force the change. The threat of coercion was alone sufficient, even the most irreconcilable opponents of removal agreeing to leave once they learned that troops had been ordered to their reservation. Unfortunately the troubles of the tribe had only begun. Such severe weather was encountered during the journey to the Territory that many died of exposure. Yet the difficulties on the road only multiplied upon arrival, for the failure of the government to prepare for reception of the tribe and the effects of the change of climate resulted in heavy mortality among the already weakened Indians. As Secretary Schurz admitted in a report concerning the removal, the tribe had been "grievously wronged" from start to finish. But outside of this official expression of regret, there was no indication that anyone had been more disturbed by the sufferings of the Poncas than by those of any previous tribe. Like many similar catastrophes, the Ponca removal promised soon to be forgotten even by the few who had been aware of the wrongdoing.[52]

The sufferings of the Poncas would not have stirred national interest, if their troubles had ended with removal to the Territory. The members of the tribe constantly begged for permission to return to their former homes, but were told to make the best of their new surroundings. When it finally became clear that the government would not consent to a change of location, a band of thirty-five led by Chief Standing Bear, escaped from the Territory. Although pursued by government troops under instructions to force their return, this group reached Nebraska early in 1879. Their dramatic flight had attracted such widespread attention to the Ponca cause that the whole country was unusually interested when T. H. Tibbles, an Omaha newspaperman, decided to prevent the return of Standing Bear and his followers to the Indian Territory by securing a writ of habeas corpus for Standing Bear. The principle to be decided in the case was of vital importance to the country and the Indians. If the courts accepted Tibbles's argument that Indians who deserted their tribes were free from governmental interference, federal control over the tribes would be at an end and any red man who left his reservation would be protected from efforts to return him to his people. There was much excitement, therefore, when Judge Dundy of the Federal District Court upheld the writ and forbade Standing Bear's return.[53] Reformers were determined that the principle must be established on a national basis by a Supreme Court decision upholding Dundy's verdict. Government officials were equally insistent that the question must be withheld from further judicial consideration. The result was a severe battle between champions of the Poncas and Indian administrators which did much to arouse interest in the cause of all Indians.

While the dispute between government officials and reformers over the Standing Bear decision ultimately advanced Indian welfare, the immediate result was a serious division in the ranks of Indian friends. Unable to agree whether Indians were ready to forego government direction, Secretary Schurz and a group of Boston reformers indulged in a long and acrimonious debate which prevented co-operation in meeting Indian difficulties. No section of the country was more aroused by Tibbles's plea for the Poncas than eastern Massachusetts. Always peculiarly susceptible to the agitation of reformers, Boston merchants and philanthropists were easily convinced that all Indians should be freed from government control. To facilitate this end, the Boston Indian Citizenship Association was formed by leading residents of the city. The group possessed a worthy opponent in the Secretary. In public letters to Governor Long of Massachusetts, Edward Atkinson, and Mrs. Jackson, Schurz explained that progress must be gradual, that sudden changes would only expose Indians to further robbery, and that government protection was too valuable an asset to be cast aside lightly.[54] With this presentation, most thoughtful reformers were inclined to agree. Meacham effectively supported the Secretary in the *Council Fire*; and Barstow of the Board of Indian Commissioners reported to a fellow member that Tibbles, who had served as Pullman car conductor, lawyer, minister, and reporter, and who was to be the Populist candidate for vice-president in 1904, was in the Ponca movement as a means of support.[55] But while personal contact with Tibbles and his Indian wife, Bright Eyes, caused Mrs. Jackson to doubt their veracity and led Senator Dawes of Massachusetts to urge that they would aid the cause of the Poncas by remaining away from Washington,[56] none of the Boston reformers relented in their criticism of Secretary Schurz. For some time all progress was checked by tactless personal abuse of a man who was equally anxious to aid the Indians.

Secretary Schurz was the target of criticism by Boston reformers from the start of the Ponca dispute in 1879 until the end of his term in March, 1881. Secretary Lincoln of the Boston Indian Citizenship Association regarded Schurz's influence upon newspaper opinion as "Mephistophilian"; an ex-agent wrote Senator Dawes that there had "never been so much ignorance and imbecility and downright dogged obstinacy in the Interior Department since its creation"; and Mrs. Jackson remarked that the Secretary was both audacious and stupid.[57] When President Hayes supported his Secretary, Lincoln exulted that his "reign" would soon be over.[58] When the chiefs of the Poncas finally announced that the tribe wished to remain in the Indian Territory, he accused Schurz of bribery.[59] Although few people were equally critical, many felt with Mrs. Jackson that there had been "a trick somewhere." [60] The most serious quarrel occasioned by excitement over the Poncas, however, arose between Schurz and Senator Dawes, director of the legislative activities of the Boston group. As Chairman of the Senate Indian Committee, the latter could not ignore the Secretary's declaration that Congress was responsible for the evils of the Ponca removal. In a letter to President Hayes, he complained that Schurz was remiss in blaming Congress for a disaster which he refused to permit the legislature to redress.[61] The Secretary remained silent, however, until Dawes delivered a speech holding him personally responsible for the death of an Indian killed in an attempted escape from Indian Territory.[62] Fortunately for Schurz, exaggerated statements criticizing his German background provided ample opportunity for an effective reply. So caustically did the Secretary attack his opponent that critics were less willing thereafter to indulge in hasty attacks lest they, too, display "the malignant unscrupulousness of the speculator in philanthropy hunting for a sensation." [63] Reform movements became more practical during the eighties largely because Schurz had exposed the evils of over-enthusiasm.

Although the Ponca dispute temporarily divided friends of the Indian, the very bitterness of the debate emphasized the need for co-operation between the government and reformers. Schurz had regretted the attitude of his opponents from the first, but as champions of the Poncas refused to trust the Secretary reconciliation was impossible. Yet once Schurz retired in 1881, both Senator Dawes and Lincoln stressed the importance of co-operation with his successor.[64] The Senator, in particular, showed that he had learned the danger of opposing the government; for he wrote regarding Secretary Kirkwood, who had energetically defended Schurz, "Of course we widely differ from him but an open conflict with this new administration, as with the last, on the Indian policy, must be avoided if possible, or we shall be very much disabled. . . . Let us, Boston and all, try to pull with Washington, but to be sure and pull the hardest!" [65] Guided by this new spirit, Senator Dawes soon became an outstanding leader in the search for a practical solution of the Indian problem and by an inevitable process drew nearer and nearer to the ideas of his erstwhile enemy. By the very act of creating serious divisions, the Ponca dispute encouraged future union by teaching the value of co-operation. Now that reformers realized the necessity for harmony, the interest aroused during the seventies began to achieve results. Less than eight years after Schurz and Dawes had quarreled so bitterly, a thorough reformation of American Indian policy was accomplished by a group of powerful organizations which united for the purpose of righting the wrongs of the past.

7. INDIAN ORGANIZATIONS

AND SECTIONAL OPINION

THE RISE OF SUCCESSFUL INDIAN ORGANIZATIONS WAS AN INDICATION that the reform movement had reached maturity. Following the close of the Civil War, occasional efforts had been made to establish societies for Indian work. Outside of the United States Indian Commission of New York, which was active in the late sixties and early seventies, however, none proved of service; and even the New York effort was of little more than local significance.[1] Only as Boston and Philadelphia assumed leading rôles in 1879 was there any sign that individual Indian workers had been able to create sufficient interest to enable the formation of prosperous organizations. Events at the turn of the decade helped to crystallize public opinion, which bore its first fruit when Eastern women not only pressed President and Mrs. Hayes for justice to the Indians, but joined on a national basis to achieve reform through the force of united effort.[2]

The Women's National Indian Association, first of the prominent Indian organizations, was established in Philadelphia late in 1879. Aided by liberal contributions from Miss Mary Bonney and by the able proselyting work of Mrs. Amelia Quinton, the organization gained influence rapidly.[3] Although the founders of the society were originally inspired by opposition to the invasion of Indian Territory, they soon widened their appeal so greatly that the directors felt it necessary to apologize for their political activities and to present a detailed explanation of their reasons for undertaking missionary work.[4] The care with which leaders described the necessity for participating in the political and religious phases of Indian reform shows that the Association was handicapped by current views regarding the proper scope of a woman's activity. Yet such prejudice was combated so ingeniously that the work was never seriously retarded.

Like other prominent Indian organizations of these years, the

Uncle Sam's Stepchildren

Women's National Indian Association supplied a peculiar need. Its task was stimulation of interest in the Indian problem through the work of branch organizations. By 1886 sixty such groups were informing the citizens of twenty-seven states about the red man.[5] In many cases, local societies rivaled in influence the national body which co-ordinated their efforts. The Connecticut branch, in particular, displayed a faculty for devising schemes to arouse interest, its plan to erect homes for Indian couples returning from Eastern schools attracting national attention.[6] The most valuable service performed by member groups, however, was the circulation of petitions. Local efforts, when multiplied many times with a final pooling of results, enabled the society to exert effective pressure in Washington.[7] The Association steadily improved its methods of operation. In a valuable report of 1886, its officers not only presented an impressive account of what had been accomplished, but advised the establishment of a central committee to act in emergencies and the placing of special emphasis upon influencing the House of Representatives.[8] Popular interest in the Indian was stimulated by pamphlets, newspaper publicity, mass meetings and the services of friendly editors and ministers.[9] Such propaganda produced results, for contributions rose from $792.75 in 1880-81 to $1,286.55 in 1881-82 and to $2,179.52 in 1882-83.[10] Members of the New York City branch of the society became so interested in the work that they encouraged formation of an Indian association among Negro women at the same time they paid tribute to Mrs. John Jacob Astor, who had "by loving sympathy encouraged them to agitate the injustice done to the Red Man of the forest."[11] At the climax of the reform movement, people of all walks of life joined in work for the Indian.

The most perplexing problem facing the Women's National Indian Association was determination of the proper attitude to be taken toward other reform groups. Although the appointment of a committee of one to co-operate with the Women's Christian Temperance Union aroused no opposition,[12] the secretary of the Eastern New York branch publicly revolted when negotiations were undertaken with leading suffrage workers.[13] Coalition with the neighboring Indian Rights Association was also contemplated.

Indian Organizations and Sectional Opinion

The organizations fortunately remained separate, each fulfilling a special function. Union was not necessary to secure singleness of purpose and independent administration enabled each society to feel a greater responsibility for the success of its own branch of the work. Both organizations played a necessary part in the work of reform, the Indian Rights Association being praised by the women because of the importance as well as the nature of its accomplishments. "As an elder sister contemplates the strength and prowess of a younger brother with grateful emotions," commented the society's president in 1885, "so may we, looking upon this organization as it masses its forces against the legal and political barriers in the way of Indian elevation, give God thanks for its stalwart arm and bravery of will." [14] Valuable as the work of the women proved, even greater contributions to the cause of Indian reform were made by the "younger brother."

The Indian Rights Association was established by Herbert Welsh of Philadelphia following a visit to the Sioux in the fall of 1882.[15] Inheriting his interest in the Indian question from his uncle, William Welsh, the founder of the new organization became impressed with the need for an agency of private citizens to combine research with pressure for advanced legislation. The new society, therefore, began by carefully studying the whole problem. Unlike the Boston Indian Citizenship Association which wasted its first years in futile dispute over the Ponca Indians,[16] the Philadelphia organization made certain of the advisability and practicality of a measure before urging its adoption. The early efforts of the Indian Rights Association were devoted to financing tours of investigation and publishing the results for the purpose of instructing both members and the general public. In pursuance of this policy, over 189,000 pamphlets were circulated between 1883 and 1887 where information and enlightenment were most necessary to stimulate reform and prevent consummation of plans which were regarded as unjust.[17] Passage of important legislation in the latter year was due in large measure to the preparatory work of the Indian Rights Association and its members.

An important factor in the success of the Indian Rights Association was the intelligent manner in which the labors of its leading officers was divided. While Welsh determined the general policies of the organization, legal problems were handled by Henry S. Pancoast and the difficult task of guiding congressional legislation was entrusted to Charles C. Painter. Each of these men became expert in his field and contributed excellent studies to an impressive list of association publications.[18] Under their direction, the Indian Rights Association gained such a reputation for discriminating criticism that evils pointed out by the society were immediately investigated. When Congress unreasonably delayed relief for starving Montana Indians in January, 1885, a letter of rebuke published in the New York *Tribune* was alone sufficient to speed action; and when President Arthur opened Crow Creek Reservation in Dakota Territory to settlement a week before the end of his administration, the energy of the Association in condemning the action led President Cleveland to revoke the order after investigation had upheld the tribe's title.[19] Such displays of strength proved that the Indian Rights Association was a powerful force in checking injustice. But while its leaders were interested in the formulation of new policies as well as in the prevention of wrong, they were generally satisfied to place their influence behind plans devised by a third important Indian organization.

Valuable as the work of the two Philadelphia societies proved, the group which contributed most to the establishment of better Indian relations was composed of Indian workers who gathered at Lake Mohonk, New York. Every fall after the first meeting in 1883, leading administrators, agents, anthropologists, religious leaders, editors, philanthropists, and legislators were invited to assemble at the hotel of Albert K. Smiley, member of the Board of Indian Commissioners.[20] A yearly opportunity thereby was provided for all interested in Indian affairs to partake in an intimate discussion of their problems. So eagerly was this chance for consultation welcomed that the conferences at Lake Mohonk immediately became a leading agency in formulation of an enlightened Indian policy. Their influence, far from being limited to those in attendance, was spread throughout the country by the publication of resolutions representing the weighed conclusions of the conferees. Both as a clearing-house for the ideas of Indian leaders and

84

as a means of presenting the public with a brief but well organized picture of the course that should be pursued by those who wished to promote Indian welfare, the annual gatherings proved a decided success.

The service of the Lake Mohonk conferences to the cause of Indian advancement can hardly be overemphasized. As disagreement concerning the aims of reform constantly threatened to check progress, a clear understanding of the Indian problem and of the best remedies to be recommended was essential. From the start, the primary purpose of the conferences was unity among Indian workers.[21] While exponents of even the most preposterous schemes were granted an opportunity to argue the merits of their causes, the final decisions of the meetings were severely practical.[22] Immediate legislation was necessary, and the directors of the conferences proposed to assist in its formulation rather than indulge in theorizing as to the red man's future. Ideals might often have to be sacrificed to necessity, but the ultimate result would be improved if Indian workers were willing to compromise with reality.

The increasingly practical outlook of the new Indian organizations was particularly welcome to the government. Whereas administrators had previously found Indian workers more apt at criticism than recommendation, the developments of the eighties greatly altered the situation.[23] The societies not only offered important information regarding the Indians, but were of much assistance in popularizing governmental measures. Administrators more and more frequently looked to Indian organizations for aid. The Indian Rights Association distributed two thousand copies of Secretary Teller's plea for an increased appropriation for Indian education in 1885.[24] The Lake Mohonk conferences supported the demand of the Indian Bureau for increased salaries for officials.[25] In these and many other ways, the organizations provided the "new voice" which Indian Commissioner Price believed necessary to arouse a Congress hardened to appeals from administrative agencies.[26] Several congressmen freely confessed reliance upon the judgment of private organizations. "You have more time and ability than we; are better able to decide the best way," Senator Dawes told a gathering of Indian workers.[27] While few legislators rated their

85

intelligence so modestly, there was general recognition that any successful Indian policy must receive popular support. The government might furnish schools, but it could not teach in them; it might provide land, but it could not insure its intelligent use.[28] Certain phases of reform depended upon the aid of practically-minded private citizens. The leading Indian organizations proved of special assistance because they surrendered much of the sentimental outlook which vitiated the efforts of the fourth prominent group of Indian friends, the National Indian Defense Association.

Founded at Washington in 1885 by Dr. T. A. Bland of the *Council Fire*, the National Indian Defense Association was composed of men having aims in direct contrast with those of the average reformer. Its members opposed rather than encouraged governmental action on the theory that Indians should be left alone. The tribes, it was argued, would not be ready to advance until their members were sufficiently interested to petition new legislation voluntarily. Any endeavor to force measures upon the tribes, therefore, was energetically opposed.[29] Yet while such intelligent men as ex-Indian Commissioner Manypenny, Samuel F. Tappan of the 1867 Peace Commission and Superintendent of Indian Schools Oberly supported this conservative position, they urged a philosophy which would have delayed progress indefinitely. Indians could not be expected to take the initiative in proposing reforms. Policies needed to be formulated with the rights of the Indians clearly in mind; but to expect changes to satisfy the race in every particular was to defeat the very purpose of reform. Members of the National Indian Defense Association allowed sentiment to obscure the evils of existing practices. They aided the red man by preventing changes from being made too rapidly, but they made no positive contribution toward introduction of a wiser Indian policy.

Eastern Sentiment

The problem confronting Indian organizations was primarily sectional in nature. A policy was wanted which would strike a balance between the hostility of Westerners and the sentimentality of Easterners by being both practical and just. Since both sections were inclined to be over emotional in considering Indian problems, the task was not easy. The widely contrasting attitudes toward red men prevailing throughout the United States aptly proved the maxim that "absence makes the heart grow fonder." The further one travelled from an Indian reservation, the more sympathy one found with the problems of the red man. Interest in the Indian, as Senator Plumb of Kansas remarked, seemed to be in exact ratio to the distance from him.[30] The greatest friends of the Indians were New Englanders; their bitterest critics were their nearest neighbors. Until both Easterners and Westerners made an effort to overcome such local prejudices the co-operation necessary for adoption of a successful policy would be lacking. But although a few reformers recognized the need for compromise in the early seventies,[31] neither section showed any desire to make concessions for several years.

In spite of frequent claims that his attitude toward the Indians was characterized by exceptional insight and impartiality, the average Easterner did not have an adequate conception of the Indian problem before 1880. Men and women, who believed that the intelligent Indians introduced on Eastern platforms were typical of the race, were naturally inclined to criticize the government as unfriendly.[32] So many people attacked administrators without adequate information that Secretary Schurz complained, "The number of American citizens 'who know all about Indian matters' without ever having given a moment's study to that large and complicated subject, has been incredibly great, and the readiness and volubility of their criticism, mostly condemnatory of everything that is done, seems inspired by inexhaustible fertility of the imagination as to facts. No story, ever so extravagant and absurd, can be told about Indian management without finding ready belief." [33] Far from contact with uncivilized Indians, the average Easterner was subject to rumors and misrepresentation. Many an Eastern community accepted without question the oft-repeated charge that the government had been to blame for every war.[34] Even after having dealt with Indians in the field, Easterners frequently suffered from over-sentimentality. The reports of agents during the period when the churches controlled Indian appointments became noted for their inaccuracy.[35] The average administrator still experienced such difficulty in adjusting himself to the Indian problem as late as 1887 that an Indian Rights Association investigator concluded there would "always be something fantastic, too much of the *a priori* element, in the conduct of Indian affairs while . . . administered almost entirely by Eastern and Southern men." [36] Seaboard residents had a concept of the Indian which did not square with the facts. Until they learned to regard Indians as human beings, their treatment of the Indian problem never approached reality.

The ultimate support of practical measures of reform by Easterners was a result of pressure by Indian organizations. Fanaticism was condemned from the first by the Indian Rights Association and the Lake Mohonk conferences. Even the sentimental editors of the *Council Fire* condemned the proposal of plans by men who had never seen an Indian.[37] The insistence of reformers upon a more realistic consideration of Indian problems produced immediate results. Unreasonable charges against frontiersmen were not only dropped, but a sincere effort was made to devise plans which would win Western support.[38] If neighbors of the tribes could be convinced that a particular measure would further the interests of both races, reform would be feasible. Such a development seemed quite possible to friends of the Indians, for if Easterners could be sympathetic without being sentimental, Westerners might learn to be practical without being unfair.

Western Hatred

In endeavoring to convince Westerners of the need for more considerate treatment of the Indians, reformers undertook a serious task. Frontier hostility, unlike the sentimentality of the East, was firmly based on practical experience with the tribes. Although organization was impossible under frontier conditions, the average Westerner was so confirmed in his hatred of the Indian that co-operative action was not necessary to instrument his views. His antipathy arose to an unfortunate extent from personal loss. Complacent Easterners, fearing for neither life nor property, need only have read a few letters in the files of the Indian Bureau to realize that contact with the Indians might prove far from a blessing. The loss of life and claims for compensation for damages resulting from Indian raids were frequently exaggerated, it is true, but government officials were equally intent on belittling outbreaks in order to preserve their reputation and conserve national funds.[39] The plea of a bereaved mother to "make them redskins smart for what tha have done," the touching lament of a frontiersman over loss of a faithful horse and elaborate plans submitted for reducing the danger of raids, leave no doubt that Westerners lived in constant fear of attack by unruly Indians.[40] Hostility to the tribes was due to much more than imagined grievances.

But while the refusal of frontiersmen to sympathize with the Indian was not surprising, hatred of the tribes often exceeded the bounds of reason. Contempt for the Indians so frequently led to abandonment of all moral scruples that reformers were justified in regarding the frontier settlers as a greater problem than the Indian.[41] The possibility that Indian rights might occasionally be superior to those of whites was inconceivable to many Westerners. Angry Montana settlers may not have fed poisoned bread to starving Indians, as the *Council Fire* charged, but the Colorado House actually did consider a bill offering rewards for "the Destruction of Indians and Skunks," and a frontiersman did refuse to sell even a portion of his cattle when a neighboring tribe was in urgent need of food.[42] To many an American, the only good Indians were still those in six-foot boxes. No better example of the intensity of this frontier hatred exists than the remarks of an Iowan, who wrote:

Sympathy with Indians is like milk spilled in the ground. It is lost. They are valueless & useless. We have 400 of them left over & domiciled in Iowa. They are tamed. But they are as worthless as so many tamed wolves. After 40 years they are, old & young, yet in their breech clouts, or some donated old clothes, hunting musk rats & fishing along the streams, literally scabs on the state. . . .

Now instead of continually removing them from reservation to reservation, and keeping off civilization; suppose you adopt the following policy which is practicable, humane and less expensive. To use a western expression 'round up and corrall' the whole Indian race, and set the land over to civilized white people. Catch as many of them dead as possible, disarm them, and put all the Bucks in one ranch, and all the Squaws in a separate ranch; and make Shakers of them by the law of necessity; and feed & clothe them there till death ends the work. That will save hundreds of lives every year, and nine tenths of the expence & help the democrats reduce the army.

Then if you want to experiment on making a citizen out of a savage or a chicken out of an owl, put in missionaries and keep out agents and whisky; always being careful to preserve the Shaker theory, and admit only females among the squaws. That will end the whole vexed indian trouble. And when the missionaries have got this generation safe over Jordan we will have done with the race.[43]

Although few Westerners were as hostile as this advocate of segregation, the rights of the race were seldom defended. But one of many Easterners to comment upon the reluctance of respectable citizens to join issue with opponents of the Indians, young Theodore Roosevelt urged Westerners to support red men from the attacks of selfish neighbors.[44] Frontiersmen aided Indians only occasionally, however, despite the growing conviction that many red men were being treated unjustly because of the misdeeds of a few. Instead, the readiness of the average frontiersman to accept stories of Indian outbreaks without investigation resulted in the spread of rumors which would have been amusing if the excitement had not so often resulted disastrously. Reformers could laugh at a Montana scare in which the only casualty was a horse shot through the ear;[45] but in other cases the shooting proved more effective and frontiersmen played upon the gullibility of their neighbors to achieve selfish ends. A few years before the Ute uprising of 1880, Agent Danforth reported that complaints against his Indians originated from a desire to create hostility and precipitate trouble which might be employed to deprive the Indians of some of their rights.[46] Similar attempts to discredit peaceful tribes were inspired by the hope of Arizona Indian contractors to check white settlement and the desire of Oregonians to prevent abandonment of a fort which was of more value as a purchaser of supplies than as a post against Indians.[47]

The uneasiness of the West was clearly reflected in Eastern newspapers. Reports of Indian hostilities were accepted so readily that within one year the New York *Herald* was completely misled by sensational reports from four different sections of the West. Thus New Mexico dispatches reporting the burning of Galeyville, Arizona, and the massacre of at least thirty settlers were published on April 27, 1882, only to be corrected the following day by an announcement that but one man had been killed three miles from the fully-protected town. Hardly a week later an item declaring that unprotected Montana posts were seriously threatened by a Snake and Bannock outbreak was followed by an article explaining that the tribes were the most peaceable under the government. But it was in July that the full susceptibility of settlers to rumors was revealed when the massacre of a party of fourteen was reported from Foulk County, Dakota Territory. Dispatches printed on the first of the month described how a lone survivor had brought word of the disaster, how General Terry had sent troops to punish the guilty Indians, and how the railroad was co-operating in moving the men to the scene of action. Yet all this excitement was caused by nothing more than the "miserable hoax" of two boys, who by whooping and firing for fun so scared an unsuspecting immigrant that he ran thirty miles for his life and reported the loss of his party "with such circumstantial details as to leave but little doubt of its truth." When reports declaring that four hundred Umatilla Indians had arisen were discovered late in the following winter to be rumors of Oregon land sharks for the purpose of forcing the tribe's removal, the *Herald* had rounded out a busy year of false alarms.[48] Only as Westerners learned to look upon the Indian question more calmly was there hope that a policy could be adopted which would benefit both settler and Indian.

Like their fellow countrymen of the East, frontiersmen became increasingly reasonable in their attitude toward the Indians. When the Osage Indians who had been expelled from Kansas were invited to return for the purpose of trading in 1877, their agent predicted that lawlessness and war would grow less and less attractive as more Westerners acquired property.[49] Neither the existence of a race of vagabonds nor the prospect of perpetual war were calculated to appeal to men desiring a stable society. Self-interest was ultimately bound to remove objections against civilizing the tribes. As Westerners, who had long hoped to live apart from the Indians, gradually realized that contact could not be avoided, their interest in the reformation of Indian affairs grew rapidly during the eighties. With increasing numbers in both sections desiring to establish a new policy, the country had only to determine what that policy should be.

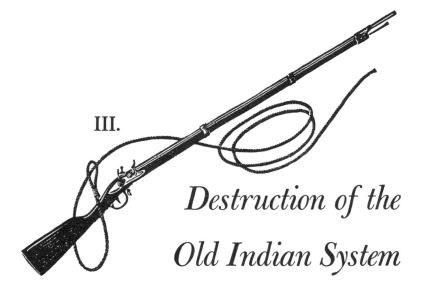

III.

Destruction of the

Old Indian System

8. THE TREATY SYSTEM
AND TRIBAL AUTONOMY

BEFORE REFORMERS TURNED THEIR ATTENTION TO FORMULATION of a new Indian program, they investigated existing policies so thoroughly that few practices of the government escaped criticism. The first practical achievements of the reform movement involved abandonment of long-established policies rather than the institution of new methods. So many features of contemporary Indian administration were disapproved that the objectives of reformers can be as clearly understood by examining the policies they condemned as by describing the changes which they ultimately recommended. Any analysis of the proposals advocated by reformers should be preceded, therefore, by a study of the successful attack upon important traditions of the old Indian system.

The first feature of contemporary Indian policy to suffer from the hostility of reformers was the treaty system which had shaped relations between red men and white since the days of the first settlers. In spite of the lapse of years and the increasing power of the whites, United States officials treated Indians during the sixties much as their colonial predecessors had done two centuries before. Long and complicated negotiations with Indian chiefs were necessary before the treatment of a tribe could be modified in the slightest detail. The practice exempted Indian tribes from ordinary legislative processes. Red men within the borders of the United States were not subject to congressional rule, but were granted a freedom from interference which placed them more nearly on the basis of foreign nations than of citizens. Theoretically, if not practically, the members of Indian tribes were free agents who might accept or reject the will of the United States according to their own choosing.

The wide discrepancy between theory and practice which existed under the treaty system was a measure of its inadequacy. The whites had long been strong enough to force their will upon the tribes, yet the fiction of Indian autonomy was retained as a cover for selfish aims.[1] As long as demands of the government could be advertised as the product of mutual agreement between the tribes and administrators, the expensive ceremonial seemed worth while. But once the weakness of the tribes became so apparent that the artificial nature of Indian consent was revealed, no reason remained for prolonging the practice.

Recognition of the futility of the treaty system first arose during the Civil War. The necessity of treating tribes which had aided the Confederacy with as much respect as if they had been foreign nations nettled America's newly-aroused nationalism.[2] Yet while the liberal extension of concessions to insurgent tribes of the Indian Territory aroused many complaints, negotiations with even the friendliest of tribes now offered few advantages. Not only was the supply of Indian land which originally had inspired the system being rapidly exhausted, but the resulting expansion of white settlements was daily rendering the necessity for powerful control over the Indians more imperative. The advisability of supplanting treaty agreements by direct legislation was so manifest that both friend and foe of the Indian urged the government to exercise its authority without consulting the Indians. With such organizations as the Indian Peace Commission and the Board of Indian Commissioners joining notorious enemies of the Indians in condemning the treaty system, the decision of Congress to abandon the policy in 1871 was not surprising.[3]

Abolition of the Treaty System

In spite of the growing unpopularity of the treaty system following 1865, the policy was so securely established that its abolition would have been impossible if a political crisis had not arisen. Far from being a deliberate move, the portion of the Indian Appropriation Bill of March 3, 1871, which declared that no Indian nation or tribe within the territory of the United States should thereafter be recognized as an independent power with whom the government might contract by treaty, was adopted as the only means of appeasing a quarrel between the House and Senate over the ratification of Indian treaties.[4] A study of the dispute, in fact, reveals not only the political origin of the change but also the reluctance with which abolition of the treaty system was accepted as a solution of the difficulty.

The dispute between the branches of Congress, which finally led to the abolition of the treaty system, first grew critical in 1868 when the House refused to appropriate the large sums of money necessary for fulfillment of treaties concluded by the Indian Peace Commission until it was consulted regarding their provisions. The representatives not only stressed their participation in passage of the act creating the Commission, but also pointed out that while the first section of the measure had declared that treaties were to be concluded "subject to the action of the Senate," the second provided that land set apart for the Indians should become permanent homes when "approved by Congress." [5] Although the Senate replied by disclaiming any intention to dispose of the public domain unconstitutionally by means of Indian treaties, it insisted upon adding over four and a third million dollars to the 1869 House appropriation of $2,312,240.12 and precipitated a crisis which forced the Fortieth Congress to adjourn without adoption of an Indian bill.[6]

The inability of the House and Senate to agree upon the Indian Appropriation Bill for 1869-70 forced consideration of the problem in the first session of the Forty-first Congress which immediately followed. As the debate progressed, the dispute over ratification soon involved the entire treaty system. A large number of representatives wished to prohibit all future negotiations and Senator Harlan actually introduced a bill to abolish the system in hope of appeasing their wrath.[7] But the House as a whole was not ready for such drastic action. The motion to forbid conclusion of future treaties was declared out of order after an attack by Representative Dawes, and the House took its stand on the ground that it should be consulted regarding the provisions of all treaties.[8] As the Senate absolutely refused to allow changes in treaties already adopted, and in sessions attended by less than half a dozen members added nearly three million dollars to the Indian bill over the protest of its own Appropriation Committee,[9] the House determined to sit all summer if necessary to defeat the bill. When the Senate even refused to consider an investigation of the system proposed by House Republicans, all possibility of agreement seemed at an end.[10] Yet action was imperative, for unless a decision could be postponed by an arrangement acceptable to both sides, the entire Indian appropriation was doomed.

The prospective disruption of Indian relations occasioned by the failure of Congress to vote an appropriation was avoided by a plan which enabled the House to vote money for the Indians without ratifying the disputed treaties. But adoption of Representative Dawes's scheme for allowing the President to spend two million dollars for non-treaty Indians was only a temporary expedient which contributed nothing to the solution of the major difficulty and which would not have been accepted if it had.[11] Even though House Democrats were appeased by strict limitations on the power of the President, and though a clause was included specifically denying ratification of any treaties concluded since July 20, 1867, a number of representatives opposed the compromise in hope of forcing immediate abandonment of the system.[12] Yet while this move failed and the immediate crisis was successfully passed, the fundamental issue between Senate and House was no nearer solution despite the long debate.

Discussions of the treaty system during 1870 only served to augment the difficulties perplexing the House and Senate. Again a measure prohibiting the negotiation of further treaties was ruled out of order in the House, and again the Senate increased the House bill over three million dollars.[13] Faced only a day before the conclusion of the session with a crisis similar to that of the previous year, Representative Dawes was forced to suggest extension of the principle of presidential discretion to the entire Indian appropriation. The acceptance of this proposal by just the necessary two-thirds vote, although even Dawes admitted that such drastic action "should be resorted to only in the last extremity," was an indication of the length to which the House was willing to go to win its case.[14] Yet the House could accomplish little in face of the Senate's determination to refuse such an exceptional measure. Despite a crucial vote of 107-55 in which the House again refused to accept the Senate bill,[15] the only concession it could obtain in the measure finally adopted was a repetition of the clause stating that treaties concluded since 1867 should not be considered ratified.[16] Since the measure specifically appropriated money for carrying out these very treaties, the House had lost another round of its fight with a stubborn Senate.

The situation facing the House late in 1870 demanded, and resulted in, a change of tactics. Discovering that they could have no voice in regard to Indian affairs unless the treaty system was abolished, the representatives finally consented to abandon the system. This decision was facilitated by a Supreme Court ruling of December, 1870. For two years leading members of the House had insisted that abolition of the treaty system would be unconstitutional. "I took up Clarks bill prohibiting Indian treaties to be made without consent of Congress to see what could be done with it. Every provision in it is probably unnecessary if not unconstitutional," a legal expert had declared in January of 1870. "It is clear that where Congress is called upon to appropriate money to carry out the provisions of a treaty that it may be refused," he added, ". . . in certain cases Congress may repeal a treaty, but has no power to prohibit the making of one." [17] But when the Court announced in the Cherokee Tobacco Case that acts of Congress might supersede prior treaties, and when the minority decision also affirmed the power of Congress to abrogate Indian treaties although questioning its intent to do so, the legality of measures to end the treaty system could be questioned no longer.[18] With the judges declaring that Congress might revoke treaties, there could be no doubt of its right to forbid their conclusion. Abandonment of the system now only waited legislative action. Yet the decision only speeded a step which would ultimately have been taken, for continuance of the futile opposition to the agreements of 1867 became absurd in view of the Senate's willingness to drop the system if previous treaties were upheld. So it was that a clause included in the Indian Appropriation Bill of 1871 to solve a serious political quarrel ended at the same time a system which had guided American Indian policy from the foundation of the government!

Significance of the Prohibition of Treaties

Discontinuance of the treaty system was an important step in the improvement of Indian relations. In the early days of the country, the policy undoubtedly had protected the tribes, but the acceptance of treaties was seldom a matter of choice as the power of the government increased. When a clause included in several treaties of 1865 provided that any modifications by the United States Senate should be considered binding upon the tribes in the same manner as if they had subsequently been presented and agreed to by the chiefs and headmen of the bands, illusions regarding Indian freedom were no longer possible.[19] Indian affairs were so completely under the control of white officials that it was only common sense to recognize the fact. Outright abrogation of existing treaties might also have been wise, as senators were constantly tampering with their provisions on the ground that the Senate and not the Indians were aware of their "true intent and meaning." [20] But assurance that future responsibility would rest solely upon Congress did remove any danger that new treaties would be used to justify further wrongs. Power unquestionably rested with the government and direct legislation offered the best opportunity for its efficient and open use. More could be accomplished to insure just treatment of the Indians by encouraging a wise application of the new powers than ever had been done by resting on the insecure basis of treaty provisions.

In addition to improving government relations with the Indians, abolition of the treaty system stimulated racial advancement. Indians needed to face the fact of their dependence instead of cherishing a false security based upon misplaced confidence in the treaty system. As long as Indians were treated as equals, they never had recognized the necessity of preparing for the inevitable contact with white civilization. Many important reforms could be instituted only after the government ceased to consult the Indians and demanded obedience to all acts of Congress. Once the full implications of abandonment of the treaty system were realized, therefore, revolutionary changes followed.

Although important readjustments should logically have occurred at once as a result of abolition of the treaty system, the decision to cease negotiations had little immediate effect. If the full significance of the move had been understood, Congress might have proceeded less rapidly. The political nature of the dispute over the status of treaties, however, caused all emphasis to be placed upon superficial aspects of the change. Certain Democrats did insist that abolition of the treaty system would be "the first step in a great scheme of spoliation," but their forebodings were easily attributed to political disgruntlement.[21] Since most legislators considered the question a mere matter of congressional prestige, the influence of their action upon Indian policy was negligible. As a result, the fears of the few who dreaded abandonment of the treaty system proved unwarranted.[22] Congressmen could not be expected to carry out immediately the logical implications of an act, regarding the significance of which they were largely ignorant.

Agreements negotiated with Indian tribes following 1871 differed from treaties only in the matter of ratification. In spite of the technical abandonment of the treaty system, commissions were still appointed to deal with tribal leaders and the resulting arrangements were considered as binding as the treaty provisions of former years. The failure of the change to produce a more realistic treatment of the Indian was especially evident when an agreement for the surrender of Sioux land promised the tribe an annuity of over a million dollars for an indefinite period following 1876.[23] This agreement was not only similar to the treaties of previous years, but was employed, as many treaties had been, to represent concessions as voluntary which had only been obtained following a war. Further evidence that tribal autonomy might still be employed to instrument concessions obtained from Indians in spite of the rule against negotiations was offered in 1880 when the government ordered Ute chiefs to surrender trespasser-murdering tribesmen under terms of a legislative agreement in which the United States had promised to prevent the very invasion which was responsible for the difficulties.[24] As long as such demands were made upon tribal authorities, the most important feature of the treaty system remained untouched. Until the United States assumed full control over its tribes, any fundamental change in Indian relations was impossible.

Tribal Autonomy

The best evidence of the failure of abolition of the treaty system to produce any basic changes in Indian relations was provided by the increasingly bitter criticism of the powers retained by tribal authorities. Objections to the consultation of Indian chieftains regarding government policies occurred more frequently after treaty negotiations had supposedly been prohibited than before. Colonel Elwell S. Otis's detailed attack upon the treaty system in *The Indian Question* did not appear until 1878, and other effective criticisms were advanced still later. Instead of supporting Senator Edmunds's contention that House consideration of Indian agreements was unconstitutional,[25] most Americans wished to increase the power of Congress to dictate to tribes even further. True reform would be impossible, they believed, until every trace of tribal independence was destroyed.

Effective arguments were presented against Indian autonomy. Red men had leaned upon a few leaders for so many years that a large majority were unprepared for the independent action required in an individualistic society. To increase the confidence of individual tribesmen, United States administrators needed to weaken the influence of Indian chiefs among their people. Such a process might be employed to the detriment of all red men; but even the sincerest friends of the tribes realized that close contact with the whites would fail as long as chiefs were allowed to remain in charge of tribal affairs. The Indians could learn the nature of white society only by submitting to its laws; and the government could protect them from approaching dangers only if it assumed full control. Too sympathetic a regard for the feelings of Indian chiefs would mean disaster.[26]

Yet despite the strength of arguments advocating an end of tribal authority, there was serious danger that the reform might be introduced too abruptly. While many Indians might be expected to profit if the power of their chiefs was reduced, the confusion certain to arise from so radical a readjustment militated against sudden change. But many people, either failing to understand Indian society or lacking a reasonable respect for the rights of the race, proposed the immediate deposition of all chiefs. J. B. Harrison, an Indian Rights Association investigator, urged that "the Indian politicians and big men should be set aside." [27] The Reverend Robert Patterson condemned Indian rule as intolerable to God, thereby expressing a belief held by many students of Indian policy.[28] In their enthusiasm for reform, such men forgot that a more adequate recognition of individual rights did not require that Indians be cast adrift by the destruction of the only society they had ever known. Indian workers needed to be constantly reminded that tribes might be ruled without being destroyed and that forced submission to the customs of a foreign race might be far more obnoxious than obedience to one's own rulers. If Indian customs were to be successfully extinguished, the process needed to be gradual.

Fortunately enough reformers realized the dangers of immediate destruction of tribal governments to protect Indian leaders from premature expulsion. The National Indian Defense Association led in this work; but as its interest in maintaining the chiefs was known to arise from its well-known prejudice in favor of the Indians, the insistence of the Board of Indian Commissioners that immediate deposition of the chiefs would result in anarchy was more effective in forestalling action.[29] An increasing number of Americans became convinced of the inadvisability of overthrowing tribal authority before the Indians were ready for citizenship. Senator Call of Florida assisted greatly in delaying moves against the chiefs when he declared:

I think that in many cases it is quite probable that the tribal relation is a better security for their protection than a direct amenability to the law and the several tenure of property. The tribal relation has some great advantages for the Indian. It interposes a barrier between him and the strong and artful man. It is an exercise of power which brings to bear upon him, for his protection or his punishment, the opinion of his tribe assembled in council. It is not inconsistent with his advancement into a higher form of civilization, nor with a love for home and family.[30]

Such respect for the tribes was not often expressed, but most reformers recognized that for the time being at least tribal rule was a necessary evil.

The decisive factor in preventing immediate destruction of tribal society, however, was the opposition of administrators. Indian leaders who were converted to reform would prove valuable colleagues in the task of stimulating racial advancement if their power was not destroyed. Although reformers frequently blamed failure to take advantage of the influence of Indian rulers for the shortcomings of American Indian policy,[31] government officials often expressed a desire to co-operate with Indian leaders and warned that chiefs should be treated with proper respect. Secretary Schurz was so thoroughly aware of the advantage of seeking the aid of tribal authorities in promoting reform that he severely condemned the "heroic treatment" recommended by advocates of tribal extinction and remarked that habits grown up in the course of centuries would not at once yield to a mere word of command.[32] Similar caution marked the policy of all government officers. Plans for gradually reducing the power of the tribal chiefs were introduced, but they were invariably accompanied by measures preparing the Indian for citizenship. Ultimate abandonment of tribal government was the goal of Indian administrators; but as late as 1885 Secretary Lamar was led by his experience with Negro emancipation to warn, "The tribal system must be adhered to. It is the normal condition of the existence of this race. It is the policy, and the only one known to the Indian race. To take him out of it is to change his social conditions, his religious and hereditary impressions, before he is fitted for higher civilization. I am a conservative, and have been made so by a costly experience." [33] Until Indians were more fully prepared to stand on their own feet, government officials were unwilling to expose them to the full rigors of white competition by destroying the tribal system.

But although the power of Indian chiefs was not seriously reduced for the time being with abandonment of the treaty system, the move was extremely important because the changes implicit in the act could be delayed but not avoided. Once Congress legislated without consulting the Indians, tribal autonomy would be adversely affected. At first ignorance, and later a realization that changes must be gradual, postponed this outcome. Yet while the chiefs still ruled in the eighties, Indian policy was moving rapidly toward an ultimate abolition of tribal rule. The confusion characterizing Indian relations before 1871 had finally disappeared. As the first step toward Indian absorption, action against the treaty system had set the course of future reforms.[34] Before further progress could be made, however, other Indian policies needed to be radically revised.

9. THE ANNUITY SYSTEM AND
CONGRESSIONAL ECONOMY

A SECOND UNITED STATES INDIAN POLICY DISTURBED MANY POST-Civil War legislators even more than the treaty system. For many years white men had pursued the practice of presenting tribes with annual gifts of food and clothing. The first treaties between colonists and Indians provided for an exchange of gifts, and appeals to the Indian eye and palate long proved the best method of avoiding hostilities. Although prevention of racial conflicts became less necessary as the strength of the whites increased, annuities continued to be important as a means of compensation for land demanded for national expansion. So much Indian territory was opened to settlement that few tribes failed to receive regular remuneration for their losses. Payments for a single cession of land were limited in duration, but before one grant was exhausted a new removal was likely to provide occasion for another. So as years passed in this fashion, a system of annuities became accepted as a settled feature of American Indian policy by both whites and Indians.

In spite of the cost of periodically supplying Indian tribes with food and clothing, the annuity system possessed many enthusiastic champions. Settlers who wished to obtain Indian land or hoped to avoid war strongly defended the policy. Indians, faced with the inevitability of white advancement, were not averse to accepting compensation for their losses and frequently pressed for increased payments. But the strongest supporters were whites who depended upon the system for a livelihood. Efforts to reduce annuity payments met strong resistance from contractors whose goods were purchased by the government, from transporters hired to carry issues to the agencies, from claims agents who assessed Indian funds for their fees, and from agency employees who hoped to benefit from the issue of goods. Modification of the system could be achieved only over the protests of a powerful group to whom annuity appropriations were furnishing a substantial compensation every year.

Government records offer considerable evidence of the selfish motives influencing many defenders of the annuity system. Inferior goods were delivered, excessive transportation rates were charged, scales were doctored, false certificates of receipt were returned. Such abuses were aggravated by the impossibility of adequately policing issues at remote agencies. The failure of administrators to overcome this difficulty became especially evident when scandals arose in spite of strong efforts to avoid irregular activities. A sensational exposure of profiteering at the Sioux's Red Cloud Agency in 1875 was even more significant as an instance of practices which were general than as an individual case.[1] The selfishness of contractors at times defied every effort at concealment. Greedy contests over whether contracts should be let in New York or St. Louis, and disputes as to the proper proportion of beef and grain or shoes and blankets often exposed the avarice of contractors and divided friends of the system.[2] But once continuance of annuities was threatened or efforts were made to divert funds to supplies which would encourage Indian self-sufficiency,[3] the ranks would mend to retain appropriations which must be maintained even if there was disagreement over how they should be spent.

Although many supporters of the annuity system opposed its abandonment because of self-interest, friends of the Indians also objected to any sudden change. As much as reformers wished to stimulate independence, they realized that a refusal to continue annuity payments would immediately lead to Indian starvation. Even the generous issues prevailing were frequently insufficient, for the bounty of the government had taught Indians that there was no necessity for economy as long as their needs were supplied. Reformers disagreed as to whether Indians were naturally improvident; but whether or not this defect was inborn or a habit acquired through the influence of corrupt Indian agents, the practice of feasting following the issue of annuities and the rapidity with which cash payments were spent proved the Indian's inability to consider future needs and embarrassed efforts to reduce annuity issues.[4] Until Indians learned to conserve their supplies, there was little chance that Indian appropriations could be lowered.

Legislators first criticized the annuity system because it encouraged Indian improvidence rather than because of its expense. The policy would undoubtedly have continued without challenge if the supply of Indian land had been limitless. But as the excess lands of many tribes had been absorbed by the government in the years preceding the Civil War, post-war legislators awoke to the fact that a large number of Indians had nothing to offer in return for extension of their appropriations. Provision of funds to maintain such tribes now clearly became a matter of charity. Although the necessity of some payments to prevent Indians from resuming their old habits was admitted, American lawmakers decided to encourage self-sufficiency by appropriating only what was absolutely essential to subsistence. As a result, Indian bills were carefully examined and only the casting vote of Speaker Colfax prevented the House from confining funds appropriated in 1867 to the payment of treaty obligations.[5] Both branches of Congress were so reluctant to grant the sums requested by administrators that the government was able to save its appropriations only by frightening legislators into respect for the red men.

The difficulty of securing funds from Congress induced administrators to revive the argument that annuity expenditures were justified as a means of war prevention. It was cheaper to feed the Indians, they argued, than to fight them.[6] If congressmen really desired economy, appropriations to provide tribes with food and clothing should be continued especially where there was danger of hostility. Confronted with such ardent appeals, Congress raised annuity funds from $1,755,830.24 to $3,713,833.85 in 1869 and failed to make any sizeable reduction until 1873.[7]

The attempt of administrators to prevent a reduction of annuity appropriations by warning of the danger of war, while momentarily successful, resulted in ultimate if not immediate injury to the Indian cause. Although temporary concessions were won by rousing fear of the Indians, the argument that annuities should be employed solely to appease hostility was used to advocate a repeal of all appropriations once the true impotence of the tribes was revealed. A still more serious objection was that wars might be encouraged rather than discouraged by offering favors to hostile tribes. Even before annuities were extensively employed in the late sixties as a means of war prevention, General Pope had warned that no nation had ever succeeded in purchasing peace.[8] The United States proved no exception. By displaying a determination to treat only the most troublesome tribes with respect, the government stimulated difficulties, as Indians had no incentive to remain peaceful when favorable treaties could be secured only by going on the war-path.[9] Use of annuities in the hope of winning peace was no longer possible once continuing difficulties with the very tribes to whom the largest sums were paid revealed the futility of attempts to buy Indian friendship.

With the impracticality of annuity appropriations for the purpose of ending hostilities proved beyond question, Congress had to decide whether payments should be continued as a matter of charity. The need of appropriations to prevent starvation was undeniable. Yet the impossibility of continuing to submit annual requests for two to three million dollars without assurance of any return was equally clear. Appropriations were maintained for a while as administrators suggested that the sums requested would decrease as particular grants expired. But when the prospect of gradual reduction was shattered by a sudden increase of over a million dollars following the Sioux war of 1876, the need for drastic action was apparent. Unless some method was discovered of reducing payments without disaster to the Indians, decreases in annuity payments would soon destroy the race.

The only means of keeping annuity appropriations within reasonable bounds was to teach Indians to support themselves. Yet little could be done in this respect if the customary payments were continued without modification. The value of self-support could not be expected to impress men accustomed to receiving help from others. But as an abrupt cessation of payments would lead to ex-termination, changes needed to be gradual. While complete abolition of the system would be highly desirable once tribes had learned to support themselves, the first task was to remodel the policy in such a way that Indian advancement would not be discouraged.

Uncle Sam's Stepchildren

The Reformation of Annuity Issues

Recognition of the need for modifying the annuity system did not solve the question of what changes should be made. The best policy to be followed was thoroughly debated during the seventies. These discussions proved unusually fruitful, for so many excellent proposals were presented that several radical readjustments were effected in less than a decade. Study of the measures which were adopted and rejected during this period permits a clear understanding of the annuity problem and the manner in which it was handled.

No feature of the annuity system was more justly criticized than the type of product given the Indians. Even a superficial examination revealed that tribes received a large proportion of their payments in goods which one commissioner declared they needed "no more than a toad needs a pocket-book." [10] Men in responsible positions had cared little whether annuity issues were of practical use as long as a tribe was satisfied. Yet once a desire to stimulate Indian independence arose, a system which permitted straw hats to be shipped to Montana and underwear to Arizona seemed inexcusable not only because of the disregard for local needs, but because even well-placed straw hats and underwear did not encourage self-sufficiency. No advancement could be expected as long as the government catered to Indian preference for knives and bracelets instead of forcing acceptance of less appealing but more useful articles.

The advisability of changing the character of annuity issues to encourage Indian independence was clearly recognized by reformers of the seventies. As an initial step, Congress followed the advice of the Board of Indian Commissioners and confined issues "more and more nearly to articles of prime necessity" in hope of encouraging Indians to secure non-essential articles for themselves.[11] Tribes were fed when an emergency arose, but were less frequently cajoled with beads and mirrors. When a band showed interest in obtaining such luxuries through their own labor, issues of seeds and tools were substituted for issues of food. Real progress toward self-sufficiency began when products of immediate use were supplanted by articles which assumed value only with the exercise of labor. By such a process, Indian effort was stimulated without withdrawing government assistance. If tribes took full advantage of the opportunity, payments of any nature might soon be abolished.

Yet despite the obvious advantages to be gained by a modification of annuity issues, serious obstacles blocked effective changes. Indian treaties often specified the exact nature of the payments or left determination of the type of article to tribal chiefs.[12] But since most treaty provisions were of short duration, and since much money was voted which was not authorized by treaties, a more formidable difficulty was the reluctance of Congress to delegate authority to remodel the system. Payments could be intelligently adjusted to the needs of individual tribes only by men in immediate contact with them. Yet while congressmen frankly admitted their inability to make the necessary decisions, they hesitated to entrust the power to any government official. Legislation concerning the annuity system, therefore, combined provisions for change with limitations upon executive discretion. But although all authority granted by such measures was carefully restricted, their passage in any form indicated that the gravity of the problem was recognized.

The desire of Congress to retain full control over Indian appropriations caused them to oppose any appropriation for which no specific purpose was provided. For many years no effort had been made to provide in detail how Indian funds should be used; but as time passed legislators looked with growing suspicion upon large unregulated appropriations and administrators experienced great difficulty after 1865 in preventing nullification of all discretion in the expenditure of Indian money. In view of this attitude, an amendment to the 1873 Appropriation Bill allowing the Secretary of the Interior to change issues established by treaty if he was able to secure tribal consent marked a striking victory for the forces of reform.[13] The Senate, it is true, urged a congressional investigation to assure that the modification power was not abused; but the House refused to insist upon even this safeguard despite the advice of its Appropriation Committee.[14] The authority was of little value, however, for Indians seldom consented to changes and the grant of power to a Republican administration rested upon the precarious support of Democratic representatives who followed the lead of Beck of Kentucky in upholding the measure.[15] Several years were to pass before any further concessions were granted.

Indian administrators had to spend so much energy in preventing reduction of discretionary funds that their power grew but slowly during the seventies. While the Senate refused to strike out all general items in 1875 by a vote of 30-20, for example, an attempt to enlarge the amounts was decisively defeated the following year. Democratic votes constituted the bulk of those opposed to discretion in each case, but the decisive factor was the strong resistance of such prominent Republican Indian champions as Senators Schurz and Dawes to every effort to reduce the control of Congress over Indian funds.[16] Administrators failed so completely in their attempt to secure wider jurisdiction that the Senate defeated an attempt to increase the Secretary's powers in 1878 by merely repeating the formula of 1873. Since even this concession was bitterly opposed by fifteen senators who wished to limit diversion of funds to $10,000, no doubt remained that Congress would continue to uphold its control over the expenditure of Indian funds.[17] Discretionary appropriations were continued into the eighties, and the Indian Office was permitted to consolidate annuity funds so that a surplus for one tribe might be used to supply the deficiency of another, but the use of such money was carefully limited.[18] Indians might have benefited if the Secretary of the Interior had been granted authority to modify annuity issues without interference, but Congress was not willing to surrender its control over appropriations that he might do so.

In spite of the refusal of Congress to vote large discretionary funds, considerable progress was made in diverting annuity issues to more practical ends. Where appropriations were not earmarked, and where treaties did not specify the exact nature of the annual payments, Indian officials instituted important changes. An examination of the contracts which the Indian Office let annually in New York City discloses important modifications in the nature of purchases. Thus while the amount of beef, coffee, flour and sugar remained fairly stationary between 1878 and 1888 (37,226,000 and

36,864,200 lbs.; 467,000 and 484,060 lbs.; 6,695,600 and 7,672,300 lbs.; and 979,400 and 939,240 lbs., respectively), the size of contracts for both wheat and corn declined rapidly because of Indian cultivation (2,160,600 to 1,151,500 lbs. and 1,730,000 to 40,000 lbs.). Similar shifts of emphasis in clothing items resulted in increased purchases of shoes and trousers (22,966 to 47,511 pairs and 10,058 to 21,148 pairs) and a reduction in the number of blankets (23,897 to 17,746). Further evidence of this progressive adjustment of annuity issues was revealed by the fact that no beads were bought after 1882 while the number of mirrors declined from 407 to 170 dozen and the quantity of bedsteads and bureaus jumped from 76 to 980 and from 16 to 350, respectively. But the most impressive proof of the government's effort to stimulate advancement was the increase in the number of plows and wagons from 721 to 1,673 and from 227 to 1,123, respectively. Purchase of such expensive items for Indian use indicated that the desirability of more practical gifts was fully realized. By continued distribution of such items, officials hoped that further issues ultimately might be unnecessary.[19]

The extent of this successful readjustment may be understood even more clearly by comparing the relationship between subsistence appropriations and funds provided for education and agriculture during the early eighties. Although the government still spent large sums to support Indians, and although the 1885 item for annuities was slightly larger than that of 1881, the proportion devoted to agricultural and educational purposes steadily mounted. While funds contributing directly to Indian advancement constituted only 14.42% of the 1881 appropriation, over 25% of the 1885 funds were intended to encourage farming and support schools. As sums voted for the purchase and transportation of annuities decreased during the same period from 70% of the appropriation to 59%, the Indian Office had required only four years to transfer 11% of the annual appropriations to more useful purposes.[20] Once successfully initiated, the substitution of educational and agricultural appropriations for annuities of food and clothing was extended as rapidly as conditions permitted.

But reformation of the annuity system was not limited to alterations in the type of goods distributed to the Indians. There were several ways of using annuity issues to encourage advancement without in the least altering their nature. One of the most important of these was to issue goods directly to the individual Indian instead of through his chief. Deciding that the power of tribal leaders was retarding individual initiative, commissioners sent to study conditions among the Sioux in 1878 recommended that annuity issues should be made only to the head of each family.[21] The advantages of establishing close personal relationship with each Indian were so obvious that, in spite of the additional expense of dealing with individuals, payment through the chiefs soon became extremely rare. Indian rulers expressed resentment at their loss of power and family issues contributed to at least one Indian outbreak,[22] but in general few tribal members expressed any criticism of a practice which was undermining the power of their leaders.

Plans to avert the evils of Indian improvidence by shortening the period between issues were suggested as still another means of employing the annuity system for Indian benefit. With this in mind, Commissioner Price tried to check the disastrous effects of wastefulness by weekly issues.[23] But although no one denied that more frequent issues would prevent the squandering of supplies, the experiment was not popular.[24] Legislators realized that the expense of storage between issues would cancel whatever savings were made through abolition of deficiency appropriations to provide for starving Indians, while reformers rejected the change because Indians would be drawn from their land so often that advancement would be discouraged. Such a measure was a concession to, rather than a correction of, an Indian weakness. If Indians were to become independent, racial failings needed to be cured, not evaded.

A desire to eradicate rather than temporize with Indian wastefulness caused many reformers to recommend that the period between issues should be lengthened rather than shortened. Believing that the consequence of improvidence could be learned only through actual suffering, legislators and administrators frequently advocated rejection of all requests for emergency supplies.[25] Some reformers, far more extreme, urged that Indians would learn the necessity for thrift only if issues were made at intervals of four

114

or five years.[26] But any considerable extension of the period between issues was impossible; for teaching tribes the value of frugality by starving them to death was an exceedingly futile method of improvement! Neither decreasing nor increasing the period between issues offered any hope of solving the annuity problem. Changes of another nature were necessary if Indians were to avoid being either pampered or annihilated.

By far the most fundamental proposal for reforming the annuity system was a demand that Indians should work for their supplies. Even the cleverest apologists for such a change did not deny that a labor requirement would revolutionize the purpose of the annuity system. Yet with Congress rebelling against voting further annuity appropriations without some return, the requirement of work in consideration for payments seemed the only alternative to discontinuance of the system. Adoption of a labor proviso was earnestly considered by the House as early as 1870.[27] The change was not officially recommended until 1873, however, when Commissioner E. P. Smith reported that an experiment with the Sisseton and Wahpeton Sioux under their treaty of 1867 had been sufficiently successful to warrant extension of the practice.[28] In line with this suggestion, Congress provided in the Indian Appropriation bill of 1874 that "all able-bodied male Indians, between the age of eighteen and forty-five" should be required to perform services on the reservations at a reasonable rate "to an amount equal in value to the supplies to be delivered." [29] While the Secretary of the Interior was allowed to issue orders exempting tribes from this requirement, repetition of the provision in 1875 proved that congressmen wished to have the new policy put into effect wherever possible.[30] Where tribes could be required to work for their supplies, annuity issues would no longer be given gratuitously but instead would be made important parts of a system for encouraging Indian advancement.

Passage of a measure requiring Indians to work for their annuity payments presented reformers and administrators with unusual problems. Most welcomed the opportunity to stimulate Indian initiative. Yet many hesitated to threaten tribes with starvation even as a means of speeding reforms, and still others were forced to admit that application of the labor requirement was impossible where rations were supplied according to treaty.[31] Legislators also recognized the injustice of forcing the labor requirement upon treaty tribes, for senators refused to withhold food from members of hostile tribes who remained peacefully on their reservations in 1876 and specifically excluded treaty tribes from an announcement of an impending annuity reduction in 1882.[32] Many friends of the Indians hoped to discover some equally effective method of civilizing Indians which could be applied more widely. In the meantime, a large majority at last recognized that if Indian advancement was to become a reality tribes must be forced to labor for their provisions wherever treaties did not stand in the way.

Since reformers had difficulty in determining how modification of the annuity system should be undertaken in cases in which the government had assumed no obligation, agreement regarding the proper method of approach when treaties provided for payments proved quite impossible. Expert opinion was completely divided as to the advisability of force when the reduction of annuities was first widely discussed in 1874.[33] A clearer understanding of the problem as time passed only emphasized earlier disagreements. Against a conviction that no action should be taken without Indian consent was pitted a belief that a strict observation of treaty provisions would injure the tribes.[34] Many Indian friends, whose sincerity was not to be questioned, advocated abrogation of all annuity provisions. Such action was too extreme for most Americans, but enough people were convinced of the need for Indian self-sufficiency to force a gradual curtailment of annuity issues whenever labor could be demanded without serious violation of previous guarantees.[35] Congress so frequently allowed its passion for economy to overcome its concern for Indian welfare, in fact, that reformers constantly had to concentrate upon maintaining appropriations rather than upon the reduction of annuities. Reformation of the annuity system was wise as long as the ultimate purpose of Indian advancement was remembered; but whenever a desire to save money became the main motive, changes were dangerous. No consideration of the annuity problem would be complete, indeed, without examination of the desire of Congress for economy which so frequently served as a motive for change.

Congressional Economy

Indian administration following the Civil War was repeatedly on the verge of collapse because of a shortage of funds. Congress seldom hesitated to appropriate money if constituents were to gain; but as few whites lived near the tribes and as the red men did not vote, there was little incentive to maintain amounts employed for the Indian at a reasonable level. Since it was useless to formulate plans without some assurance of obtaining funds for their execution, administrators and reformers had to battle proposed reductions at every session. Legislators, in their desire to prevent unnecessary expenditures, were inclined to forget that the expense of a policy should be judged by its ultimate rather than its immediate savings. A wholesale reduction of Indian appropriations, for example, not only enhanced the danger of a costly war but indefinitely delayed the day when the tribes would be able to support themselves. But in spite of constant advice that a wise policy should aim at saving men rather than money, a large number of legislators consistently struggled to reduce Indian appropriations.[36]

Without exception, the annual battles over Indian appropriations found the House of Representatives and the Democrats acting as the special champions of economy.[37] The yearly figure was kept near the five million mark almost solely through the efforts of Republican senators from New England and the West. Indian appropriation bills advanced through Congress in a regular routine. First, the House would adopt a measure providing funds well below the figure requested by the Indian Bureau; then the Senate would increase this amount materially, approaching if not surpassing the aim desired; and finally a bill would emerge from conference providing somewhat less than administrators had asked, but also well above the original figures of House economizers. Crises over Indian appropriations were usually very similar in nature and often arose over apparent trivialities. Thus House Democrats joined with a small majority of House Republicans in 1874 to allow but one-fifth of a $250,000 Apache increase voted by a large majority of both parties in the Senate. When the same subject was discussed by the Senate during the following year, the Democrats nearly succeeded in abolishing the entire appropriation.[38] Five years later a session marked by many attacks on Indian appropriations displayed a similar division on the significant question of non-treaty appropriations. Yet a leading issue was whether the Cheyenne Indians should be given a mere $5,000 worth of seeds not provided for in any treaty. As Senate sponsors of the proposal frankly admitted that the appropriation was not obligatory, the 29-24 vote in favor of the provision revealed that Eastern Republicans and senators of both parties in states containing the wildest Indians were more willing to exceed treaty requirements than a large majority of the Democrats and a group of mid-westerners of both parties who lived further from hostile tribes. The successful resistance of the House to including even this small appropriation in the conference report makes particularly clear the powerful resistance which all non-treaty proposals encountered.[39]

The opinions expressed by individual congressmen during debates regarding Indian appropriations were the results of both sectional and party considerations. Since most Democrats advocated the fulfillment of treaty obligations, their stand against supplying additional funds may be attributed to reluctance to appropriate large sums for the use of Republican administrators. The opposition of the House, on the other hand, arose because of the large number of Easterners who were willing to vote money when their own constituents were involved, but who showed little concern when Western needs were concerned. The Senate, with a greater proportion of Western members than the House and so better fitted to take a national point of view, understood the necessity for appropriations more fully. Under the leadership of Republicans from New England and the West, the Senate was the main ally of Indian administrators. But neither the enthusiasm of reformers nor the desire of Western senators to secure large appropriations for local expenditure led even the most favorable senators to support every request of the government. With constituents condemning employment of their money to support an idle race, all legislators considered Indian appropriations with unusual care. Certain Republican senators were noted as champions of the Indians not because of any great enthusiasm for the cause, but because they demanded less reductions than most.

The congressional practice of providing as little as possible for the conduct of Indian affairs seriously impeded reform. As Colonel Dodge and other students of the Indian question complained, large funds voted in days of plenty were being abolished at the very time extinction of the buffalo made the need for assistance especially great.[40] There was no relation between the miracles Congress wished the Indians to accomplish and the means it provided to help them do so. Plans for stimulating advancement included in the Appropriation Bill of 1875 were nullified by a section which forced a reduction of personnel by allowing but $6,000 annually to be spent for an agency's employees just as additional workers were needed.[41] While the Secretary of the Interior was permitted to increase the figure to $10,000 wherever necessary, even the higher amount was far from adequate for most reservations. Administrators constantly stressed the impossibility of encouraging Indian advancement with such a limited personnel, and after five years of agitation finally obtained clauses exempting Indian employees and white teachers from the maximum salary requirement.[42] As there was an imperative need for instruction outside of the schools, however, such concessions were insufficient. Even when Congress at last voted $25,000 for employing farmers in 1884, the inadequacy of a measure enabling assignment of but one farmer to every three agencies was widely noted.[43] More employees and men of considerably greater ability were necessary if annuities were to be reduced, for while anyone could distribute rations in one day, farming instructors had to exert intelligent effort over a long period.[44] A large but temporary increase in appropriations might have produced surprising results if well administered. Congress did spend increasing amounts for Indian civilization during the eighties, but the total was comparatively small and constant pressure from Indian administrators and reformers was necessary to prevent sudden reductions.

Congressional economy retarded the advancement of many

tribes; but to have gone to the opposite extreme and immediately paid all annuity funds in cash, as some reformers desired, would have destroyed them completely. Overconfidence in Indian ability caused certain friends to recommend a plan which was advocated with equal enthusiasm by selfish whites.[45] Indians were not ready for such responsibility. The speed with which money paid to the Indians found its way into the hands of white men was notorious. Yet there were many people who felt that independence would be worth serious losses. The leading Indian Rights Association investigator wrote of the Omahas, "The Indians want all this money at once, and I think it would be in every way a good thing to let them have it and expend it and have done with it. They may waste some of it, but if they waste it all, it is still better that they should have it and exhaust it, and then have to depend wholly upon themselves." [46] Indians were not slow to back such proposals. The prospect of immediate riches was intriguing, and with their usual lack of foresight red men failed to consider how inconvenient the absence of future help might prove. Some of the more intelligent members of the race foresaw sufficient personal gain to warrant suffering for other Indians.[47] But only an inadequate appreciation of the value of government assistance caused people who had the Indian's interest at heart to support the demand for immediate surrender of all money to the tribes. Full payment of all obligations was suggested in hope of stimulating advancement and enabling future economy, but with little thought of what would happen when penniless Indians returned to ask further aid of an inconsiderate Congress. Many features of the old system, in spite of fundamental weaknesses, did provide protection from dangers which reformers were too inclined to discount in their enthusiasm for progress. Such policies could be safely abandoned only after equally successful methods of defending the Indian had been devised. The annuity system could not be abolished at once and problems of a similar nature confronted reformers who wished to terminate a third policy of long standing, the reservation system.

10. THE RESERVATION SYSTEM

WHETHER INDIANS SHOULD BE CONFINED TO LIMITED AREAS UNDER government supervision has always been one of the most important questions confronting United States officials. Although no one denies that administrative problems are ·simpler and interracial difficulties more easily avoided when tribes are located on such reservations, the policy has been frequently opposed. Reformers of the seventies and eighties, in particular, regretted that isolation was preventing Indians from learning the ways of white society. Yet today the results of forcing a strange method of life upon the red men are condemned by Indian officials, and the government is attempting through the Wheeler-Howard Act of 1934 to stimulate native customs by re-establishing separate Indian communities. Such a move is undoubtedly retrogressive, if cultural assimilation is an ideal. With the growing tendency to question the benefits of private ownership, however, many Americans have learned to regard Indian ideas more tolerantly and see less need for forcing Indians to conform to alien habits. This attitude is new. While Indian isolation was frequently defended in the years following the Civil War as a means of protecting the frontier, there was little suggestion that preservation of Indian society was itself desirable. Once the danger of inter-racial warfare disappeared, the reservation system seemed hopelessly out-of-date and no step was considered more essential to Indian advancement than abolition of a policy which was separating the races.

Although an awakening interest in Indian affairs soon revolutionized public opinion regarding the reservation system, segregation was especially popular following the Civil War. In colonial days Indians remaining among the settlers were frequently ordered to stay within specified limits, but so many tribes preferred to move West instead of living near white settlements that little land outside of the Indian Territory had been set aside for Indian occupation before 1850.[1] Only as large numbers of Americans began to cross the plains in the fifties was there serious need for restricting

Indian movements. Once interest in Western travel mounted, however, the inadvisability of allowing tribes to roam at will became so evident that officials at last endeavored to end the wanderings of all Indians. The reservation system, instituted to achieve this purpose, reached its climax in the decade after the Civil War.[2] By 1870, all but the wildest Indians had been induced to accept treaties in which they agreed to stay within established boundaries. In return, the government promised to punish white invaders and provide the tribes with food and clothing until they were able to supply themselves. Through such agreements both races pledged themselves to do everything in their power to avoid inter-racial contact. So fully was the principle of isolation embodied in the provisions that relations between the races were not only subject to strict regulation, but almost extinguished.

Even though the reservation system closed large areas of the West to white men, it possessed enough advantages to win favor for several years. Not only were many sections opened to settlement by Indian removal, but the danger of raids was reduced by the strict regulation of tribal activities. With the number of conflicts between the races rapidly declining, frontiersmen concurred with officials who maintained that the erection of Indian barriers was "shrewdly devised to meet the known weaknesses of the Indian character."[3] Until greed for land exceeded fear of war, there was no demand that the system be abandoned.

While Westerners supported the reservation system because of its success in reducing the number of raids, Easterners were more interested in the policy as a means of protecting the Indians. The Indians rather than the frontiersmen had been the greatest sufferers from unregulated racial contact despite the distress occasioned by Indian attacks. As long as red men had been required to defend themselves, opportunities for fraud had proved unlimited. Conditions improved tremendously once the government regulated intercourse with the tribes. Although this policy necessitated racial isolation, the dangers of contact were so great that friends of the Indians long opposed any modification. Until Indians were ready to compete with whites on equal terms, the reservation system provided invaluable protection.[4]

122

The Reservation System

Isolation, which protected the life and property of both Indians and whites, was equally beneficial in its effect upon character. Reformers had long noticed the alarming fact that racial contact spread evil habits more rapidly than good.[5] Thus Indians learned to gamble and drink without becoming ambitious, while border whites grew more stealthy and cruel without appreciating the value of stoicism or communal life. Racial segregation was the only way to prevent such evils. Most administrators, it is true, realized that isolation could not be continued indefinitely; but they also knew that a temporary establishment of reservations would enable the Indians to prepare for future contacts without interference. Only after Indians had learned to live in white society would unregulated contact be safe. Until that time reservations would prove of benefit if used as training grounds and not merely in a foolish hope of postponing the inevitable meeting between the races.

The Rise of Opposition to Segregation

The impossibility of adopting the reservation system as a permanent policy was generally recognized. A significant sample of opinion regarding the utility of isolation was obtained in 1874 when the Board of Indian Commissioners asked a group of agents, "Does your experience lead you to believe that they [your Indians] will prosper and support themselves among whites or will they become vagabond beggars & thieves?"[6] Answers to this query revealed that interest in segregation was already beginning to wane. Fifteen observers, it is true, felt that reservation Indians were less exposed to corruption than they would be under any other system; but three correspondents from Michigan and Minnesota believed that contact with white neighbors would be of benefit to their tribes.[7] As Indians living west of the Mississippi had opportunity to become as well prepared to live among nearby settlers as those of Michigan, Minnesota, and Wisconsin, opposition to the reservation was certain to increase. But for the moment Secretary Whittlesey of the Board was forced to confess that while he believed a Minnesota correspondent supporting contact had presented the "wisest view of the whole case" there was no "good ground to hope that Congress would adopt it & enact it into an 'Indian policy.' " [8] The reservation system was securely established for several years to come.

While isolation had many energetic defenders in 1874, even the most conservative reformers considered the policy of limited use a decade later. Secretary of the Interior Lamar still dreaded the evils of unregulated contact in 1885; but realizing that Indians must meet the whites on an equal basis sooner or later, he admitted the wisdom of opening portions of all reservations.[9] His desire to have a section of each reservation retained for exclusive Indian occupancy, however, did not win popular favor. Americans had become too interested in establishing close contacts with the Indians to allow the change to proceed gradually. Arguments against the reservation system, which had convinced Lamar of the need for establishing closer inter-racial relationships, led less cautious workers to demand the immediate abandonment of all segregation.

Opposition to Indian isolation had been expressed at the very height of the reservation system's popularity. As early as 1862, General Pope urged the government to move Indians nearer white settlements to enable more frequent contacts.[10] But the first systematic attack on the reservation system occurred when a small but determined group of Western congressmen leveled repeated charges against segregation in the years immediately following the Civil War.[11] Still more persistent complaints were registered during the early seventies by senators and representatives from Nevada and Northern California. As the Indians of both states had associated intimately with neighboring whites for many years, congressmen from the area saw no reason why the tribes should be placed upon reservations.[12] In endeavoring to thwart effective national control of local tribes, these men developed arguments which were increasingly employed as opposition to segregation grew. For a time, few people believed that contact with the whites was essential to Indian advancement. But as each year passed, more and more Americans became convinced that progress would be impossible unless inter-racial relationships were increased by relaxation, if not outright abolition, of the reservation system.

A widespread desire to obtain additional Indian land undoubtedly

124

played a major part in stirring public criticism of the reservation system. As many people whose friendship with the Indians was unquestioned argued that the government had authority to employ any section of the country it pleased for purposes of public welfare,[13] the eagerness with which frontiersmen advocated opening the land of neighboring Indians was not surprising. Many men honestly believed that reservations were barriers to progress, but a large number made no effort to cover their selfish designs. Statements issued by opponents of the reservation system often displayed an astonishing disregard for Indian rights. Thus Governor McCook of Colorado announced that because "God gave to us the earth, and the fulness thereof, in order that we might utilize and enjoy His gifts," occupation of the best portions of his territory by indolent Indians would no longer be tolerated.[14] To men who considered themselves divinely chosen to dispossess savages, the humanitarian principles upon which segregation was based could have no appeal. Standards of honor and justice meant nothing to men seized with a hunger for land. Even many Indian officials forgot their responsibilities under stress of opportunities for personal gain. A tribe could expect little sympathy from an agent who urged that its land should not be withheld from the public "merely because a rude agreement called a treaty, placed it within the boundaries of a described reservation."[15] With men intimately connected with the Indians frequently recommending that acquisition of Indian land should be considered paramount to protection of tribal rights, the public was easily persuaded that the welfare of the country depended upon immediate destruction of a system which reserved large areas of the West for Indian occupation.

Although a craving for land was responsible for much of the criticism of the reservation system, opposition also resulted from considerations of a less selfish nature. In the opinion of many Americans, Indians would benefit from inter-racial contact as well as whites. Since red men in the Indian Territory and the East had profited from intercourse with their neighbors, similar progress might be expected if other tribes were exposed to the influence of white civilization.[16] Even reformers who were far from certain regarding the superiority of white institutions admitted that the inevitability of ultimate contact rendered attempts to secure tribes in the possession of large areas of land unwise.[17] Since illiteracy would never be conquered by concentrating the forces of ignorance, reformers urged that "the expiring embers of savagery and heathenism should be scattered."[18] Indians would be exposed to serious dangers once reservations were abandoned, but such risks had to be faced if they were to advance.

The greatest threat to successful intercourse between Indian and white was the unscrupulousness of settlers residing in the vicinity of reservations. Close contact might be beneficial if Indians were assisted by their neighbors. Since most frontiersmen were merely interested in exploiting the tribes, however, the prospect of satisfactory relations was not promising. Many enthusiastic champions of assimilation hesitated to abandon segregation until conditions surrounding the reservations offered a greater possibility of success.[19] But the advocates of caution were outnumbered. Failure to appreciate the complex nature of adjustments which had to be made in shifting from one society to another caused most Americans to believe that all efforts to postpone destruction of the reservation system were only unjustified attempts to preserve the Indians as a separate race.

In spite of the varied motives which inspired friends and foes of the Indians to demand abandonment of the reservation system, both factions condemned isolation as an obstacle to national unity. Whether a citizen was more interested in securing land or in aiding the red man, he was invariably impressed by the impossibility of achieving national solidarity as long as the segregation policy was continued. Realizing that a unified society required complete racial equality, many Americans advocated revocation of all privileges possessed by the tribes.[20] The racial distinctions upon which the policy of segregation rested seemed out of place to most citizens in a country noted for its championship of equal rights and its ability to absorb alien peoples. Many Americans insisted that Indians had no more right to have a special government bureau than members of any other race.[21] Although such critics disregarded the peculiar nature of the government's obligation to the tribes, even reformers who recognized the nation's responsibility for Indian welfare sometimes demanded an end of isolation.

Whether selfish or charitable motives predominated among opponents of the reservation system is difficult to determine. Men's motives are usually mixed; and as self-seeking was easily disguised, the average declaration of purpose was seldom reliable. Yet one conclusion is clear—if either enemies or friends of the Indians had unitedly resisted the change, a tendency to cling to established customs would have enabled the system to survive. The demand for abandonment of the reservations was overpowering only because the change promised to benefit both Indians and whites. If whites had lost by the opening of reservations or if ultimate contact had been generally considered detrimental to the Indians, defense of segregation would not have been largely confined to the unpopular Indian Defense Association.[22] As it was, many friends of the tribes were so thoroughly convinced of the need for change that the evils of isolation were frequently exaggerated. In declaring that "Satan himself could not have devised a better plan" for checking Indian advancement, President Gates of Rutgers College was only slightly more outspoken than other members of the Board of Indian Commissioners.[23] But although Dr. Gates's frequent outbursts against "the sinks of iniquity" were so exaggerated in rhetoric that he once urged reformers to burn the reservation system like a fever-infected hospital, the impracticality of his suggestion did not impair the popularity of his cause.[24] Americans objected to segregation so strenuously that the question engaging public attention during the eighties was not so much the advisability of the change as the manner in which it should be effected.

Plans for Abolishing the Reservation System

The decision of administrators to abandon the reservation system did not solve the problem of what policy should be substituted. Although a few reformers believed that the race could be absorbed without difficulty, most realized that unusual care was necessary to prevent disaster, As a result, numerous suggestions were offered for avoiding the dangers of unregulated contact. A final selection was made only after the relative expediency of several schemes had been thoroughly investigated.

One of the most popular plans introduced as a substitute for the reservation system proposed that tribes should be moved to locations where contact with whites would prove more beneficial than on the frontier. The suggestion had an unusually wide appeal, since frontiersmen were just as anxious to get rid of their Indians as reformers were to secure satisfactory neighbors for the tribes. Return of the red men to states east of the Mississippi was frequently recommended on the ground that civilization would be more easily encouraged because of the larger number of whites and the greater cultural refinement.[25] Elaborate plans for distributing Indians among the states were submitted to President Grant in 1870 and 1873 and to Secretary of the Interior Schurz in 1878.[26] But although reformers professed interest in racial advancement, none rushed to provide facilities for settlement in his own community. When Delegate Downey of Wyoming suggested early in 1880 that tribes should be moved to the East, his measure was quickly ruled out of order.[27] Easterners were always ready to lecture frontiersmen regarding the proper treatment of Indians but were unwilling to sanction any measure which would force them to apply their principles at home. Further Indian removals would be too expensive, they complained, glad of an excuse to avoid close association with their beloved wards. The refusal of Easterners to bear any portion of the burden of adjusting red men to white society checked any chance that tribes might be moved among more sympathetic neighbors. With no section ready to assume responsibility for the care of additional Indians, administrators were forced to admit that tribes must make the best of their surroundings rather than hope to be civilized under more pleasant conditions.

Realization that civilization of the red man must be undertaken on existing reservations caused certain legislators to urge that Indian affairs be administered locally. Western states and territories had long hoped to secure jurisdiction over their tribes. A bill introduced in 1870 by Representative Axtell of California had provided that all federal funds appropriated for local Indians should be spent by the Governor of each state instead of the Secretary of the Interior; and during the next session Representative Fitch of Nevada had declared that "the best Indian policy would be no policy at all, except to place in the hands of the settlers on the frontier the means of settling the Indian problem in their own way and that way would be very simple and very economical and very just." [28] But while frontiersmen always proclaimed their intention to handle Indians fairly, a majority of United States legislators realized that too many selfish interests were at work to enable satisfactory local administration. And since the reservation system was the only effective obstacle to local control, Indian officials and reformers hesitated to expose tribes to frontier rule by abandoning segregation. Occasionally selfish considerations caused professed friends of the race to recommend state administration, as when a Catholic author advocated an end of federal control in hope that his Church would receive better treatment from local authorities.[29] Enthusiastic championship of local rule, however, was generally confined to Western legislators, who even suggested that reservations should be leased to private individuals to relieve the government of further expense. But neither the fact that such a rash proposal received twenty-four votes in the House in 1880 nor the earnestness with which schemes of this nature were pressed altered the government's decision to proceed slowly.[30] As any attempt to civilize Indians by removing them from federal jurisdiction would invite disaster, United States administrators were determined to retain their authority over the tribes indefinitely.

Having concluded that the United States could not remove tribes to more favorable localities and should not surrender control to Western officials, reformers sought some means by which interracial contact might be encouraged without endangering Indian welfare. This aim might be accomplished, it was hoped, by reducing the size of reservations instead of abolishing them entirely. If Indian titles were carefully defended at the same time tribes were required to live within more restricted areas, administrators might preserve the advantages of the reservation system while avoiding its evils. Students of Indian affairs frequently urged, therefore, that the holdings of each tribe should be diminished by opening its reservation to white settlement after a specified acreage had been set aside for every Indian. Most features of this important proposal can be discussed to better advantage later. But the portion of the plan which provided that whites should be allowed to enter alternate sections of every reservation was a fundamental part of the campaign for encouraging racial contact.

Little improvement in the red man's ability to acquire strange customs could be expected if reservations were reduced without providing more opportunities for contact. But when Ottawa lands were allotted in 1862, Congress had declared that all assignments "be made adjoining, and in as regular and compact form as possible." [31] Only as the evils of isolation were more thoroughly understood did reformers recommend that the allotment policy should be utilized to mix the races. Yet once the nation awoke to the need for encouraging contact, many plans were offered for opening reservations to white settlement.[32] While land left in Indian hands was still protected every effort was made to abandon the policy of isolation and to place whites on land adjacent to Indian holdings. In the opinion of Captain Pratt of the Carlisle Indian School, this tendency was not carried far enough; [33] but administrators had at least decided that racial contact was to be encouraged rather than avoided.

Although the decision of administrators to discontinue the reservation system established the course of future reforms, many adjustments were necessary before segregation could be completely abandoned. The relentless advance of white settlement gradually forced even the most ardent champions of Indian rights to admit the impossibility of avoiding racial absorption. Secretary of the Interior Schurz, who at first defended the reservation system, soon changed his mind and shortly after his retirement in 1881 declared that "a stubborn maintenance of the system of large Indian reservations must eventually result in the destruction of the red men" however careful the government was to protect their rights.[34] But although this warning was justified, successful contact would have been impossible if isolation had been abandoned immediately. Indians needed to be trained to support themselves before government protection ceased. If the reservation system was discontinued prematurely, unscrupulous whites would take advantage of

Indian ignorance. Whether planning to abandon reservations, adjust annuity issues, or abolish treaties, reformers were forced to conclude that little progress could be made until Indian educational facilities had been substantially improved.

11. THE PROBLEM OF
INDIAN EDUCATION

ALTHOUGH EDUCATION SHOULD HAVE BEEN RECOGNIZED AS AN ESsential part of any intelligent Indian policy, the United States did not offer satisfactory opportunities for instruction until late in the nineteenth century. Adequate schooling had been so rare that few red men of 1880 spoke English in spite of their century of contact with United States officials. Numerous treaties promising schools and teachers had been concluded before the Civil War, but in only a few instances were such pledges even partially fulfilled. Treaties of 1855 with the Yakima and Nez Percé Indians, for example, stated that the United States would establish "within one year of ratification hereof, two schools, erecting the necessary buildings, keeping the same in repair, and providing them with furniture, books, and stationery"; yet aid to a school founded on the reservation of the former in 1860 was quickly withdrawn and no effort was made to supply a school for the latter until 1867.[1] The story of post-war efforts was equally dismal. Neglect of treaty obligations was less flagrant in these years only because Congress cautiously provided that tribal opposition might be used as an excuse for inaction.[2] As Indian hostility was inevitable, the reluctance of legislators to permit compulsory instruction prevented establishment of an adequate educational system. The unfortunate effect of such indifference did not escape reformers, the Board of Indian Commissioners insisting in 1875 that the Indian problem would already have been solved if promised schools had been provided, and the House Indian Committee reporting as late as 1880 that only one child in twelve was being instructed.[3] In spite of America's exceptional interest in public education, training of the Indian was so neglected that any one examining educational facilities on the reservations in the seventies would hardly have imagined that the United States had even the remotest responsibility for Indian welfare.

132

The Problem of Indian Education

In explaining the failure of their government to foster Indian education, Americans emphasized the difficulty of conducting schools in the face of tribal resistance. Critics of the race naturally believed that inadequate schooling could be attributed to the red man's aversion to change; but many close friends of the race were equally insistent that Indian indifference was responsible for the collapse of educational efforts.[4] Representative of such disillusionment was a Western doctor, who wrote the Indian Bureau that he wished to dispose of a young Indian prisoner whom he had endeavored to train for ten years without success.[5] Many advanced Indians did write the Indian Bureau for money to finance additional education, one correspondent actually enclosing elaborate drawings as samples of his qualifications for aid.[6] But as such applications were confined to the most intelligent red men, administrators were extremely discouraged. The average Indian rebelled against any education for himself and sent his children to school only when he was forced to do so. Such an excellent Indian worker as Captain Pratt of the Carlisle Indian School needed every ounce of his extraordinary diplomacy to secure Indian students and often considered his efforts at conversion futile.[7] Even Bland of the *Council Fire*, who hoped tribes would advance voluntarily, reluctantly confessed that the reaction of Indians to offers of instruction was generally unfavorable.[8] Having been encouraged in their indolence for years, Indians refused to accept any system demanding exertion. If Indian education were to be successful, reformers needed to disregard tribal objections and insist upon instruction whether it was welcomed or not.

While Indian opposition to education placed formidable obstacles in the path of racial progress, the reluctance of tribes to take advantage of their educational opportunities was understandable. A race could not be expected to accept passively a civilization which demanded surrender of its dearest traditions. From the vantage point of later years, in fact, some authors contend that the red man's attitude was not only understandable but wise. Thus Stanley Vestal recently upheld Sitting Bull's opposition to remodeling his way of life by writing:

Uncle Sam's Stepchildren

If one believes that the world has made no mistake in scrapping most of what passed for civilization in the '80's, then one cannot deny that Sitting Bull was wise. But the old Indian Bureau wished him to take it over, as it was, lock, stock and barrel. No man of intelligence could or would do that.[9]

One need not concede Sitting Bull superhuman insight into the ways of mankind, however, to admit that enthusiasm for education among members of his race would have been surprising. As tribes knew only the rough ways of frontier society and were uninformed concerning the more attractive aspects of civilization, they had little incentive to expend the effort necessary to acquire new customs. A decision to labor was not made easier by the growing inclination of officials to place Indian offenders at work on the reservations.[10] Nor was advancement encouraged by the lack of confidence in Indian integrity displayed when schools were erected with bullet-proof shutters and educators declared that every pupil would be a hostage.[11] Failure of educational efforts could not be blamed upon the red man until after Americans had made a sincere effort to overcome the Indian's natural hostility to a change of culture.

White Neglect of Indian Education

The complaint that Indian indifference was retarding advancement would have been more effective if congressmen had shown a reasonable amount of interest in providing educational appropriations during the seventies. While large sums were voted annually for the "civilization and sustenance" of certain tribes, little of the money was spent for instruction. Congress itself recognized the need for additional efforts in 1870 by appropriating $100,000 to support schools for which no specific provision had been made.[12] Even this modest sum was spent so cautiously that $40,000 still remained for reappropriation in 1874. The Senate, in view of the surplus, not only refused to add over $10,000 to the fund, but two years later joined the House in limiting an appropriation setting aside Indian money for educational purposes to a mere $20,000.[13] Although administrators frequently protested that such paltry

134

amounts were of little value, Congress refused either to increase or decrease most appropriations. Desertion of nine Republican senators in 1875, for example, defeated a committee proposal raising the education fund of the Central Superintendency; yet a motion to strike out the entire appropriation was also defeated by the return of all but one of these senators to the party fold.[14] As a result of such tactics, appropriations for Indian education was never sufficiently large to enable establishment of an adequate system. Frequent debates arose concerning the relative significance of inadequate educational appropriations and Indian opposition in explaining tribal ignorance. Among those best qualified to judge there was little doubt; for of forty-eight agents who were asked whether the deficiencies in the Indian's educational equipment were caused by lack of facilities or aversion to education, thirty-three accused the government, six blamed the Indians, and nine held that both were at fault.[15] Responsibility for delaying tribal advancement, at any rate, could not be shifted entirely upon the Indians.

While no section of the United States was exclusively to blame for the neglect of Indian education, Western legislators were unusually active in opposing plans to train the race at government expense. Such representatives did not agree with reformers who held that frontier communities would be the first to benefit from Indian advancement.[16] They insisted, instead, that education would only enable Indians to combat white interests more intelligently. To prevent such a disaster, Westerners defeated educational appropriations and forced agents to abandon plans for speeding tribal advancement in order to retain their posts.[17] Occasionally a desire for financial profit caused citizens of certain frontier areas to ask establishment of an Indian school, but although the Albuquerque Board of Trade requested $75,000 for a school in 1883, the project was severely criticized once local workers realized that they might lose their positions to government-educated Indians.[18] A few Westerners did foresee the advantage of mollifying the red man's savagery, but neighbors of the tribes were not conspicuous in the Indian educational movement.

Even more effective than Western opposition in delaying establishment of a satisfactory educational system was a common conviction that Indians were incapable of progress. Frontier legislators would not have been able to defeat educational projects if citizens of other sections had believed that such efforts would succeed. Sufficient respect for Indian qualities to stir interest in large educational appropriations was not to be expected from Westerners, who loved to quote opinions of Spencer and Buckle as evidence of the impossibility of Indian advancement or to ridicule the disgust of agents whose Indians insisted upon cutting a circular section from their trousers "at the point where the Government reinforces for cavalry service." [19] But similar skepticism regarding Indian abilities was expressed by men intimately concerned with Indian affairs. General Sherman took the occasion of acknowledging Bishop Whipple's condolence upon Mrs. Sherman's death to express a conviction that Indian work was futile! [20] A surprising number of Indian officials and legislators seemed to share this opinion. Not only did one agent write that he would send his superintendent a coat as soon as he could "keep an Indian sober long enough to make it," but another bitterly condemned his Indians for being lethargic, selfish, superstitious, and conservative.[21] Despite years of service for the red men, Senator Windom of Minnesota announced that no liars and vagabonds equal to the Indians could be found on the face of the earth.[22] Wherever a tribe's accomplishments threatened to disprove such scornful conceptions of the red man's ability, the exception was declared the consequence of a large admixture of white blood or of some other factor unrelated to native intelligence. Such unfavorable opinions were undoubtedly justified in the case of certain Western tribes. But more striking distrust of Indian ability could not have been expressed than when a New York agent announced that government training would only further corrupt his Indians.[23] As long as administrators believed that even the most advanced tribes would not benefit from education, efforts to elevate the race could not be undertaken with any enthusiasm.

Even close friends of the Indians shared the pessimism of frontiersmen and administrators regarding tribal ability. General Hazen, who frequently expressed sympathy for the race, declared the Indian "a dirty beggar and a thief" standing "in the way of natural evolutions of progress." [24] A poet, who had been especially critical of American Indian policy, confessed that "a more intimate acquaintance with Mr. 'Lo' served to take out a large amount of the starch of poetry from the linen of his imagination." [25] Even Bland of the *Council Fire*, instead of emphasizing his belief that the tribes would be the greatest sufferers from reform movements, preferred to intimate that proposed changes would turn 200,000 untamed Indians loose upon the country.[26] Belief in the desirability of reform and in the worthlessness of red men were not incompatible. They were often so closely joined that General Sanborn concluded a speech on the need for education by declaring:

> Little can be hoped for them as a distinct people. The sun of their day is fast sinking in the western sky. It will soon go down in a night of oblivion that shall know no morning. . . . No spring-time shall renew their fading glory, and no future know their fame.[27]

The sentiment was general.

As Indians needed the very assistance which even their best friends refused to give without proof of Indian intelligence, the possibility of establishing a satisfactory educational system long seemed very remote. Confidence in Indian ability, so completely lacking in the seventies, was absolutely essential to inauguration of a successful program of training. Indians could not be expected to welcome educational opportunities as long as they were taught to regard themselves as incompetent.[28] Nor could Americans be asked to undertake work requiring the expenditure of much time and money without reasonable assurance of success. Reformers of the eighties would have accomplished little if they had not been able to remove doubts concerning Indian ability. But once the public was convinced that Indians could progress, half the battle was won.

The Rise of Interest in Indian Education

Few developments in Indian history have been more remarkable than the sudden shift in public opinion regarding Indian capability which followed 1880. Many Americans, who ridiculed tribal accomplishments during the seventies, were equally impressed by the possibilities of advancement a few years later. To a great extent this change was the result of an increasing sympathy for the Indian stimulated by intelligent study of his problems. Yet this broader understanding would have been comparatively ineffective, if it had not been accompanied by concrete evidence of the Indian's ability to adapt himself to civilized life. Interest in reform spread rapidly as information regarding Indian aptitude became available.

While lack of publicity was partly responsible for the widespread ignorance of Indian accomplishments, red men had had few opportunities to prove their worth. Where independent effort had not been discouraged by providing Indians with food and clothing they should have learned to supply for themselves, inadequate protection had taught ambitious tribes that their improved land was more subject to invasion than the holdings of less industrious neighbors. There was little incentive for Indians to improve their condition as long as each accomplishment increased the danger of removal.[29] Indian laziness could not be justly criticized until opportunities for advancement had been provided and protection assured. Fortunately, once the need for generous assistance had been emphasized by President Hayes in his first annual message of 1877,[30] there was no abatement in the campaign to increase appropriations for Indian civilization and growing confidence was expressed that success would be assured if Indians were furnished adequate facilities.

Public interest in Indian education was stimulated by knowledge that many tribes had advanced with little or no encouragement from the government. An overwhelming demand for official action arose as mounting evidences of Indian ability awakened citizens to the possibilities of formal instruction. Popular imagination was stirred by the realization that many Indians were not unintelligent. In innumerable ways Indians revealed unforeseen abilities which caused Americans to recognize for the first time that even slight assistance from the government might produce surprising results.

One of the most encouraging manifestations of Indian ability was the successful employment of red men as reservation police in the early seventies. Although Agent Lightfoot of the Iowas reported the appointment of tribal policemen in 1869, the first regular employment of Indians took place in 1872 when a thousand Navajos were selected by General Howard to guard reservation boundaries, arrest thieves, and recover stolen stock.[31] While this force was responsible for the recovery of sixty head of stock during its first three months, its discontinuance was ordered from Washington.[32] This decision was successfully resisted by Agent Arny, however; and by the following year the satisfactory operation of forces among Winnebagoes, Santee and Red Cloud Sioux, and Navajos led Commissioner E. P. Smith to recommend formation of other groups at the Secretary of the Interior's discretion.[33] So widely did this suggestion appeal to men in the service that thirty-nine out of sixty-two agents favored immediate establishment of forces on their reservations.[34] But Indian policemen received no compensation until Congress finally sanctioned the system in 1878 by appropriating $30,000 to pay fifty officers and 430 privates. This sum was doubled the following year and continued to mount thereafter along with the size of the forces and the pay for service.[35] A few agents objected to a scheme which granted so much power to their Indians.[36] Such opposition was impotent in face of the overwhelming popularity of the system. Although the necessity of confining activity to reservations impeded the efficiency of the forces,[37] Indian police performed such valuable services in checking liquor consumption, reducing the number of Indian raids and preventing trespassing by whites that opposition to aiding the tribes could no longer be based upon the inability of Indians to profit from government appropriations.

Tribal attainments in purely civilian activities were even more impressive than those of the Indian police. Accomplishments of the seventies were too numerous to be described at length, but brief reference to a few of the outstanding performances will indicate the nature of developments which ultimately convinced the public of the adaptability of the Indian race. Among these achievements none was more remarkable than the freighting of agency supplies by Indians in the last years of the decade. As late as 1877 supplies were transported from railroad to reservation by white contractors who demanded large sums for their services. It was the exorbitant rates demanded by these men, in fact, which led agents to urge that Indians should be allowed to do the hauling in return for a small wage. So satisfactory were experiments conducted in accordance with this plan among the Cheyenne and Arapahoe in 1877, and with the Spotted Tail and Red Cloud Sioux in 1878, that contract transportation had been abandoned on twenty-four reservations by 1880. As during that year four tribes alone hauled eight million pounds over an average of 150 miles for but $115,900, officials decided to encourage further reductions in freighting charges by giving two thousand wagons to Indians who wished to transport supplies. So Congress, alarmed at the cost of Indian administration and at the difficulty of finding ways to facilitate racial advancement, discovered that both problems could be simplified by a single policy! [38]

Enthusiasm regarding the red man's future was also spurred by the rapid progress of certain tribes toward civilized existence. Many branches of the race shared in this advancement. The Santee Sioux of Nebraska, however, not only made the most striking gains, but received by far the most publicity. The tribe, but one of several forced to move from Minnesota following the massacres of 1865, settled in northern Nebraska apart from the majority of the race. Although over a third of the group was wiped out by disease during the early years, the eight hundred Indians remaining worked to establish a permanent home. Aided in this purpose by the efforts of three missionary schools, the tribe advanced rapidly. Large farms were successfully cultivated, and homes erected; an elective chieftainship was established, and a native paper printed. Such accomplishments attracted wide attention as a result of the publicity work of both the missionaries and government officials. With publication of detailed information regarding increased cultivation between 1873 and 1878 and the resulting reduction in government expenditures, Santee achievements became the leading example of what might be accomplished with sufficient encouragement.[39] As similar, if less spectacular progress was being made by other tribes, doubt regarding Indian ability was gradually dispelled.

The Indian experiment which stirred most interest in the possibilities of education was the attempt of tribes to govern themselves. The Five Civilized Tribes of the Indian Territory were frequently condemned for their insistence upon managing their own affairs, but their accomplishments were appreciated even by those who wished to supplant Indian authority with national rule. Interest also was expressed in the governmental institutions of Pueblo Indians and the executive ability displayed by officers of Indian police forces. Officials became so convinced of the ability of Indians to bear governmental responsibilities, in fact, that several attempts to train the Indians in self-government were initiated during the early eighties. Not only were native courts for the trial of Indian offenses established by the Indian Bureau in 1883, but an inter-tribal council was satisfactorily inaugurated among the Apaches by Agent Clum and a complicated system of self-rule was instituted among the Yakimas by Agent Milroy.[40] But again these were only the most prominent of several efforts; and more remarkable than any particular accomplishment was the unanimity with which reports from all sections of the country portrayed a steady advancement. Since the average Indian had been able to progress in spite of governmental indifference, citizens were justified in hoping that establishment of proper educational facilities would solve the Indian problem.

While Indians provided much evidence of their ability to learn, adequate educational appropriations could not be secured until the public was informed of their accomplishments. A leading task of reformers was to spread knowledge about the achievements of leading tribes. Hoping that readers would be converted to the cause of reform, Indian workers filled such publications as the *Commissioner's Reports*, the *Board Reports* and the *Council Fire* with statistics of racial progress.[41] But far too few people consulted publications of this nature to make the campaign effective. Even when such evidence was read, the most accurate facts and figures were frequently attributed to the bias of administrators and reformers. Americans had been skeptical of Indian qualifications for so many years that only some direct and sensational proof of ability could alter their opinion. Without the successful work of General Armstrong and Captain Pratt at Hampton Institute and the Carlisle Indian School, interest in Indian education might never have been effective.

Establishment of powerful Eastern institutions for Indian education was largely an outcome of the work of Captain Richard Henry Pratt.[42] As a young lieutenant, Pratt was directed in the spring of 1875 to select a group of Cheyenne and Kiowa captives for confinement in Fort Marion, Saint Augustine, Florida. Determined that the seventy-two Indians chosen for this punishment should profit from their experience, Pratt trained them industrially in their Saint Augustine quarters. This instruction so completely transformed the Indians that a majority begged permission to settle in the East when the government ordered their return to the West three years later. This request was rejected by the Indian Bureau; and even when the younger members of the group asked if they might continue their education at Eastern schools, consent was obtained only on condition that their expenses should be privately borne. As Pratt's work had stimulated great enthusiasm among wealthy winter residents of Saint Augustine, this requirement was met by subscription of $115 for each of the twenty-two students desiring to remain. When the prisoners left for home in April, 1878, therefore, seventeen of the twenty-two remaining headed for Hampton Institute, a Virginia Negro school operated by General Samuel Chapman Armstrong. There, under the watchful eyes of the two army men, began the first serious effort to educate the Indian.

Initiation of Indian education at Hampton was only the first of several efforts to train the race. Before the first year was over, General Armstrong secured Secretary Schurz's permission to train fifty additional pupils at government expense and Captain Pratt gathered forty boys and nine girls from Sioux tribes to add to the Indians already at Hampton. But Pratt had still more ambitious plans. Dissatisfied at the prospect of educating Negroes and Indians jointly, he requested permission to open an Indian school in the deserted Army barracks at Carlisle, Pennsylvania. Although General Sherman condemned Indian education as "old woman's work," Secretaries Schurz and McCrary supported the proposal and introduced a bill for transfer of the property to the Interior Department. Pratt's lobbying failed to force consideration of the measure, however, in spite of a favorable House report.[43] Only when Army officers agreed to permit tentative transfer pending congressional action was the experiment able to proceed; and it was without assurance of legislative support that Captain Pratt set out for the West to collect pupils for his school in the summer of 1879.

Work at the Carlisle Indian School began with the arrival of eighty-two Sioux in October, 1879. Collecting the students had proved difficult because of the objections of Chief Spotted Tail, but once his opposition had been overcome more children applied than could be accommodated. Forty-seven Pawnees, Kiowas, and Cheyennes completed the first year's enrollment. The difficulties of the experiment were many; but so much had been accomplished with the aid of eleven of the boys trained in Florida, and of a few white assistants, that when a group of government investigators visited Carlisle three and a half months later the question of an appropriation became only a matter of time.[44] With provision of $67,500 in May, 1882, Carlisle was safely launched.[45] Enrollment figures had jumped by that time to 195 Indians from twenty-four tribes and expansion was to continue until in 1900 there were over 1,200 from seventy-nine tribes. To men seeking evidence of Indian ability, Carlisle's success offered convincing proof.

Captain Pratt's work at Carlisle revolutionized public opinion. Americans had become so accustomed to picturing Indians as an inferior race that they were impressed by even the most modest accomplishments.[46] As Indians trained in the East quickly advanced beyond fundamentals, old prejudices dissolved. When an Indian graduated from Roanoke College in 1883, even the editors of the New York *Herald* surrendered an habitually contemptuous attitude toward the race long enough to exclaim, "What man has done man can do." [47] The success of the Eastern schools had placed opponents of Indian education on the defensive for the first time in many years.

Few people questioned the possibility of Indian advancement after 1880. Effectually prevented from interfering with educational appropriations, the inveterate critics of the race who remained were forced to concentrate on such side-issues as whether Captain Pratt should receive more than his regular Army salary for his work at Carlisle.[48] Knowledge that the Captain had aroused faith in the Indians angered men who had hoped to profit from the unpopularity of red men. The wrath of Senator Plumb of Kansas, who headed the depleted ranks of the opponents of education, was clearly revealed in the summary of an interview between the Senator and Captain Pratt reported by Mrs. Wilkinson, wife of the headmaster of the Forest Grove Indian School. Angrily recalling her humiliation at the Senator's violence, Mrs. Wilkinson wrote:

He said they [all officers carrying on Indian education] were all frauds and they knew it; that they did it to shirk military duty, and get soft places, and that Capt. Pratt was a swindler and he knew it, that his school at Carlisle was a farce and that the post was secured by fraud and was held illegally, that the extra allowance of $1,000. pr. annum was illegal, that he voted against it, and should again, and that he should break up the school if he could. Capt. Pratt was the worst enemy the Indians could have; his posturing before the country was ridiculous, and only done to make for himself notoriety, and gain credit for doing great things; that the articles in the papers commendatory of this work were the most silly twaddle and made him sick. He repeated over and over again the epithets of swindler and fraud, disputing in the most offensive manner every word that was said, would not admit of any explanation, but insisted that he knew all about the Indian question, and the Capt. nothing at all, and if he said he did, he was either a fool or a fraud.[49]

No better indication of Captain Pratt's place in the history of Indian reform can be given than the bitter invective which poured from the mouth of Senator Plumb. The Captain was a fool to the Senator; but to those who hoped for Indian reform he was a hero. Lack of confidence in the red man, which had delayed progress for years, was no longer to be feared. Once Captain Pratt had conclusively demonstrated that Indians were not hopelessly unintelligent, the Indian problem never again seemed quite so discouraging.

144

The Problem of Indian Education

Assimilation as a Solution of the Indian Problem

An immediate result of the newly acquired confidence in Indian ability was the sudden popularity of another proposal for settling the Indian question. There was little interest in racial admixture as long as red men were regarded as inferior beings; but once the adaptability of the race had been demonstrated many people expressed a hope that the Indian problem might be solved by assimilation. Peculiar tribal customs had been tolerated for years only because peaceful absorption seemed impossible. Now that reformers were convinced of the ability of Indians to master the intricacies of white society, they were determined to facilitate closer racial relationships by forcing abandonment of long-established habits of the red men.[50] When dissenters objected that such traditions as tribal government and communal ownership were natural conditions of an Indian's life, the Board of Indian Commissioners retorted, "So are superstition and sin. But that is no reason against trying to improve his condition by instruction and wise legislation."[51] If advocates of assimilation had their way, every aspect of Indian life would be revolutionized.

Incorporation of the red man into white society was most frequently defended as an indispensable means of preventing Indian annihilation. Most reformers believed that peace would be impossible as long as tribes led a separate existence. The only way to overcome racial antipathies, they maintained, was to eliminate the hostility produced by contrasting ways of life. As wholesale extinction of the red men would be the inevitable outcome of any fight to retain native customs, destruction of all practices marking the Indians as a separate race seemed advisable even though many perished in the process. The dictates of civilization might seem harsh; but with fifty million whites facing only a quarter million Indians, nothing was to be gained by ignoring them. To save the individual Indian, the race must be destroyed.[52]

In spite of efforts to create an impression that their position was a result of compassion for the Indian, most champions of assimilation supported the policy because they believed no feature of Indian life was worth preserving. For supposed friends of the race, advocates of absorption were surprisingly reluctant to admit that Indian civilization had any advantages. Praise, such as Agent Llewellyn lavished on a Mescalero custom providing that a Mescalero mother-in-law and son-in-law should never meet, was extremely rare.[53] More frequently, reformers insisted that Indians would never contribute anything vital or distinctive to American life.[54] Interest in the Indian was seldom extended to his institutions.

Although a surprising number of Americans desired racial absorption, there was serious disagreement regarding the proper method of effecting the change. In many instances immediate extinction of Indian customs was recommended. As early as 1870, field officials asked permission to outlaw antiquated Indian ceremonies on the ground that red men would not change their mode of living until they were forced to do so.[55] But while such requests were frequently repeated in the following years, no systematic effort was made to uproot tribal customs until an order of April 10, 1883, instructed agents to appoint leading tribesmen as judges of courts to act against such practices as sun dancing, medicine making, polygamy, and the sale of wives.[56] The courts, intended to encourage Indian participation in the task of reform, were often successful.[57] But many tribes were unprepared for the move. Considering that few Indians had been trained for such responsibilities, it is not surprising that a Mescalero "judge" begged permission to accompany his drunken defendants to jail if allowed to consume the remaining evidence![58] Although Commissioner Atkins declared this complaint the only failure of the system officially reported in 1885,[59] voluntary surrender of Indian customs was not as successful as optimistic departmental reports represented.

Two influences were chiefly responsible for the failure of Indian courts to banish evil customs. Both the refusal of Congress to pay the judges and the hostility of the red men to a change of culture greatly reduced the chance of success. If Indians had been well remunerated for service on the courts, more might have willingly defied tribal opinion by accepting judgeships; but Commissioner Price's request for an appropriation of $50,000 was defeated by Congress in 1883. As a result, members of the Nez Percé court received a portion of the fines they collected, and on several reservations Indian policemen served as judges because they were already receiving pay. Although administrators pointed out the inadvisability of making salaries contingent upon assessments for misbehavior and of allowing policemen to try their own prisoners, Congress still declined to provide the necessary funds even when only $5,000 was asked in 1886.[60] The repeated demands of officials for financial assistance finally succeeded in 1888,[61] but the persistence of administrators could not conceal the fact that Indians were neither prepared for the responsibility of running the courts nor willing to admit the error of their ways. Coercion might have been employed, it is true; but the public was not willing to risk war over such an issue.[62] As long as force was opposed, Indian courts offered the only hope of remodeling Indian customs by direct action.

Since many advocates of assimilation did not believe that Indians should be goaded into rebellion by over-zealous insistence upon change, the slower but more effective method of racial admixture was frequently recommended. Many people naturally viewed intermarriage with the same dread which led Commissioner Walker to consider extermination preferable to racial union as a solution of the Indian problem.[63] Yet in spite of the hardships of half-breeds, who often felt that they belonged to neither race and who were rejected and scorned by both, many reformers looked with less and less alarm upon the prospect of intimate racial contacts.[64] Their fear was further allayed when an article in the *Popular Science Monthly* announced that nature was doing more to solve the Indian problem than statesmen had ever accomplished.[65] Most reformers were less enthusiastic regarding the merits of miscegenation.[66] But while few joined the correspondent who recommended that United States citizens should emulate the bee by gathering honey "from every opening flower," [67] close contact with the Indian was urged in other respects. Numerous disputes arose concerning the manner in which absorption should be achieved, but there was remarkable agreement regarding the desirability of the final end.

So overwhelming was the popularity of assimilation that criticism was limited almost entirely to members of the National Indian Defense Association. An occasional reformer advised the

147

public not to "underrate the cost to the Indian of abandoning the customs of his ancestors," [68] but only Bland and his associates consistently condemned interference with tribal life. Instead of supporting schemes which were intended to "crush out the Indians as a typical race," members of the Association urged Americans to capitalize upon Indian qualities.[69] Bland and his friends not only were unperturbed by Indian communism, but believed that many other features of tribal society might also be retained. Yet they were also sufficiently realistic to admit that the race must ultimately conform to white customs. Their primary aim, therefore, was to prevent changes which would destroy Indian individuality by their suddenness. This purpose could not have been more clearly explained than when Judge Willard wrote of the Indians:

> They should be permitted to reach civilization through the development of their own institutions under the motives afforded by advanced surrounding civilization. An act of Congress cannot lay the basis of civilization, that exists in antecedent conditions and institutions. While there should be a general conformity to the conditions and habits of the nation at large, there is abundant room for Indian individuality to display itself in the growth of these institutions. It is also essential that time should be allowed for the consumation of these transformations. . . . Sudden changes in methods and manners are contrary to the course of nature.[70]

Beyond such modest ends, opponents of assimilation could not go, for hatred of Indian institutions had become so acute that no halt was possible in the campaign to abolish them.

Indian Educational Problems

The enthusiasm with which Americans welcomed assimilation as a solution of the Indian problem stimulated still further the reviving interest in Indian education. Since racial contact would be disastrous if the red men were not prepared to associate with whites on an equal footing, educational appropriations were immediately increased. Congress, which had never provided more than $130,000 a year for Indian schools before 1880, initiated a long series of increases in that year by appropriating over $150,000. Educational expenditures, which had constituted but 1.8% of the Indian disbursements of 1875, now rose to 3.6% and but five years later reached 17.1%. As these increases were achieved at the expense of subsistence and annuity items, the effectiveness of educational appropriations in promoting racial independence was clear. Congress accepted this opportunity to encourage racial progress so enthusiastically that although Indian appropriations remained in the neighborhood of five and a half million dollars more than a million dollars was spent for education in 1887 in contrast to a mere quarter of a million five years before.[71] Much of this amount was intended for Carlisle and Hampton; but the West received a share following establishment of similar institutions at Chilocco, Indian Territory, Genoa, Nebraska, Lawrence, Kansas, and Forest Grove, Oregon, and still another portion of the fund was used to finance instruction in private schools. Education on the reservations was of equal importance, however, as over half of each year's money was spent among the tribes. Just what proportion of the increasing educational appropriations should be applied to one type of school or another stirred more congressional debate, in fact, than the size of the appropriation itself.

Whether the United States should devote particular attention to developing boarding schools in the East or day schools on the reservations was an important question. Disagreement over the respective merits of the two methods of instruction was as complete as the contrast between them. No debate could have been more significant, since whether Indians should be taught in small schools among the tribes or in special institutions established in centers of white civilization involved questions which penetrated to the heart of the Indian problem. The nature of the dispute was clear as early as 1881 when congressional investigations disclosed a fundamental difference of opinion regarding the purpose of Indian education. Reformers could not agree whether thorough training of a few Indians or slow advancement of the entire race was preferable.[72] All agreed that progress would be retarded if Indians stayed on the reservations; but since less could be trained in the East, many people opposed a system which left the major portion of each tribe in ignorance. As advocates of Eastern education insisted that returning Indians would ultimately be able to reform their tribes more rapidly than white educators working entirely on the reservations, they were particularly disappointed when graduates of Eastern schools showed an inclination to resume old habits instead of assuming tribal leadership.

The difficulties experienced by returning students seriously jeopardized the success of Eastern schools. Not only did life on the average reservation provide few opportunities for civilized labor, but the Indian who endeavored to apply his knowledge was subject to the ridicule and often the enmity of his fellows. Although Miss Helen Ludlow reported in the fall of 1885 that but four of seventy-three Carlisle graduates had reverted to savage life, Representative Cannon announced that none of the Indians had been able to succeed without government assistance.[73] Both undoubtedly misrepresented the true situation. While the record was much less impressive than optimistic Indian teachers liked to believe, it was somewhat less black than rabid opponents of Eastern schools intimated. The letters of Indian graduates clearly revealed that complex problems had to be faced; but in view of the difficulties, their achievements were frequently remarkable.[74] Reformers soon realized, nevertheless, that Indians returning to their reservations must be steadily encouraged if even a majority were to succeed. Although Captain Pratt made little effort to assist these Indians and advised that "the aim of educating the young Indians should be more directed to preparing and encouraging them to enter the organized industries of the country, rather than preparing them to return to their former places," [75] General Armstrong worked incessantly to ease the difficulties of Hampton graduates. Not only did he insist that Indian education would be worthless unless opportunities were provided on the reservations to apply knowledge gained in the East; but he also complained bitterly that plans to supply such work were discouraged by government agents.[76] The General's fight to limit Eastern training to practical subjects and to provide places for returning Indians helped many students to make a commendable showing,[77] but the discouragements which the students encountered even with his help emphasized the fact that boarding schools alone could not solve the Indian problem. Although a House investigating committee failed to its attempt to abolish boarding schools in 1886, both General Armstrong and Captain Pratt were forced to admit that the work of Eastern institutions would be more effective if supplemented by a system of day schools.[78]

Reservation schools provided several advantages which Eastern institutions did not possess. As boarding and transportation expenses were negligible, more students could be trained. Civilization, which needed to rest firmly upon tribal support, was more permanent once it developed.[79] But the greatest merit of local training was that students did not have to be won from unwilling parents. Indians were extremely reluctant to part with their children. When several pupils died at Eastern schools and those who returned seemed unfitted for either tribal society or life among the whites, therefore, opposition to sending more boys and girls became formidable.[80] Yet the refusal of an Indian to surrender his children to Eastern educators did not always signify hostility to education itself. Spotted Tail, who aroused national attention by withdrawing his children from Carlisle in 1880, joined his tribe the following year in requesting a reservation school.[81] As Congress welcomed the opportunity to economize by reducing transportation costs and recognized the value of imparting practical training in the region where it was to be applied, such petitions were usually effective.[82] Education on the reservations had been so generally accepted as an essential part of any satisfactory school system by 1886 that J. B. Harrison of the Indian Rights Association regarded the failure of Superintendent of Indian Schools Riley to recommend the establishment of day schools as evidence of incompetency.[83]

Even if the superiority of day schools had never been challenged, the problem of whether such schools should be conducted by the government or private individuals would have remained. For several years both types of operation were encouraged. Thus while Carlisle was administered by government employees, Hampton was privately owned; and the building of such government schools as Forest Grove and Lawrence was balanced by the appropriation of funds for the education of Indians at Lincoln Institute in Philadelphia and the Saint Ignatius Mission School in Montana. Private work was still further encouraged in 1882 when Congress provided a fund of $17,000 to assist any institution or family educating Indians. The appropriation, which reached a peak of $90,000 in 1884, enabled the government to give substantial aid to private groups.[84] As less was paid per pupil than in the case of government schools, however, there was much debate as to whether the contribution to private institutions should be raised to $200 or that to government schools reduced to $167.[85] But establishment of a common figure would not have rendered administration of Indian schools by both government and private agencies any less haphazard or subject to criticism. General Armstrong accepted government funds for Hampton for only a short time before he discovered that national aid weakened his work for the Indians by discouraging private contributions;[86] and legislators soon realized that both types of school were handicapped by the division of responsibility. Conduct of a policy which depended upon outside assistance for success had proved so unsatisfactory by 1887 that an Indian Rights Association investigator reported:

There is, as yet, no coherent or comprehensive system or plan for the education of the Indians under Government supervision. . . . The existing arrangements, machinery and methods are highly inorganic, incoherent and inefficient. They involve vast waste of force, and do not include any practical provision for development or improvement which is not negatived and neutralized by some other feature.[87]

Even the appointment of a Superintendent of Indian Schools produced no worthwhile result until the dual system was gradually abolished after 1891 by placing all schools receiving congressional appropriations under the Indian Bureau.[88]

A final problem confronting the friends of Indian education was whether instruction should be made compulsory. Administrators had not proceeded far before they discovered that progress would be unbearably slow without the use of force. No friend of the race desired to use coercion unnecessarily; but as few tribes showed any intention of accepting educational facilities willingly, the necessity for forceful methods was increasingly admitted. Indians, who refused educational facilities because they were unconquered invited conquest.[89] Yet resistance was natural. As President Seelye of Amherst College wisely observed, education by consent was impossible because acceptance of opportunities for advancement would mean that a tribe was already civilized.[90] Since compulsion seemed essential to success, men normally opposed to coercion on any ground often resolved that for once the end would justify the means.[91] Even Meacham of the *Council Fire* abandoned his customary objection to projects interfering with tribal independence and declared that Indians "must conform to the new condition of things, or cease to be." [92] Educational problems, it seemed, had taught reformers that force was an indispensable constituent of any successful Indian policy.

In spite of the apparent necessity for compulsion, resistance to the use of force was not confined to Indians. Senators and representatives, although unaccustomed to upholding Indian rights in other respects, expressed considerable alarm at the separation of children from unwilling parents. As early as 1880, Army criticism of methods employed in the collection of Cheyenne pupils inspired senators to investigate the need for legislation to protect Indians in the possession of their children.[93] Eastern educators were able to postpone action for a time by denying that pupils had been taken without permission.[94] But despite persistent attempts to prevent congressional interference, the opponents of compulsion finally won a decisive victory by securing a provision that no money in the 1886 Indian Appropriation Bill should be used to educate children removed without consent of their parents.[95] For the moment congressmen rather than reformers were the champions of Indian rights!

Education of the red man would have been more successful if instructors had been more willing to adapt their methods to Indian character. Early workers, it is true, had made the mistake of exaggerating Indian peculiarities.[96] But once the researches of Lieutenant Garrick Mallery assured Americans that Indians could survive the process of civilization, distinctive characteristics of the race were intentionally disregarded.[97] Educational experiments of the eighties suffered from the failure of reformers to capitalize upon

Indian qualities. With Captain Pratt and his disciples insisting that Indian students must be treated like whites, critics of Eastern boarding schools justly condemned the refusal of administrators to adjust education to Indian conditions.[98] Indian education was bound to prove unsatisfactory until racial peculiarities were employed to advantage. Much had been accomplished in stimulating interest in the problems of Indian education, but much remained to be done in expanding facilities and improving methods.

While inauguration of an adequate system of Indian education introduced many aggravating problems, preparation of the tribes for future responsibilities was a vital part of any reform program. Disappointments were unavoidable when such a complex question was handled for the first time. But Bishop Hare furnished both an excellent analysis of the inevitable defeats and a philosophy for facing them when he wrote:

Indian youth, like white young people, when they come back to their homes from school or college, are apt to have an exaggerated sense of their own importance and want to have their own way. They have ideas of their own and are harder to manage than ignorant Indians, a disagreeable thing to incompetent guides. They know too much to be easily cheated, and they have too much independence to submit to being treated like dogs. To some this is inconvenient.

In a word, these students are in their green-apple stage. People who bite them of course make faces. But let them alone or give them the sunshine of a kind and considerate friendship and they will become ripe and mellow.[99]

Friendship and tolerance were prime requisites for successful Indian education. Some mistakes were inevitable. But since alert reformers profited from each error, educational experiments were welcomed by everyone interested in tribal advancement. The accomplishments of Indian educators of the eighties, modest though they were, greatly aided the cause of reform; for as Secretary Kirkwood remarked, it was "better to move in the right direction, however slowly and awkwardly, than not to move at all."[100]

12. THE LAST STAND OF SUPPORTERS
OF THE OLD INDIAN SYSTEM

Discussion of the mounting popularity of plans to revise American Indian policies should not obscure the fact that important groups opposed any alteration of existing methods. Men, who depended upon maintenance of the old system for their livelihood, naturally resisted innovation.[1] Traders vigorously defended the annuity system as the source of a substantial annual income. Whites living on Indian reservations as the husbands of Indian squaws demanded preservation of the authority of tribal governments in hope of retaining their influence with the race. Cattlemen opposed abandonment of the reservation system to protect their leasing privileges. Not a single policy, in fact, lacked support from individuals who hoped to profit from its retention. Self-interest made the resistance of such men unusually determined. Although their numbers were small and their rivalries intense, defenders of the old Indian system succeeded in delaying reform until their opponents learned the value of organization. Once reformers united to press reform, however, the champions of contemporary Indian policies were subjected to scathing criticism.

The growing contempt expressed for supporters of existing Indian policies was stirred primarily by the monopolistic nature of the privileges they possessed. Indian traders, for example, were assured that other dealers would be prevented from entering the reservation to which they were assigned. Such a practice, while permitting the fortunate individuals to make huge profits, enabled the government to regulate inter-racial contacts with a minimum of confusion. Yet as early as 1866 Secretary of the Interior Harlan inquired why such trade should not be opened to all loyal citizens who promised to obey official regulations; and a decade later Secretary Chandler perceived "no legal objection to licensing any number of traders to trade at the same Agency."[2] Only officials directly connected with the Indian Office apparently understood the advantage of restricting trading privileges. If some Indian reformers were conscious of the dangers of unregulated intercourse, their opposition to monopolistic trading was nonetheless persistent. The first Mohonk conference condemned the policy of exclusion and the Women's National Indian Association denounced restrictions upon the Indian's right to sell in an open market.[3] As the ranks of opponents were swelled by traders who wished to share in the gains of their more fortunate rivals,[4] protection of the Indians by means of trade regulation became increasingly difficult.

Indian Traders

The unpopularity of traders was not due entirely to hatred of monopoly. If all merchants had been allowed to deal with the tribes, those including arms and ammunition among their goods would still have been condemned. Most Americans had no desire to serve as a target for rifles obtained from greedy traders. Yet efforts to regulate such traffic were unsuccessful.[5] When Congress prohibited the sale of arms in 1872, General Sheridan correctly predicted that means would be found to supply the Indians secretly.[6] Prohibitions against selling arms on reservations were usually effective, but Indian officials could not prevent such trade at Army posts and frontier towns.[7] When merchants of Caldwell, Kansas, sold rifles to freighting Kiowas in 1882, Commissioner Price reluctantly confessed that he had no authority to prosecute the offenders.[8] As arms traders did not hesitate to supply even the most hostile tribes, agents frequently urged that Indians should not be forced to resort to illegal armament sources because of restrictions upon the right of Indian officials to issue rifles.[9] But the government continued to discourage the trade from any quarter and placed full responsibility for the illicit traffic upon individual merchants.

Traffic in liquor as well as arms helped to discredit Indian traders with the public. All intelligent Americans realized that racial advancement would be delayed as long as merchants cultivated the Indian's weakness for intoxicants. Yet officials encountered great difficulty in checking the trade. Even the mildest penalties proved impossible to enforce because most frontiersmen considered liquor sales legitimate. Especial alarm was caused in 1882 when a California judge criticized Agent Lawson for bringing liquor cases before his court; [10] but the problem was continuous and confined to no particular area. Even where members of Western communities opposed the traffic, little could be done to counteract the opinion of the majority. While agents were especially critical of the silent consent which respectable Westerners bestowed upon the liquor trade, such opposition could have accomplished nothing in face of the overwhelming belief in the legality of liquor sales. Many methods were employed to circumvent government restrictions. A physician to the Blackfeet Indians discovered that his predecessor had prescribed abnormally large amounts of alcohol for supposed patients. [11] Traders did a thriving business in tonics with a high alcoholic content, few having the scruples of the Peru, Kansas, pharmacist who wrote:

Seeing your order conserning seling liquors to Indians I am drugest in this place and wish to aske you ef I have the wright to selle them medcsons such as McLane Strengthing Congal or Shermans Prickely ash bitters or any other Patten medesons I am a law biding man and dont wish to doo any thing that is contayer to our lawes of our government please let me know [12]

Instead of revealing a desire to uphold the laws, most correspondents asked just what could be done without becoming amenable under federal statutes. [13] Such men had little cause for alarm, as Congress steadily refused the desire of administrators to instrument laws prohibiting liquor traffic by establishing a minimum penalty. Although a majority of the 1885 House finally voted a fine for liquor dealers after considerable debate, the Senate continued the practice of judicial discretion on the ground that the provision constituted new legislation out of order in an appropriation bill. [14] So administrators had to fight the evils of drink without adequate support from frontiersmen, courts or Congress. Yet a growing number of citizens were becoming disturbed at the violation of laws governing Indian trade. The indifference, which had enabled traders to employ the old Indian system for private gain, was rapidly being replaced by an increased sense of responsibility for the protection of Indians from the plots of selfish men.

Squaw Men

The animosity which Americans displayed toward Indian traders was equally evident in public opinion regarding squaw men, as all whites who married Indian women were disparagingly labeled. Sentiment against individuals who disregarded racial barriers is often overwhelming. But Americans of the eighties were especially disturbed because intermarriage with the Indian was employed to manipulate tribal policy for personal advantage. Such men not only were able to enter Indian reservations at will, but assumed commanding positions in tribal government and shared annuity payments. While squaw men opposed any change in Indian policy which would interrupt their life of ease, Americans were equally determined to force abandonment of a system which enabled men to prosper without exertion. A few individuals who married Indian women worked for racial progress rather than self-aggrandizement, but most were not sufficiently interested in Indian welfare to justify Vestal's suspicion "that the term 'squaw man' was invented by some spinster from the East, who came west to find a husband, only to discover that the Indian women had married all the best men." [15] Instead, intrigues against the government and resistance to the will of Indian agents made squaw men so unpopular that they were officially accused as late as 1887 of primary responsibility for delaying reform.[16]

Strict government regulation of inter-racial relations was the only possible way in which the evil influence of squaw men could be arrested. Even Bland, who shared their interest in preventing interference with the Indian and insisted that the choice of a man's wife was his own business, urged adoption of severe penalties for insubordination.[17] Less convinced of the desirability of upholding tribal authority than Bland, administrators fought strenuously to reduce the influence of men they believed were doing more harm to the cause of civilization in one year than American missionaries could counteract in ten.[18] Determined that no one should profit from being a citizen one moment and an Indian the next, officials asked Congress to prohibit the issue of rations to the wives and children of squaw men and to expel from the reservations all whites not employed by the government.[19] Proposals of this nature were defeated by the House in 1876, however, as congressmen were not sufficiently interested in the problem to sanction drastic measures.[20] Legislators awoke to the necessity for checking the activities of white men who married Indian women only after they became convinced that intermarriage was retarding rather than speeding more normal racial contacts. Even then little was done, for by the time action was possible cattlemen had replaced squaw men as the chief menace to reform.

Cattlemen and the Leasing Problem

While regulation of the intercourse of American Indians with squaw men and traders introduced complex administrative problems, the most important question involving inter-racial contacts was whether unoccupied Indian land should be leased to whites. Long before cattlemen requested permission to enter reservations in the late seventies, officials had been urged to permit use of Indian property. Thus a telegraph company secured permission to cut poles on the Sioux reservation in 1871 and the Indian Bureau was forced to reject innumerable plans for exploiting the mineral wealth of reservations.[21] The danger of allowing whites to occupy tribal holdings might have been already accepted as a general principle, if more Americans had been aware of the experience of the State of New York where Seneca land had long been used not only for farming but for the erection of towns. The very existence of the community of Salamanca depended upon the prompt payment of rent for the land upon which it was established. Under such conditions, disputes between the Indians and whites were inevitable.[22] So many perplexities had arisen by 1874 that plots to secure permanent possession of the land, the small number of Indians receiving payments, and the idleness encouraged by existence of a steady tribal income caused an investigating committee of the Board of Indian Commissioners to question the value of leasing.[23]

But since few people knew of the Senecas's difficulties, no government policy was formulated until pressure from cattlemen forced action in the eighties.

The original reaction of the government to requests for grazing privileges on Indian land was indecisive. Several agents had asked permission to lease portions of their reservations before the first department ruling was issued in July, 1880.[24] Even after the government announced that tribes would be allowed to lease their land for one year in cases where assistance was needed, little effort was made to enforce the rule.[25] So, although Secretary Teller wrote that he regarded leasing proposals as merely schemes for seizing Indian land, he admitted that cattlemen might enter reservations at their own risk.[26] Failure either to protect or to fight the cattle interests angered both the friends and foes of leasing. Since leasing was either right or wrong, a positive stand was necessary. Efforts at compromise, whether due to doubt as to the proper course or to a desire for harmony, aggravated rather than quieted the problem.[27]

One method of avoiding official responsibility for Indian leases was to refer the decision regarding each request to the tribe concerned. Although Attorney General Devens ruled in 1880 that tribes could not dispose of their surplus lands without permission from the United States,[28] administrators tried to avoid embarrassing situations for a time by making Indian consent the deciding factor.[29] Yet the true opinion of a tribe was generally difficult to ascertain. The *Council Fire* declared that Pawnees signed a contract only after they were threatened with death if they refused; and J. B. Harrison of the Indian Rights Association found neighbors of the Klamaths prepared to fight because of the tribe's refusal to lease its land.[30] While such threats were exceptional, leasing fees were so often employed as bribes rather than legitimate payments that support of proposals by tribal authorities could seldom be held the result of sufficient deliberation. Responsibility for accepting or rejecting contracts could not be shifted to tribal leaders. However troublesome, some conclusion regarding the advisability of leasing had to be reached by United States officials.

Superficially considered, the leasing of Indian land to cattlemen appeared to offer important advantages. Not only could extensive areas be profitably employed without impairing tribal titles; but the money obtained could be used to encourage Indian advancement.[31] Closer racial contact would result from the policy and tribes might ultimately even relieve the government from the necessity of further support by learning to raise cattle of their own.[32] If such potentialities had not been associated with equally important disadvantages, excess Indian land would quickly have been placed in the possession of cattle companies.

The wisdom of leasing Indian land, seldom questioned when the arguments of cattlemen were first presented, appeared less certain after more thorough study. Although prospective lessees pretended unusual sympathy for the Indians, realistic reformers realized that the concern was only a cover for less admirable purposes. Cattle companies were more interested in securing the use of large areas of land at rates as low as one and a half cents an acre than in advancing the Indian race.[33] Even if funds received from leases had not completely discouraged Indian labor, cattlemen admitted to reservations were too careful of their own interests to stimulate competition by assisting Indians to establish tribal herds.[34] Prospects of increased racial contacts were no more favorable than those for self-support as lessees endeavored to obtain as much land as possible by crowding Indians close together.[35] Everyone who secured Indian land hoped to delay opening of the reservations indefinitely. Possessing exclusive privileges certain to be terminated once contact became an ideal, cattlemen led the opposition to reform. Occasionally some Indian worker advised acceding to the wishes of cattlemen, but few recommended such action once the full implications of the policy were understood.

Opposition to leasing Indian land united groups otherwise at odds regarding the proper course of Indian reform. Thus, while most reformers objected to leasing because racial contact would be delayed, Bland of the *Council Fire* charged that cattlemen were plotting to open the reservations![36] Glad to receive help from erstwhile opponents, reformers did not regret Bland's failure to comprehend that cattlemen were lessening the danger of wholesale intrusion rather than acting as agents for trespassers. The *Council Fire* and the Indian Defense Association, as a result, inadvertently helped Indian reformers instead of joining the cattle companies in their effort to preserve the reservation system. A fundamental difference of outlook did not prevent frontiersmen from reaching similar opinion regarding leasing. Every man who wished reservations to be opened for settlement was naturally disturbed when cattle companies promised the government to "employ reliable men in such numbers as would effectually repel without trouble any attempt at occupancy by others." [37] Westerners could not accept a policy depending upon exclusive use of land which they hoped to make available to all. Faced with possible occupation of the Indian Territory by cattle concerns, they resolved that "interested and powerful individuals, corporations and combinations should no longer be permitted to stand in the way of the best interests of the great mass of the people." [38] Reservations should either be open to general settlement or closed to all.

Faced with a rapid growth of opposition to leasing in all sections of the United States, government officials were unable to postpone a definite stand for long. Soon after President Cleveland's inauguration in 1885, an incident occurred which forced the government to act. Cheyenne Indians, who had leased large sections of their land in western Indian Territory to cattlemen, objected that the agreement had been violated. With the dispute threatening to produce hostilities between the Indian and cattlemen at any moment, General Sheridan was sent to investigate the need for government action. As he reported that immediate cancellation of the leases seemed the only solution of the problem, President Cleveland issued a proclamation on July 23 ordering cattlemen to leave the Cheyenne reservation within forty days.[39] This order, backed by a decision that Indians could not lease any portion of their land without government consent, marked the first straightforward resistance of Washington officials to opening reservations to white occupation.[40] Indecision regarding the advisability of leasing had at last given way to outspoken hostility.

President Cleveland's proclamation against leasing played a significant part in the ensuing collapse not only of Indian Territory grazing but of the entire range cattle industry. Yet its effect can easily be exaggerated. A series of severe winters and the growing antipathy of settlers were fully as responsible for the decline, while range cattlemen contributed to their own downfall by intercompany feuds. Attempts to exclude rivals, disputes as to whether the Indian Territory should be used for trails or as a range, and attacks upon successful companies by groups which had been outbid seriously injured the cause of the grazers. Though cattle companies blamed the President for their collapse, the leading student of their affairs concludes that "the decline of the ranching industry had already begun, and the removal of the herds from the Indian lands was only an added but comparatively minor factor in the general depression which was past due." [41]

The plight of the cattlemen aroused little sympathy in Congress. Instead of criticizing Cleveland for expelling the herds, senators and representatives rebuked the President for failing to act with greater dispatch. A consideration of the difficulties involved in removing from the reservations caused Cleveland to extend the time in which cattlemen must comply with his order. Congress revealed no such patience. Instead, the legislators condemned the President for subservience to the cattle interests with such rancor that Representative Rogers was forced to explain the delay at length. Cleveland, he pointed out, had been authorized rather than required to remove the cattlemen and three months still remained to carry out Congress's request for action. Cattlemen were not being tolerated as temporary occupants of the Territory, he assured, with any intention of stirring demands for the admission of permanent settlers. But while Rogers insisted that Indians could lease their land as long as no terms were included conflicting with the prior right of the United States to utilize the land if it desired, Congress was in no mood to brook favoritism toward cattlemen under any circumstances. Any possibility that leasing might be allowed was clearly at an end once the hostility of congressmen toward efforts to monopolize Indian land was evident. [42] As long as Congress had a say, the leasing of Indian reservations would not be permitted for any purpose.

The failure of cattlemen to force adoption of leasing as a government policy was of tremendous assistance to the cause of reform. If officials had consented to rent Indian land, the establishment of a better Indian system would have been indefinitely delayed. But instead of retarding advancement, pressure for leasing accelerated reform. Westerners would have refused to sanction any change in Indian policy for many years to come, if fear that cattlemen might be granted exclusive permission to occupy reservations had not wakened them to the need of joining Easterners in devising a plan for a more general utilization of Indian land. By forcing frontiersmen to accept many proposals of the Eastern reformers, the desire of cattlemen to obtain exclusive use of Indian reservations was in large measure responsible for the passage of the revolutionary Severalty Act of 1887. Senator Dawes, as leader of the reform movement, saw clearly that the selfish manipulation of the cattle interests would prove more beneficial than at first apparent. "There is one result not altogether to be deplored which is likely to follow this wretched business," he wrote the New York *Tribune* in 1885. "It will hasten action and force the United States to settle the Indian question." [43] Reform would ultimately have been achieved, but the process was greatly facilitated by the defeat of the cattlemen. Once these powerful defenders of the old Indian system were routed, reformers needed only to determine the details of the policy of the future.

IV. *Formulation of the New Indian Policy*

13. PRECEDENTS FOR REFORM

The thoroughness with which reformers repudiated the old Indian system becomes especially evident when precedents are sought for the plans which they proposed. American experience offered little encouragement to those who sought a worthy method of dealing with the Indians. As General Armstrong declared, no one could study the Indian problem in the late seventies without being humiliated at the extent to which the country depended upon the common sense of those in power for the initiation of new plans.[1] Since officials seldom recommended changes and Congress hesitated to inaugurate any program for which few arguments were advanced other than a need for change, there was little experimentation. Reformers would have cited evidence that their proposals had proved successful if they could have done so; but American Indian policy had been so barren of accomplishments that Senator Dawes exclaimed, "What has been done in the past is of no use, except to teach us that something different is needed in the future." [2] Canada rather than the United States provided inspiration for those who hoped to secure from the past at least a few suggestions regarding the course that a wise Indian policy should follow.

Canada's Example

The successful management of Canadian Indians was a constant topic of discussion during debates concerning American Indian relations. While patriotic pride rendered praise of Canada's methods unpopular, international rivalry made such admiration a powerful argument for the improvement of American policy. Most reformers realized that many Canadian customs were worthy of emulation, even though they refused to agree that the Indian problem would be solved if American Indians were treated precisely as those of the Dominion.[3] Conditions in the two countries were sufficiently varied to make such a simple method possible. But although Canadian methods were not directly applicable in many instances, the average American believed that many practices might be employed to advantage, and almost every reformer took time to discuss the lessons of Canadian experience at length.

Indian reformers quickly noticed the unfavorable contrast between the Indian policies of the United States and Canada. As early as 1869, General Sanborn declared that the success of the Hudson's Bay Company in dealing with Canadian Indians proved that the United States and not the Indians had been responsible for American hostilities.[4] Although the government undoubtedly resented such criticism, a desire to profit by Canada's example was displayed officially in 1870 when Consul Blake reported favorably upon the Canadian system. Many policies which the United States might well have adopted sooner—the success with which Hudson's Bay Company officials kept liquor from the Indians, the long tenure of Indian Superintendents, the wise administration of Indian funds —were heartily praised. A refusal to annex land without Indian consent was recommended as an excellent method of winning friendship, while opposition to leasing showed a wisdom not shared by American administrators for many years.[5] Blake was most interested to learn, however, that every aspect of Canadian policy was undertaken with the purpose of rendering the Indians independent of governmental support. Although progress in this direction was necessarily slow, the Indians had already shown enough capacity for self-government to promise ultimate success. As this ideal particularly appealed to Americans, the efforts of Canadians to improve their Indians were followed with great interest by reformers who hoped to profit by their example.[6]

Although many factors were responsible for the success of Canadian Indian policy, each was related to the justice with which the race had been treated. Canada had had less trouble with the Indians than the United States because she had not hesitated to punish whites for crimes against Indians.[7] The interests of the red men were so safeguarded that tribes were not even permitted to sell land unless the government considered the transaction to their advantage, and the possibility of fraud was lessened by providing tribes with full accounts of their funds.[8] The unpreparedness of American Indians for responsibilities of this nature was certainly not due to racial characteristics, for their Canadian brothers had been trained to uphold their interests with comparatively little trouble. Canadian workers had encouraged advancement by making "their own civilization the pioneer, instead of gathering a mass of discontented savage humanity on their border." [9] While the United States faced difficulties of long standing, the sooner an effort was made to correct the faults, the sooner American Indians could be treated like those of Canada. The secret of Indian progress lay in combining justice and practicality after the Canadian example. As American policy had been conspicuous for neither, there was much to learn.[10]

While many reformers agreed that American Indian policy was contemptible, criticism originating outside of the United States was keenly resented. A United States senator might remark that the heart of Canadian Indians swelled with pride at their British citizenship, but such a suggestion was not welcome if it came from an Englishman.[11] The truth of foreign jibes at the administration of United States Indian policy merely made them less easy to bear. Only the radical editors of the *Council Fire* dared to publish the attack of a Britisher, who declared, "We in England keenly observe the Republic's dealings with the weak and helpless, and I am sorry to say we are compelled to own that our monarchy is greatly superior in true charity and justice to the so-called emblem of freedom and justice—the Republic." [12] For further criticism and comparison, foreigners had to rely upon European magazines.[13] United States citizens frequently admitted that American Indian policy was faulty, but they preferred to discover their errors for themselves. Only a few denied that Canadian experience offered a valuable guide, and in most instances these men merely hoped to prove that Canada had no lessons to teach because she had no problem to face.

Attempts to belittle the arguments of reformers who urged the United States to copy Canadian Indian policies were a failure. Certain Western senators fought every reference to Canadian experience. But while Senator Teller declared that there was "nothing learned from English history to be applied," Senator

Ingalls was able to use his extraordinary knowledge of Canadian policy to demonstrate that allotment of land in severalty had proved worthless.[14] No great harm could result, certainly, from intelligent study of Canadian experiments. Skeptics who felt that Canadian experiences were of no significance to Americans could point to the contrasting pressure upon the two frontiers;[15] but Western tribes composed far from all the Indians in either country. Critics of the American system, who attacked Canadian policy because of its similarity to that of the United States, were much closer to reality than those who denied that there was any inter-relationship.[16] Thus an editorial in the *Nation*, which argued that the United States should not emulate a system established to meet different conditions, admitted that the policies differed only in execution.[17] The problem of dealing with subject races was of such a universal nature that the experience of one nation was certain to be of assistance to another. If Americans could not hope to have matters of detail answered, Canada could at least throw light upon methods of improving the general policy.

The close ties between American and Canadian Indian policies are evident even after only cursory examination. United States methods have tended to follow Canadian developments. A common purpose underlying the legislation of each country has given their acts a similarity which varying details can not obscure. American Indian reformers of the eighties might have found an able summary of their goal in the title of an act of 1857 which announced as its purpose "the gradual removal of all legal distinctions . . . and . . . the acquisition of property, and of the rights accompanying it, by such individual members of the . . . tribes as shall be found to desire such encouragement and to have deserved it."[18] Furthermore, at the very time the United States was discussing the advantages of citizenship and property rights, Canada passed "an Act for conferring certain privileges on the more advanced Bands of the Indians of Canada, with the view of training them for the exercise of municipal powers," which contained ideas of corporate rule not introduced into United States Indian legislation until fifty years later![19] Only when Canada sent a special investigator to study American Indian schools in 1879 did the policy of the American government inspire emulation.[20] The similarity of the problems faced by the two nations should have resulted in many studies, but so few were undertaken that the mistakes of one provided no lesson for the other.

Canada and the United States showed an amazing inability to profit from each other's errors. Similar problems resulted in similar mistakes. Canadians were the last people to claim that their policy was without fault. But while one speaker condemned the meager contributions of the government to education and the employment of inefficient Indian farmers, both difficulties had been faced in the United States.[21] Similarly, complaints against government grants to denominational schools were the product of a prejudice with which American officials had long been familiar.[22] But the most remarkable example of the inability of each country to learn from the experiences of its neighbor was the failure of the United States to profit from the collapse of Canadian efforts to encourage Indians to abandon their tribes. The provisions of the act of 1857, which American reformers considered so worthy of emulation, were admitted to be unsuccessful by Canadians as early as 1868! To have been disabused of any expectation that tribal dissolution would solve the Indian problem, Americans need only have turned to Consul Blake's comments on the policy and read:

It appears that all . . . plans for enfranchisement and absorption are likely to prove nugatory, and that the actual elevation of the Indians might be better attained by considering the right to dispose of their land as a question apart and distinct from enfranchisement, to which either the test of property or intelligence might be applied, thus admitting the most thrifty of them to the ordinary political rights of white men, without at the same time offering any inducement or opportunity for them to renounce affiliation with their own people, whose prospects of advancement would undoubtedly be injured if legislation should result in the withdrawal of the best men from the Indian communities.[23]

The main error of the Indian reformers could not have been more clearly presented. Insistence upon rushing reforms too rapidly and indifference toward Indian rights had been the cause of much trouble in the United States, and were to be the cause of more. American reformers of the eighties respected tribal rights in practice even less than their predecessors.

In spite of the widespread interest which Americans displayed in Canadian Indian policy during the years following the Civil War, the basic reason for Canada's success escaped the notice of all but a few writers. Those who did approach the fundamental difference between the methods of the two countries usually failed to appreciate the significance of the contrast. Captain Butler was quite correct, for example, when he stated in his prize-winning essay, "The British method may be the wiser one, so far as keeping the Indians in subjection is concerned, but is certainly much less generous than ours." [24] Any suggestion that the generosity of America's policy had been largely responsible for its failure, however, was not advanced. J. R. Thompson did sense the reason for Canadian success when he wrote in the Puget Sound *Weekly Courier* of January 30, 1880:

We talk about the Indian policy of the British government being superior to ours, as though all the wisdom in regard to this matter were over on the north side of our national boundary line and foolishness all on this side. The fact is, John Bull's policy is not as good, essentially, as ours. But he carries out *his* policy, and we do not.[25]

Instead of continuing to explain that American theories were too impractical to be enforced, the author weakened his emphasis upon the more realistic nature of Canada's policy by adding, "The British government recognized the Indians as the original 'lords of the soil,' and never pretends to own it until it has been bought and paid for. Not so with us." That an author could hit upon the reason for Canada's success only to revert to the customary explanation of contrasting treaty policies shows that even the most discerning writers missed the main significance of Canadian policy. It remained for later historical studies to reveal that Canada's policy was successful because it was severely practical as well as kind.

Although contemporary students have not attempted to analyze the reasons for the success of Canadian Indian policy completely,

172

all acquainted with the subject agree that Canada was more liberal than her legislation required. While the United States recognized Indian rights theoretically but was forced to violate them, the Dominion granted the Indian less but lived up to her bargains. Canadian Indian agreements, as one author declares, were carried out with the utmost good faith except that much more was often done for the Indians than had been stipulated! [26] By refusing to promise anything impractical, Canadian administrators were able to please their Indians with unexpected concessions. Canadian authority was not only firmly established, but intelligently utilized. As only two deputy superintendents directed Indian affairs during the thirty-one years following 1862, Canadian policy profited from a continuity which that of the United States can never achieve. Superintendents Sprague and Vankoughnet might easily have abused their power, but the policies of both were tempered with good intentions. [27] Canadian Indian policy was a success not because Canadian Indians were treated more liberally than those of the United States, but because they were treated more fairly.

Canada's successful Indian administration was due to her insistence upon possessing sufficient power to enable her to assume full responsibility for the conduct of Indian affairs. Although the Indian's right of occupancy was recognized in every province but British Columbia, Canadian officials stressed the right of Indians less than United States administrators. One author actually declares that in granting land to Indians "the Dominion doubtless thought it was conveying its own domain." [28] While the theories which shaped Canadian treaties are difficult to determine precisely, all agreements contained outspoken declarations of tribal subjection to the central government which were omitted in American treaties. Yet the greater obedience demanded of Canadian Indians was more than repaid by the excellent treatment they received. Whereas the United States government found difficulty in carrying out the innumerable promises of educational facilities made in Indian treaties, Canadian educational efforts were based on "an interpretation of all promises which went far beyond the letter of the compact." [29] Even in British Columbia, where the Indians were not protected by treaty rights, Canadians made a much better

173

record than that of their American neighbors.[30] Behind Canadian insistence upon law and order lay a determination to consider Indian prejudices and customs. Despite the generous aims of American Indian policy, the need for adapting measures to racial traits was never learned. Canada granted all that she could to the Indian without destroying her power; the United States weakened her control over her Indians without making any concession to their prejudices. Canada offered a precedent, but the true significance of her lesson is only now being learned as a result of bitter experience rather than intelligent study.

The Indian and the Negro

While Americans looked to Canadian Indian policy for inspiration, they failed to profit from an experience of their own which offered fully as many suggestions concerning the proper course of reform. Negro emancipation presented more than enough related problems to merit serious study by all interested in Indian advancement. Yet the two movements were so completely divorced in the minds of most contemporaries that the difficulties of adjusting Negroes to white society made little impression. Many citizens, it is true, unconsciously became more conservative than they would otherwise have been. But although opposition to immediate Indian citizenship was an inevitable result of the unsuccessful experiment with Negro suffrage, there was too little conservatism in the ranks of Indian reformers to prove that the lessons of emancipation had been well learned.

United States citizens with few exceptions have believed that the problems of the American Indian and the Negro must be solved separately. For a time, reformers held that Indians had been granted citizenship by the Fourteenth Amendment. But once the fervor of the war period died, extension of the privilege to Indians was opposed and Indian Commissioner Walker suggested that the red men might bear restriction as well as the Negro had borne emancipation.[31] The cause of Indian reform had gained nothing as a result of the successful crusade against slavery. Instead, Indian workers were forced to cultivate an entirely new public opinion because appeals for the support of men interested in the Negro were no longer effective. Although one author felt that emancipation had aided the Indian movement by fixing "the attention of thoughtful persons upon our relations to all dependent people," such an influence played a minor part in the rise of the new movement.[32] So firmly had the distinction between Indians and Negroes become established as early as 1870 that an agent censured Americans for worshipping Negroes at the same time they crucified inoffensive Indians.[33] A long time passed before advocates of Indian freedom were powerful enough to demand equal rights for the Indian with any effect.

In considering the relation between the Indian and Negro problems, it must be remembered that emancipation was far more attractive to the slave than citizenship to the Indian. Negroes had much more to gain because they possessed fewer rights. Indians, on the other hand, exercised so many important privileges as a result of their independent status that any extension of citizenship would entail considerable sacrifice. Indian leaders consequently opposed inclusion under the Fourteenth Amendment and pointed out that the eagerness of many whites to grant citizenship to Indians arose from a knowledge that many barriers protecting the tribes would thereby be removed.[34] While many reformers resented the favoritism shown to Negroes and in growing numbers advocated extension of civil rights as a solution of the Indian problem, immediate citizenship would have exposed red men to dangers for which they were unprepared.[35]

The experience of the United States with emancipated Negroes enabled friends of the Indian to comprehend the danger of granting political rights prematurely. Their ultimate decision to extend similar privileges and responsibilities to the Indian was not made without an understanding of the risks involved. Only a belief that tremendous benefits were to be derived from political independence caused reformers to advocate citizenship in the face of the difficulties with the Negroes. The outlook of the average worker was that of a friend who wrote Carl Schurz, "It was an awful experiment to try with the negroes, & a good deal that is wretched has come of it. But I believe it is worse not to try it at all with the Indians." [36] Yet Indians were even less prepared for responsibility than the Negroes had been. Slaves, as Captain Pratt pointed out, had been in close contact with civilization; Indians, never having been enslaved and having had relations with only the most backward Americans, still had to learn the wisdom of subjection.[37] Fear of the consequences of granting suffrage to the Indians made some reformers hesitate. Most, however, continued to express faith in the miracles of citizenship. But the methods proposed for Indian advancement showed that the unconscious influence of the experience with Negro emancipation had been strong. What catastrophes might have developed, if measures for Indian citizenship had not been hedged with safeguards made possible by the lessons of Negro suffrage, one can only imagine. Certainly the problems which did result were serious enough to make one appreciate that the difficulties with the Negro had been heeded at all.

14. THE FAILURE OF EARLY

SEVERALTY PLANS

The most frequent suggestion advanced by men desiring to improve United States Indian policy recommended a distribution of tribal property among individual Indians. This proposal arose because reformers recognized that satisfactory inter-racial relations would be difficult to establish unless similar methods of land holding were in force. Although the comparative merits of communal and several ownership were open to dispute, practical requirements dictated that the custom of the less numerous race should be abandoned. There was no need to insist upon the change as long as the government protected red men from contact with their neighbors; but once close relationships were in prospect, most reformers believed that Indians could learn the self-reliance essential for survival in a competitive society only by an allotment of reservation holdings. Excellent as joint ownership of Indian land might be in theory, it could no longer be safely allowed to prevent preparation of the race for the responsibilities of life among the whites.

Allotment proposals of the eighties were not the first of the sort to be made. As early as 1816, Secretary of War Crawford had recommended apportionment of Indian holdings among tribal members, and his advice was repeated six years later by Secretary of War Calhoun. Several years passed before any attempt was made to apply the suggestion. Occasional experiments were undertaken during the thirties and forties, but allotment was not employed widely until a series of treaties concluded by Commissioner Manypenny in 1854 provided for individual ownership in enough instances to enable the first real test of the severalty principle.

Early experiences with land allotment were disheartening. The Wyandott Indians of Kansas lost so much property to whites when they were granted individual titles in 1855 that restoration of tribal ownership proved the only remedy for their troubles. Nearby Pottawatomie allottees, in spite of a reputation for prudence, were soon forced to seek refuge in the Indian Territory with fellow tribesmen who had wisely refused 1861 assignments. Life among Kickapoo, Shawnee, and Stockbridge Indians was so disrupted by land disputes that agents recommended cancellation of all individual titles. Reports from Michigan were equally unsatisfactory, as over four-fifths of all allottees hurriedly disposed of their holdings and purchased land which they cultivated in groups. Even the most advanced tribes often opposed the plan, because individuals could be more easily deprived of their holdings than tribes. So it was that when a House committee investigated the history of land allotment in 1879 but two of fourteen instances were found in which the practice might be judged successful.[1]

The failure of early severalty experiments effectively hampered consideration of further allotment legislation. Before severalty was tried again as a means of solving the Indian problem, legislators demanded full information as to why the first experiments had failed and why early difficulties no longer bore weight. Pessimism regarding the likelihood of successful allotment was so great in 1885 that ex-Commissioner Manypenny severely criticized himself for having directed the negotiations which led to the earliest allotments. "Had I known then, as I now know, what would result from these treaties," he exclaimed, "I would be compelled to admit that I had committed a high crime."[2] In spite of the refusal of certain severalty advocates to admit that early legislation had proved unsatisfactory,[3] Manypenny's discouragement was general. Severalty legislation had been so thoroughly discredited that the first important task of reformers was to prove that factors other than land allotment itself had been responsible for the disastrous outcome of early measures.

Defects in Early Severalty Legislation

In assigning responsibility for the failure of the first severalty experiments, reformers pointed to many errors in previous legislation. The absence of any provision prohibiting sale of allotted land was especially criticized, as everyone studying the problem soon realized that severalty would prove unsatisfactory as long as Indians were allowed to dispose of their allotments. A few Eastern tribes had been in contact with white civilization long enough to appreciate land values, Massachusetts Indians having successfully operated farms since 1834; [4] but as most others seized the first opportunity to exchange their holdings for a little ready cash, land was hardly assigned to Indians before it was owned by whites. The rapidity with which the Pottawatomie Indians lost their land especially dismayed the noted Catholic missionary, Father. de Smet. [5] Yet the evils of which he complained were repeated wherever similar experiments were tried. The inability of Indians to retain allotments convinced many Americans that Indian welfare required continued communal land holding. [6] A much greater number insisted that both tribal ownership and the errors of early severalty legislation could be avoided if all allotments were made inalienable.

Although the failure of the government to retain control over land allotted to Indians was the chief defect of early severalty measures, hardly any provision indicated that administrative problems had been sufficiently considered. Even in the important matter of arrangements for the disposal of surplus land, little care was taken to assure that receipts were collected and credited to the Indians. [7] Legislators, instead of retaining portions of the reservation for common use, insisted that all unassigned land should at once be opened to white settlement. While administrators denied that land allotment necessitated surrender of excess land and occasionally defended Indians who opposed its loss, [8] Congress not only removed valuable land from tribal jurisdiction but left no property for assignment as young men became eligible for full allotments or the membership of a tribe increased. [9] Related complications involving the rights of minors and heirs constantly plagued the government. Additional trouble was caused when officials granted land to half-breeds on the ground that Congress had failed to specify who should receive allotments and although such allotments were plainly of more value to land sharks than Indians. [10] Provisions prohibiting division of an individual allotment among different sections of a reservation made assignment of plots of equal value impossible and led to monopolization of the best land by a few Indians or its reservation for whites. [11] As many of these severalty problems remained unsolved even after the policy had been thoroughly studied by experts, the failure of the original measures is hardly surprising. Fortunately the perplexities encountered in administering the original acts enabled reformers to remedy many defects which had contributed to the collapse of early efforts. Legislators of the eighties at least had the advantage of knowing that land allotment involved problems of which their predecessors had not been even vaguely aware.

The Extension of Homestead Privileges to Indians in 1875

Even if severalty measures had been perfectly drafted, successful land allotment would have been hampered by a general lack of interest in promoting Indian ownership. More often than not, legislation intended to advance the Indian discouraged rather than fostered acceptance of individual responsibilities. The sacrifices demanded of all red men who endeavored to become self-sufficient were particularly burdensome in the case of acts governing the status of Indians on the public domain. By depriving such Indians of annuity payments, Congress withdrew aid from those who were most worthy of encouragement.[12] Few red men could be expected to settle outside reservations as long as efforts to be independent involved the surrender of large sums of money. Individual effort, whether on or off the reservations, entailed the loss of valuable privileges.

An important step toward a better Indian policy was taken when Congress finally adopted a measure encouraging individual initiative. By providing in the deficiency bill of March 3, 1875, that all benefits of the Homestead Act of 1862 should be extended to Indians, legislators enabled red men to join the whites in receiving title to 160 acres of the public domain after five years of occupancy and payment of a small entry fee.[13] As Indians taking advantage of this opportunity to become independent of their tribes were allowed to retain their share of tribal funds, the concession was rendered particularly attractive. A further provision that land granted to Indians should be inalienable for five years after issuance of the final patent, while less welcome, offered a necessary protection against improvidence. But although the new measure remedied major defects of previous legislation and was hailed as solving the Indian problem,[14] officials realized that still other safeguards were imperative. Since Indian homesteads were protected from sale only temporarily and no provision was included regulating the expenditure of annuity payments, Commissioner E. P. Smith immediately requested legislation to protect Indians from speculators and insure a strict examination of the ability of all applicants.[15] Rigid eligibility rules would reduce the number of Indians receiving land;[16] but until red men were taught how to utilize their holdings and how to comply with homestead rules, administrators were justified in discouraging legislation which failed to offer full protection. As it was, complicated requirements for completing title enabled whites to turn the Indian's ignorance of land rules to his disadvantage on so many occasions that the complex severalty law of 1887 was hailed for its relative simplicity.[17]

Influential as the principle of rewarding initiative was to prove in the development of a new Indian policy, the true significance of the legislation of 1875 was unrecognized by contemporaries. Instead of being the result of deliberate and well-considered action, the clauses extending homestead rights were added on the last day of Congress to a bill intended merely to provide for deficiencies in previous appropriations.[18] As debate was impossible under such conditions, a conference committee rather than the legislators as a whole vetoed a provision granting citizenship to allottees and added the section continuing annuity payments.[19] The extension of homestead privileges was of unusual importance, but the effect of the legislation was seriously limited by its rapid passage. Only the absence of debate upon the measure and its obscure position at the end of an unrelated statute can account for the widespread ignorance of its existence. Many people intimately connected with Indian affairs displayed an amazing lack of knowledge regarding the act. One agent wrote that two of his Indians wished to secure homesteads by becoming citizens and by renouncing their annuities only to be told that neither act was necessary under the law.[20] Yet even this was hardly surprising when one considers that the House actually debated in 1879 whether such a law existed![21]

In view of such ignorance, red men can not be blamed for failing to avail themselves of opportunities of which even their superiors were unaware. A better-publicized measure was necessary if individual ownership was to be satisfactorily established; but success depended above all upon officials and legislators encouraging individual ownership so enthusiastically that there could be no doubt concerning their intention to aid every Indian who showed an interest in self-advancement.

In spite of the law granting homestead privileges to Indians, interest in promoting allotment activities did not increase. Treaty provisions contemplating individual land holding were still unenforced and only in 1884 did Congress even consent to appropriate funds to aid Indians in selecting land and filing claims.[22] Government officials explained their failure to act on the ground that such assistance had not been requested by the Indians, but their argument neither explained why they had waited so long to stimulate advancement on their own initiative nor why the few Indians who did wish to receive title to private holdings were refused patents. With aggravating inconsistency, officials threatened to force individual allotments upon the tribes of Indian Territory, but refused to make assignments at the request of Oregon Indians.[23] Severalty, one soon discovered, was popular solely where its advantage to whites was clear. True reform could be achieved only if legislators accepted the policy for unselfish reasons. If Indians were to prosper, officials and legislators needed to throw enthusiastic support behind some consistent, definite and farsighted program of reform.

The Need for a Definite and Inclusive Indian Policy

None of the lessons gained from a study of early American Indian policy was more important than the need for instituting a definite plan of operation. For years the purpose of administrators had shifted so frequently that establishment of any permanent method of dealing with the tribes seemed impossible. With one course of action succeeding another with lightning rapidity, Americans had had no means of judging a policy's merits. Nor was there any hope for successful reformation of Indian policy as long as Congress could be accused of acting "in variable and irresponsible mood, without reference to precedent, or even to right and justice, intent only on getting rid of the special vexing question of the hour in the quickest way, and with the least possible trouble." [24] Legislators needed to look beyond the needs of the moment, if they ever hoped to reach any permanent solution of the Indian problem.

The need for clarifying the aims of American Indian policy became especially evident during the administration of President Grant. The so-called "peace policy" of these years was more a product of confusion regarding the proper course to pursue than of an intelligent effort to solve Indian problems. Instead of setting a goal, administrators drifted aimlessly, meeting difficulties as they arose without thought of the future. So purposeless and confused were the actions of contemporary Indian officials that Commissioner J. Q. Smith attributed most difficulties to the absence of "a well-defined, clearly-understood, persistent purpose on the part of the Government." [25] In the opinion of both contemporary and modern observers, even the most heartless system would have been less cruel in its operation and less disastrous in its results if steadily pursued.[26] Indians needed to know what was expected of them; administrators, what they were to achieve. Although many Americans did not wish to tie themselves to any particular policy, there was no use in continuing Indian work until the country had some conception of what should be accomplished. "So long as we travel without having a point at which we are purposing to arrive, and raise no questions as to the directions," warned Painter of the Indian Rights Association, "we are in danger of mistaking simple movement for progress, and, feeling the jostle of this ongoing, give ourselves no concern, though we reach no place in particular." [27] Since there could be no progress without a goal, Indian friends joined President Cleveland and legislative champions of reform in demanding that before further effort was expended a suitable purpose should be established as an end toward which all energy might be directed.[28]

The determination of reformers to formulate a definite program for the conduct of Indian affairs did not settle whether all tribes should be included under a single system. As the entire nature of projected legislation depended upon the comprehensiveness of the policy desired, no action was possible until administrators had decided what exceptions should be allowed from a rigid enforcement. There was no denial that Indian tribes varied greatly. The problem was to decide to what extent such differences should be considered in drafting reform legislation. Since contemporary policies were unusually haphazard, establishment of a more comprehensive Indian program seemed especially desirable. Only a brief study of previous relations revealed the danger of making too many concessions to tribal peculiarities. Legislation adapted to particular needs had been primarily responsible for the indefiniteness which had characterized United States Indian policy. Now that the final subjection of hostile Indians enabled Americans to consider the race as a whole for the first time, concern with the problems of specific tribes was less necessary. Although Board members reported in 1872 that three years of experience had convinced them of the inexpediency of superseding laws regulating the Indian service with any general legislation,[29] administrators and reformers of the late seventies looked with increasing favor upon proposals urging a program of racial advancement to be applied to all Indians alike.

The contest between the advocates and opponents of general legislation ended in compromise. While President Cleveland in referring to the Indians in his first annual message urged that "no attempt should be made to apply a fixed and unyielding plan of action to their varied and varying needs and circumstances," he pointed out the following year that "inequalities of existing special laws and treaties should be corrected and some general legislation upon the subject . . . provided."[30] Realizing that any system which could not be adapted to varied circumstances was unworthy of consideration, Cleveland demanded flexibility. Yet he also insisted that such adjustments should be related to a common policy. Reformers, also, were determined that every concession should be a development of, rather than a variation from, a general plan. Although Indians might be permitted to advance at different rates

184

of speed, the final goal was to be the same. Congressmen could not hope to prescribe every detail of a reform program, but they did insist upon setting the direction of future policy by establishing aims which were to govern all relationships.[31]

As the first measure in American history giving definite direction to American Indian policy, the Dawes Severalty Act of 1887 was justly hailed by the Indian Rights Association as "the beginning of a new order of things."[32] Congress hoped to solve the Indian problem by adopting a policy which had failed previously because of poor legislation and governmental indifference. Individual ownership, citizenship, and sale of surplus land were finally accepted as the only possible means of improving American Indian affairs. But this decision was not reached immediately. A long debate over the advisability and the proper method of correcting the errors of previous acts was necessary before the measure was passed which at last definitely set a program for general application.

Legislative History of the Dawes Severalty Act

As most events leading to passage of the Dawes Act can be treated most satisfactorily in discussing their relationship to outstanding features of the reform program, a brief chronological resumé of progress will be sufficient to cover the legislative history of the bill. The campaign began early in 1879 when Representative Scales and Senator Allison introduced the first general allotment proposals. Scales's House bill received a favorable report and early in the next session was again introduced, again favorably reported, and again failed to be reached before adjournment. In the meantime, while the House bill waited consideration, Senator Coke of Texas took charge of a Senate bill, which although introduced only a month before the end of the second session of the Forty-sixth Congress (May 20, 1880) was thoroughly discussed during the last of January, 1881.

The Senate debate on the Coke bill was the first detailed consideration of severalty as a general Indian policy by either legislative branch. Need for a more careful examination and pressure of other business finally caused postponement of further discussion until the Forty-seventh Congress opened in the following December. Then, as one of the first bills introduced into the Senate, the Coke bill was reported in revised form and after slight amendment passed without debate on April 24, 1882. But although a House bill was introduced the following year, neither this measure nor that of the Senate was considered during the second session. Bills were immediately introduced in both Houses, however, at the opening of the Forty-eighth Congress in December, 1883. Again the Senate bill passed after a brief debate (March 26, 1884); but while it was reported favorably by the House Indian Committee on January 9, 1885, following minor amendments, it was not debated on the floor.[33]

Although the House failed to consider the Senate severalty bill for a third time in early 1885, the first favorable report of the Senate's measure marked progress which continued until the bill was adopted before the end of the following Congress. Persisting in its purpose, the Senate passed a bill proposed by Senator Dawes on February 25, 1886, after a very brief debate. This measure was recommended by the House Indian Committee on April 20th in preference to the bills of three House members,[34] but an amendment was added providing that the consent of two-thirds of a tribe should be required before enforcement and the bill was not debated until after the summer recess. Finally, on December 15, 1886, the House passed Dawes's bill with three important changes—a reduction of the time allowed for selection from five to two years, a provision that disposition of money from the sale of surplus land should be left for the future determination of Congress, and a clause stating that the measure must be accepted by a majority of each tribe before being applied. This was the last stand of the House, however, for on January 21, 1887, they accepted a conference report which allowed four years for selection, provided for disposal of money from the sale of surplus land, and dropped the clause insisting upon Indian consent. In this form, the bill also received approval from the Senate and with the signature of President Cleveland became law on February 8, 1887.

It is remarkable that all essential information concerning the congressional history of such an important measure as the Dawes

Act can be given in such little space. Not once was a record vote taken on a subject relating to the bill. The attitude of Congress toward allotment can be discovered much better by examining debates on the bill of 1880 extending severalty to the Utes of Colorado than in the unusually restricted discussions of the more significant Dawes bill. Yet there was a reason for this lack of congressional debate. Detailed consideration of the bill at Board meetings, by the various Indian associations, and during Mohonk conference meetings took the place of the usual hearings and debates. Congress trusted the ability of specialists in Indian policy to devise a satisfactory plan. In discussing the major features of the severalty act, the debates of Indian organizations as well as those of Congress will be considered in order to shed as much light as possible on the origin and purposes of the most important Indian legislation in the history of the United States.

15. SEVERALTY DEBATES OF THE EIGHTIES

ALTHOUGH OWNERSHIP OF LAND IN SEVERALTY WAS NOT WIDELY proposed as a solution of the Indian problem until the eighties, its advantages had been expounded by leading reformers for several years. Even in the midst of the Civil War, Bishop Whipple urged President Lincoln to issue land patents and his appeals were renewed frequently after the war.[1] Similar interest in severalty was displayed by the Society of Friends, whose representatives championed land allotment as early as 1869.[2] In Congress, also, allotment possessed an energetic exponent in Senator Stewart of Nevada; while Representative Clarke of Kansas introduced a bill in 1870 providing for division of tribal land, sale of unallotted areas and issuance of patents rendering all assignments to Indians inalienable for ten years.[3] So the severalty proposals of the eighties can not be regarded as startling or novel. For several years, however, interest in severalty was not sufficient to draw attention to these plans. Land allotment schemes became important only after both the peace policy and transfer movement had collapsed.

Credit for inaugurating the program which finally resulted in the Dawes Act of 1887 has frequently been awarded to Secretary of the Interior Schurz. But while the Secretary's *Report* of 1879 helped to publicize the cause, his ideas were more remarkable for their organization than their originality. In fact, Schurz was not the first administrator to advocate severalty officially, Commissioner J. Q. Smith having urged allotment three years previously.[4] Yet by drawing attention to the subject Schurz did perform a valuable service. Consideration of allotment proposals would ultimately have been necessary because of the failure of other plans, but the Secretary's energetic advocacy sped the process and brought congratulations from as far as Rio de Janeiro.[5] Ideas, lightly regarded before the eighties, were discussed seriously once the views of America's leading reformer were known.

188

Severalty Debates of the Eighties

The Ute Bill

The measure responsible for the first extended discussion of the desirability of land allotment was drafted in January, 1880. Secretary Schurz had hoped for some time to present a severalty bill to Congress. When settlement of an uprising by the Ute Indians of Colorado required conclusion of an agreement in the fall of 1879, therefore, the Secretary seized the opportunity to force acceptance of a provision for a division of tribal land. Called upon to implement this arrangement with legislation, congressmen recognized the significance of the central proposal so clearly that the measure was considered at great length.[6] So fully were the advantages and disadvantages of allotment discussed that subsequent debates on the subject merely developed further arguments already presented.

The varied reasons advanced by legislators in ratifying the Ute agreement are an excellent indication of the wide appeal of allotment as a method of handling the Indian problem. For once, a measure passed the Senate concerning which there was neither sectional nor party agreement. Not only did the Colorado senators, Hill and Teller, split over this issue,[7] but those representing nine other widely distributed states failed to agree despite similar party affiliations.[8] Both parties cast substantial majorities for the bill, yet in neither case was there unanimity of purpose. Thus a Maine Republican and a Missouri Democrat backed the bill only as a means of war prevention, while a Rhode Island Republican and a Kentucky Democrat felt allotment necessary as a sad but inevitable result of the defeat of transfer.[9] Most supporters, on the other hand, held that severalty had advantages of its own, but there was little agreement as to the nature of the benefits. Several senators felt that the measure offered unusual opportunities for Indian advancement,[10] yet many others, including the sponsor of the bill, urged that the land opened to white settlement would be of value even if the measure proved unsatisfactory for the Indians![11] Severalty appealed to many individuals, but to feel that its adoption in the Ute agreement was a result of either great enthusiasm for the policy or wide sympathy for the Indians would be a serious error. Its success was due to the fact that widely divergent schools of opinion had found a policy from which each expected to obtain the end it was seeking.

Opponents of the Ute agreement disagreed less violently than its supporters only because they were outnumbered. The two leading enemies of severalty in the Senate not only represented different parties and sections, but advanced contrasting arguments. Both Teller of Colorado and Morgan of Alabama wanted the United States to dictate to the Utes; but while Teller was unalterably opposed to severalty in any form, Morgan confined his criticisms to technicalities.[12] To add to the confusion, neither man was logical in his attitude toward allotment. Thus Teller, after condemning the government for surrendering to Indian desires, stated almost immediately that Indians did not want severalty; while Morgan, who opposed the Ute bill as specific rather than general, proceeded in the next Congress to criticize the Coke severalty bill as general rather than specific![13] Opponents at the other end of the capitol approached the problem from other and equally varied points of view. The three outstanding critics of the Ute bill in the House were an Arkansas Democrat who claimed Indians were already sufficiently advanced, a Pennsylvania Republican who announced that Indians were not ready for responsibilities, and a Mississippi Democrat who opposed dictating to the Indians as strongly as it had been advised by Teller and Morgan![14] As proponents of the bill in the House backed severalty with arguments varying from extreme selfishness to unrealistic humanitarianism, discussions of the Ute bill clearly revealed land allotment as a proposal of such wide appeal that a realignment of forces was bound to result once the policy was clearly understood.[15]

The Leading Arguments of Opponents and Advocates of Severalty

Ratification of the Ute agreement did not signify congressional acceptance of land allotment as a general solution of the Indian problem. Not only was the plan limited in application to a single tribe, but several legislators announced that they supported the bill merely because war seemed the alternative. A less satisfactory reception awaited measures providing for severalty on a wider scale or where no emergency existed. When no particular need for rapid action could be cited, the policy was forced to stand upon its own merits. This was for the best, as severalty needed to be judged according to its suitability in normal situations. Debates concerning the wisdom of allotment continued with little interruption until passage of the Dawes Act in 1887. As the issues became clearer following repeated discussion, severalty proposals gradually won friends. But even though arguments became less confused as the policy was better understood, neither the opponents nor the supporters of severalty were ever in complete agreement among themselves.

Harmony among the opponents of severalty was more apparent than real. All critics of land allotment argued that Indians were unprepared for the change. But while Easterners feared that frontiersmen would take advantage of unprotected Indians, Westerners were primarily interested in preventing association with ignorant tribesmen on a basis of equality. Between men regarding the Dawes Act as "a cunningly devised scheme of our covetous, heartless element to rob" and those attacking its sponsors as fanatics who hoped to improve upon the Almighty by eradicating habits of mind and body which had existed for centuries, there was a tremendous gap.[16] Many frontiersmen, it is true, complained that severalty would result in racial extermination; but in contrast to colleagues from the East they felt that the disaster would be due to Indian weaknesses rather than selfishness on the part of the whites.[17] By displaying a respect for Indian institutions in complete contrast with the contemptuous attitude of frontiersmen, Eastern opponents of severalty agreed with their Western cohorts only in their ultimate aim. As both factions desired to postpone allotment measures, however, they were able to unite effectively for some time in spite of their differing points of view.

While conflicting motives handicapped the opponents of severalty, advocates of land allotment were equally at odds. In most cases, reformers believed that a distribution of tribal holdings among individuals would solve the Indian problem permanently. Yet many others considered the measure more necessary than desirable. The advantages of land allotment appealed with equal force whether men were critical of communal life or merely felt a change of customs inevitable. But a fundamental difference in outlook separated the reformer who believed severalty "a measure correspondent with the progressive age in which we live" from the one who urged the plan only as the lesser of two evils.[18] To hold that Indians "must either change their mode of life or . . . die" was not to admit that "the bane of our Indian system and the prime cause of its failure was the fact of communing tribes upon reservations like herds of cattle in fenced pastures."[19] Yet whether severalty advocates welcomed the plan or merely accepted it as inevitable, they soon combined in sufficient numbers to rout the opponents of reform.

Although the contrasting arguments of severalty advocates were both employed with great success, neither stands careful analysis. Much trouble was to arise because reformers regarded land allotment as a panacea instead of realizing that no measure could provide an absolute cure for the evils of Indian policy. Severalty was hailed by too many Americans as an end in itself instead of but one means of reaching the true goal of Indian advancement. Yet those who simply regarded the plan as inevitable were equally incorrect. Allotment was the result of deliberate choice, not a mere product of fate. Although Senator Dawes referred to severalty as "a new and startling idea forced by sheer necessity," and declared that the problem could be solved "in no other way,"[20] legislators might either have allowed conditions to continue or have adopted entirely different methods of reform. But while land allotment was neither a cure-all nor a necessity, the fact that advocates regarded it as such was of tremendous importance. If more reformers had been aware of the problems introduced by severalty or had realized that the change was not indispensable, the course of American Indian history would have been far different.

As the eighties progressed, the arguments in favor of severalty gradually resulted in joint action by Eastern and Western legislators to force acceptance of the policy. In 1882 party ties failed to prevent eleven out of twelve Western representatives from supporting an allotment measure opposed by Democratic leaders.

Severalty Debates of the Eighties

As but five other Democrats revolted and the eight Republican representatives opposing the proposal resided east of the Mississippi, the effect of the severalty campaign upon Western opinion was already evident.[21] Frontiersmen, who had opposed granting definite title to any Indian land as long as there was a possibility of removal, were now nearly unanimous in their support of allotment as the only method of obtaining more Indian land. Although they hesitated to extend the privileges of white men to Indians, the advantages of contact and the prospective opening of large areas of surplus land were felt adequate compensation for such concessions. A few Westerners continued to lead the fight against the reform, but their influence rapidly declined.[22] At the same time, an important change of opinion was taking place among Eastern reformers who had regarded land allotment with suspicion for several years. Now, as the possibilities of the policy were increasingly realized, the opportunity to use allotment as a means of initiating important reforms was at last admitted. Eastern champions of severalty did not subscribe to the policy without careful thought. Land allotment was favored only after reformers had become convinced that tribal holdings might be broken up without danger if sufficient protection were offered. Even this decision was reached only after a long period during which confidence gradually grew. The process by which Easterners finally joined Westerners supporting land allotments is unusually well reflected in the changing views of Senator Dawes, sponsor of the successful severalty measure and the leading authority in the country on Indian affairs.

Senator Dawes and Indian Reform

Henry Laurens Dawes had had a long congressional career before he became interested in Indian affairs during the Ponca dispute of 1879. As a member of the House of Representatives from western Massachusetts, he had expressed a desire to have Indian lands allotted in 1871,[23] but only after becoming chairman of the Senate Indian Committee in the late seventies did he have opportunity to devote much attention to Indian problems. Dawes's views were not stated at length until the Ute bill debates of 1880 when he revealed his conservatism by insisting that nothing was to be gained by abolishing tribal government. Feeling that the Utes could not profit from such a complicated process as land allotment until they were better educated, Dawes warned his colleagues:

> You might as well turn loose the inmates of an insane asylum and impose upon them the restraints of law and require at their hands obedience to the obligations of citizenship as to undertake by this process to make citizens self-supporting, obedient to the law of the land, of these Indians.[24]

Already a leading figure in Indian affairs, Dawes was not prepared to accept radical methods. Yet seven years later he was to play a major part in securing adoption of the very policy he so severely condemned!

Senator Dawes changed his opinion in regard to severalty only after painstaking deliberation. During discussion of the first general allotment bill in the year following the Ute debate, he still confessed "a great deal of difficulty in coming to the conclusion" that land allotment would "do the Indians much good." [25] He expressed similar uncertainty early in 1882 by declaring tribal dissolution "an undertaking beyond our power," which, "if practicable," would "perhaps" be wise.[26] But by far the best evidence of the serious thought which Dawes bestowed upon severalty problems is contained in a letter to Secretary Teller late in September of the same year. The difficulties which had to be faced by advocates of land allotment were never more clearly expressed than when the Senator wrote:

> What can you do with them? We may cry out against the violation of treaties, denounce flagrant disregard of inalienable rights and the inhumanity of our treatment of the defenceless and all that but the fact remains the same and there will come of this outcry, however just no practical answer to this question. We are all talking about 'land in severalty' for the Indian, treating him as white men are treated by giving him the benefit of and making him obey the laws like any other citizen. All this is well in theory but you and I know that it will not

194

meet the present practical difficulty. Two hundred thousand savages who cannot read a word of any language or speak a word of English, who were never taught to work and dont know how to earn their living nor care to learn, who cant read or be made to comprehend the laws they are expected to obey as citizens or know what is meant by a Court of Justice instituted to enforce them, or even the law of *meum et tuum*, the foundation of society, cannot be set up in severalty and left to stand alone any more than so many reeds. Can no more be turned loose on society and bid to confide in and respect an unknown and invisible power relied on to enforce right and punish wrong than so many wild beasts. Without doubt these Indians are to be somehow absorbed into and become a part of the 50,000,000 of our people. There does not seem to be any other way to deal with them. But how? This is what troubles me and this is what I want you to answer in your annual report to Congress. It does not seem to me that the answer can be delayed another session, and you are the only one from position and power and knowledge of Indian character who can do it. There will be all sorts of plans impractical and visionary introduced into Congress, and we shall drift no one can tell where. The Administration and you as its organ should take command of this question and be the first with a well considered measure adequate to the exigency and be prepared to push it. You may depend upon my co-operation in Congress and my readiness to do whatever is necessary there. I do not write this because I have any plan of my own but because I have none and at the same time see a combination of irresistible forces driving the Indians in upon us a great deal faster than we shall be prepared to deal with them. Feeding them in reservations is bad enough. You cannot wait for the children to be educated at Carlisle & Hampton for you are going to have the adults on your hands with no land in reservation worth anything to put them on. All ordinary processes of absorption are slow and scarcely perceptible in their effect upon the whole. They will prove as impotent to solve the problem as colonization was to exterminate slavery. Nor can absorption, any more than amalgamation be forced. The whole subject is surrounded with difficulties but if I can induce you to take hold of it in earnest I am sure of a practical solution. There is no escape from it and it is the part of wisdom to be found prepared for it when it comes.[27]

The doubts regarding severalty, which Dawes expressed in the early eighties, were not forgotten when he became convinced that the policy must be adopted. Having decided to support land allotment only after a serious study of its difficulties, the Senator was determined to provide every possible protection for the tribes. Not only did he constantly seek advice in attempting to improve his bill; but failing to share the dangerous optimism of reformers who had studied the problem less carefully, he forced the adoption of many important amendments. Fully aware of the need for caution, Dawes told the Mohonk conference of 1885, "The more I have to do with the Indian, the greater become the perplexities, and the more distrustful I become of myself." [28] Yet despite his recognition of the dangers of inadequate severalty legislation, Dawes's interest in the policy never flagged. When the advent of the Cleveland administration might easily have delayed reform, Dawes co-operated so closely with Democratic officials that Secretary of the Interior Lamar wrote on the occasion of a re-election battle that he depended largely upon the Senator to do something for the Indian.[29] The concern of leading reformers for the Indian transcended partisanship to such an extent that the great reform measure was sponsored by a Republican senator and signed by a Democratic president. In large measure because of Dawes's personal efforts, victory was achieved only seven years after serious agitation for severalty had begun. Although the Senator received invaluable assistance from large numbers of helpers, few begrudged him credit for his remarkable success.

Victory in the campaign for land allotment confirmed Senator Dawes's reputation as the country's outstanding Indian friend. Much evidence exists in the Senator's papers of the extent to which he was considered the leading reformer in the nation from 1880 until his death in 1903. When chapters describing the Indian question were rejected by Colonel Dodge's publishers in 1881 as of little interest to the general public, for example, the author of *Our Wild Indians* enclosed the manuscript of the omitted portions for the Senator's use.[30] Realizing that the conclusions of an Army officer would be more effective if expressed by another, Dodge immediately selected the Massachusetts Senator as his best spokesman. Similar honors were received frequently in the years following. Thus a friend of the Winnebagoes, when refused a hearing by both

Wisconsin senators, sent his complaint to Dawes.[31] Such applications were only natural, for Dawes was publicized by the president of the Indian Rights Association and by General Armstrong of Hampton as having "more power over the fate of the Indian than any man in the country." [32] Only the inveterate fault finder, Bland, questioned the Senator's sincerity by writing:

> Senator Dawes courts, and in certain quarters, he has achieved, the reputation of a champion of the Indians, but his record does not entitle him to be so regarded. He has been the special champion of every corrupt agent and other official of the Indian service which *The Council Fire* has exposed.[33]

Dawes's record belied such criticism. From first to last, he gave evidence of an effort to treat Indian problems carefully and wisely. Although some may question the opinion of the eulogist who held that no one in the history of the nation had done more for the protection and advancement of the Indian, few will deny that Henry Laurens Dawes must be placed high on any list of Indian friends.[34]

16. INDIAN CITIZENSHIP

Even after reformers decided to employ land allotment as a means of encouraging Indian advancement, several important matters remained to be settled. Three questions in particular had to be answered before severalty legislation could be finally drafted —should allottees be granted citizenship, should their land be subject to sale, and should acceptance of the plan be made compulsory. In reaching conclusions regarding such details, Congress had to determine the extent to which new methods should be instituted. Legislators had questioned the wisdom of racial segregation and tribal autonomy for some time. Now specific decisions regarding citizenship, land tenure, and coercion modified practices which had long been fundamental features of United States Indian policy.

The provisions of the Dawes Act which shifted the course of American Indian relations most drastically were, like the act itself, the product of compromises between Eastern and Western reformers. The diversity of outlook which divided inhabitants of the two sections whenever Indian problems were discussed has already been described. Although a majority in all parts of the country finally supported reform, Easterners hoped for a measure which would aid the Indians while frontiersmen pressed for plans beneficial to themselves. Since neither faction had enough power to dictate provisions of the final bill alone, decisions were reached on debatable subjects only after considerable adjustment. Certain sections of the Dawes Act, it is true, were the result of pressure by the less selfish element, but in an equal number of cases the effect of concessions to Western demands is evident. Product of a balancing of interests by hostile forces, the Act possessed both the benefits and defects of compromise legislation. The nature of the agreements, which enabled both factions to support land allotment, may best be understood by examining the debates of legislators leading to decisions regarding the three problems most open to controversy—the Indian's legal status, the provisions for land distribution, and the question of force.

Recognition of the Need for Law

Long before 1887 wise reformers realized that determination of the proper legal status of Indian allottees was a necessary prerequisite to successful allotment. Any weakening of tribal ties would lead to disaster, most Americans recognized, unless some effort was made to regulate relations between Indian land holders and their white neighbors. Whether such legislation should include an immediate grant of citizenship to Indian allottees, however, was debatable. If citizenship could have protected Indians without requiring intelligent co-operation on their part, no problem would have existed. But as the possession of legal rights established responsibilities as well as bestowing benefits, agreement regarding the status of allottees proved extremely difficult.

The failure of Congress to insist upon the application of American legal principles among Indian tribes had not been entirely due to ignorance of the problem. As early as 1867 the *Nation* dwelt at length upon the advantages to be gained by treating Indians and whites alike.[1] Warned in 1871 that any extension of white jurisdiction over the tribes would destroy Indian rights, reformers insisted that interference with savage customs was in the interest of Indian advancement.[2] Delegates at the Church-Board meeting of 1872 urged the necessity for establishing governmental authority among Indians by a rigid enforcement of American judicial rules on all reservations. Only Chairman Brunot of the Board questioned the wisdom of this suggestion, and even he admitted that certain tribes would benefit from a knowledge of legal practices.[3] Two years later Commissioner E. P. Smith officially supported the campaign for law extension by declaring that United States Indian policies had failed largely because the Indians had not been made amenable to law.[4] While frontiersmen generally were reluctant to have the rights of red men more clearly defined, many supported law extension in hope that Indian abuses might be more effectively punished.[5] So for one reason or another large numbers of Americans had become convinced by 1880 that Indians should no longer be allowed to occupy a position incompatible with the national ideal of equal privileges and responsibilities for all.

In spite of the nationwide interest in establishment of a common judicial system for Indians and whites, legislators of the seventies hesitated to disturb existing racial relationships because the advantages of a change which appeared clear in theory seemed of less value when considered from a more practical standpoint. Equality was a worthy ideal. But as few tribes were sufficiently educated to understand white customs, immediate introduction of a new legal system threatened to expose Indians to exploitation without providing protection. Any exact definition of the red man's status, furthermore, was just as undesirable from a purely selfish point of view. The United States had capitalized for many years upon the uncertainty regarding the status of Indians by treating tribes as independent or dependent according to the needs of the moment.[6] Since this tactical advantage would cease once Indian rights were clearly established, and since most Indians were unprepared for responsibilities, legislators saw no reason why a gradual adjustment of relations would not be preferable to placing Indians and whites upon an equal plane at once.

Officials approached the problem of the Indian's legal status cautiously.[7] Admitting the ultimate, but not the immediate necessity of racial equality, administrators began to prepare the tribes for future responsibilities without exposing them at once to unnecessary evils or taking the drastic step of granting local courts jurisdiction over Indian cases. Care in training Indians in the exercise of one or two fundamental rights was regarded as much more important than a wholesale extension of privileges which would neither allow time for adequate administration nor permit concentration of purpose.[8] Thus federal authorities limited their attention for several years to employing a few elementary legal principles upon the reservations. This purpose was best accomplished through Indian agents, whose regular administrative duties involved many cases of a judicial nature. But although Commissioner E. P. Smith became so enthusiastic regarding the possibilities of agency courts in 1873 that he urged establishment of a code of law based on agents's decisions,[9] no rules were ever announced. Nothing more comprehensive than local regulations was ever possible, as agents had insufficient legal training and were forced by varied local circumstances to meet difficulties without reference to precedent.[10] Something more substantial than the will of an agent was necessary if Indians were to learn obedience to law. Indian courts were established in 1883 as a more direct method of instruction; [11] but before these new agencies had been adequately tested, the case of *ex parte* Crow Dog in December of the same year caused the government to abandon caution and recommend that no further delay be tolerated in plans to apply American legal principle upon Indian reservations.

The case of Crow Dog was unusually well suited to arouse an overwhelming demand for law extension.[12] The plaintiff, a Brulé Sioux chief, had been sentenced to death in the territorial court of Dakota for murdering a fellow tribesman, Chief Spotted Tail. On the ground that the United States possessed no jurisdiction over crimes committed by an Indian against an Indian within Indian country, the Supreme Court was asked to release Crow Dog. That body, after a careful examination of existing law, concluded unanimously that in view of the failure of Congress to provide for national jurisdiction over Indian crimes Crow Dog should be freed immediately. Until federal officials were granted legal authority over reservation Indians, the judges ruled, even a murderer could not be punished.

So dramatic an announcement of government impotence forced Congress to act, even though Justice Matthews's decision bitterly condemned all who wished to apply white laws to Indians. The necessity of permitting Crow Dog to return to his tribe in spite of his murder of a fellow chief was generally regarded as a dangerous precedent. Since Indians would have no respect for law until such acts were punished, many legislators recommended that all Indians should be made amenable to criminal law at once. Less than four months after the decision, the House of Representatives amended the pending Indian Appropriation Bill to make Indians subject to United States criminal jurisdiction. This provision was defeated in the Senate and struck out by the conference committee, but only because legislators felt that more time was necessary to formulate a satisfactory measure.[13] This excuse was not possible the following year.

The question of law extension was a subject of major importance during 1885 debates on Indian problems. By this time, legal experts of the Indian Rights Association had had an opportunity to study the matter thoroughly and were recommending the establishment of special courts with jurisdiction over Indian reservations.[14] Such a creation of new agencies seemed only a temporary expedient to many reformers, including Secretary Whittlesey of the Board of Indian Commissioners. "If our judicial system is write enough & good enough for all other tribes & kindreds, & people," Whittlesey wrote Painter of the Association, "it is write & good enough for a few thousand Indians. And they are no more ignorant of the proceedings of justice than millions who are now subject to the laws of the land." [15] As a vast majority of Americans were of like mind, Congress discussed the removal of all legal distinctions separating red men and white. A section of the 1885 Indian Appropriation Bill, adopted by the House with only two dissenting votes, stated that Indians should be subject to criminal laws and that civil courts should be opened to tribal members on the same basis as citizens. As such legislation was not properly part of a financial measure, and as the provision had not even been considered by the House Indian Committee, the section was deleted by the Senate.[16] With neither branch of Congress willing to desert its position, a second conference committee was necessary before the House permitted the Senate to write a compromise measure extending only criminal jurisdiction and exempting the tribes of Indian Territory from the provisions.[17] Even in this form, the action of Congress vitally affected existing relations between the races, for at last the disastrous theory of tribal responsibility for crime had been dropped in favor of the accountability of the individual Indian.

Although the refusal of Congress to extend civil law to the tribes enabled critics to charge that legislators "sought to exact justice from the Indian while exhibiting no justice to him," [18] application of criminal statutes to Indian cases was only the first of more fundamental adjustments in racial relationships. Congressional action on the matter not only allowed the Supreme Court to reverse its Crow Dog decision denying government jurisdiction over Indian crimes (United States vs. Kagama, 1886),[19] but also stimulated further discussion of the Indian's legal status. Reformers, refusing to accept the defeat of plans to bring Indians within the jurisdiction of civil as well as criminal courts, pressed for additional legislation. Faced with opposition from men who felt many tribes unprepared for responsibilities, advocates of legal equality agreed to limit law extension for a time to the most advanced red men. As the pending act for distributing land in severalty provided that Indians undergoing the change should be carefully selected by the government, a decision that Indians receiving allotments should also be amenable to civil law followed as a matter of course. So it was that section six of the Dawes Act marked the first step toward full legal equality by providing:

Each and every member of the respective bands or tribes of Indians to whom allotments have been made shall have the benefit of and be subject to the laws, both civil and criminal, of the State or Territory in which they may reside; and no Territory shall pass or enforce any law denying any such Indian within its jurisdiction the equal protection of the law.[20]

This was not the only revolution in the Indian's legal position, however, for the section also contained a statement upon the closely related and even more significant subject of Indian citizenship.

The Problem of Indian Citizenship

Consideration of the Indian's legal status had inevitably introduced the question of citizenship. If red men were to be subjected to the laws of white society, it seemed only just that they should be allowed full political privileges as well. Real equality could be achieved only if both Indians and whites shared the rights and responsibilities of citizenship. Yet the advantages to be gained through participation in the political life of whites were not without corresponding losses. Any grant of citizenship threatened to destroy privileges which tribes had exercised for years. Whether Indians should be made citizens or allowed to continue as a peculiar group with special rights and disabilities was a serious problem, the answer to which was certain to be of great importance to the future of the race.

The exact position of the Indian in the American political system remained in doubt for several years after the Civil War. Legislators could not decide whether Indians were affected by the citizenship provisions of the Fourteenth Amendment. As the question of including Indians had evenly split the Senate committee reporting the amendment and as the Senate itself had voted against referring to the problem specifically, the matter was left unsettled.[21] Even after a special Senate committee announced in 1870 that Indians were not citizens under the amendment,[22] the question of citizenship was not decided. Many reformers insisted that Indians could not become citizens under any circumstances, but the Senate Indian Committee of 1870 declared that individuals need merely leave their tribes to become eligible for citizenship and a House committee denied that even this action was necessary.[23] With those best informed upon the problem unable to agree, some time passed before a definition of the Indian's position was generally accepted.

Although no single theory regarding Indian citizenship won overwhelming support during the seventies, the opinion that red men automatically became citizens upon leaving tribal jurisdiction became increasingly popular. Many reformers continued to insist that separation from tribal life should not be required; but since many who urged unrestricted citizenship also attacked the validity of Indian treaties, more and more friends of the red men were willing to limit citizenship to individuals who abandoned their tribes.[24] This view of the matter was accepted so widely by the turn of the decade that it was supported by legal authorities. The principle was explained in the *American Law Review* of January, 1881, by G. F. Canfield, who wrote:

Congress may prevent an Indian leaving his reservation, and while he is on a reservation it may deprive him of his liberty, his property, his life; but as soon as an Indian has severed his tribal relation, the supreme power of Congress over him ceases,—he then becomes a person within the meaning of the Constitution, and under the protection of its restrictive clauses, and every executive officer and every legislative body in our country must respect his rights.[25]

Under such a theory, Indian relations with the government were not like those with immigrants. The contrast was well described by an anonymous author of the late seventies, who stated:

> The Indian differs from an alien in this, that he is not born wholly foreign to the jurisdiction of the Nation, but to a certain extent within it. His disability consists only in the incompleteness of this relation, not in a birth antagonistic thereto. He therefore has, if we may so speak, an inchoate right of citizenship, which may be perfected by bringing himself wholly within the relations upon which citizenship depends.[26]

So it was that by the early eighties most Americans believed either that all Indians were citizens or that they could become so by leaving their tribes.

While contrasting opinions were expressed regarding Indian citizenship, not even the slightest disagreement would have been possible if Congress had consented to define the position of the red men. Citizenship measures were introduced annually following 1873 in efforts to end confusion regarding the rights and duties of Indians, but in every case the legislators refused to act. So although the ire of Bishop Whipple and other reformers was aroused in 1873 when the Supreme Court ruled that Indians could not sell reservation timber,[27] neither revelation of the red man's dependence nor the pressure of his friends led senators to consider a citizenship bill reported favorably by the Indian Committee.[28] When homestead rights were extended to Indians the next year, a provision granting citizenship to all individuals who abandoned their tribes to accept public land was eliminated by the conference committee.[29] Similar reluctance to act was shown in 1876 when the Senate refused to consider a citizenship bill for fear of imposing on the Indians, and the House defeated a similar measure by failing to pass the transfer bill to which it was attached.[30] Not until

Uncle Sam's Stepchildren

Senator Ingalls of Kansas introduced a bill in 1877, which would have enabled Indian land holders to become citizens while continuing to receive annuity payments and hold inalienable land, was a citizenship proposal discussed at length. Then it became clear that with one group of legislators complaining that no special privileges should be granted and another arguing that insufficient protection was provided, action was impossible.[31] There were too many disputes regarding Indian affairs among legislators of the late seventies to permit agreement upon so controversial a subject as Indian citizenship despite the need for clarifying the red man's status.

The increased interest in Indian affairs, which marked the early eighties, did not influence the attitude of Congress toward Indian citizenship. Senator Hoar of Massachusetts proposed to extend full citizenship to all Indians accepting allotments under the severalty bill introduced by Senator Coke of Texas in 1881, but Senator Call of Florida joined Coke in expressing fear that adequate protection would be impossible even if the grants were made inalienable as Senator Hoar desired. Combined with the less openly expressed reluctance of Westerners to accept Indians as equals, this fear that Indian citizenship would prove disastrous again delayed action. Only eight senators supported Hoar's proposal, and of these six came from New England and but one from west of the Mississippi.[32] With frontier legislators all but unanimous in opposing any change in the Indian's legal status, no political analyst of the early eighties had any premonition that an act providing for Indian citizenship would be passed before the decade had ended.

Just as the Crow Dog decision of late 1883 was immediately followed by the extension of criminal law to Indian reservations, so the Elk-Wilkins decision of a year later speeded action on the matter of Indian citizenship.[33] This important case arose when John Elk, a non-reservation Indian, was refused the right to vote in a local election by registrar Charles Wilkins of the Fifth Ward of Omaha, Nebraska. Statements that the plaintiff had separated from his tribe and was therefore under the jurisdiction of the United States were accepted by the Court. Claims that he thereby became a citizen with the right to vote, however, were rejected by a majority of the tribunal on the ground that an Indian could not "make himself a citizen without the consent and co-operation of the government." A mere surrender of tribal allegiance, in other words, did not constitute a formal admission to the privileges of American citizenship as long as Congress had not so provided. Even if Indians did come under the jurisdiction of the United States upon leaving their tribes, the majority declared, they were no more "born in the United States" within the meaning of the Fourteenth Amendment than were the children of ambassadors born in this country. Two justices dissented from these statements on the ground that the majority opinion strained the intention of citizenship clauses of the Fourteenth Amendment, but all agreed in emphasizing that United States laws on the subject of Indian citizenship were unsatisfactory. Unless determination of an Indian's status was to be referred to the Court whenever such problems arose, legislative action was imperative. Congressional reluctance to define Indian rights disappeared rapidly once Americans were told that Indians gained no privileges by deserting their tribes. While legislators had hesitated to state their views, most had felt that Indians could become citizens by placing themselves under United States jurisdiction. Most Americans were deeply shocked to learn that citizenship was possible only after naturalization. The widespread feeling of disgust which caused Senator Dawes to declare that the Elk-Wilkins ruling was the strangest, if not the wickedest decision since the fugitive slave cases, was soon replaced by a determination to remedy the evils growing out of the decision by new legislation.[34] As the Court's decision upheld the right of Congress to grant citizenship to the Indians, prompt legislative action seemed the best way of providing for Indians who were neither tribal members nor citizens. Caution, which had often been considered essential in introducing Indian citizenship, was less frequently recommended after John Elk was denied the right to vote.

The Early Opposition to Immediate Citizenship

The extraordinary effect of the Elk-Wilkins decision upon American thought can be fully understood only by examining the contrasting views regarding citizenship which prevailed before and after 1884. Few people denied that Indian citizenship should be an ultimate goal once the rights of minority races had been emphasized by the Civil War. But prior to 1884, the dangers of extending citizenship prematurely also were stressed by men interested in Indian welfare. If reformers had not insisted that training was necessary, red men might have been mentioned as citizens in the Fourteenth Amendment. Instead, those most responsible for the tribes exerted every effort to have their wards excluded. Commissioner Walker classified advocates of citizenship as enemies of the race, prophets of despair, and impractical idealists.[35] The strange union between men who were sick of the Indian problem and those who believed citizenship would be a blessing to the race, which characterized these years, could not have been more accurately described. But in spite of the varied nature of the groups interested in citizenship, little progress was made for several years.

Although many Americans opposed Indian citizenship for selfish reasons, the advantages of extending political rights following the Civil War were not sufficiently obvious to win the support of even a majority of the best known friends of the race. Leading reformers constantly emphasized the evils of premature citizenship. The suffering to be expected as a result of advanced political position could be stressed with unusual effect in the case of Indians residing in territory acquired from Mexico. While the Mission Indians of California and the Pueblo Indians of New Mexico were treated as citizens in accordance with treaty provisions of 1848 promising that they would be granted the same rights they had possessed in Mexico, equality with neighboring whites proved more of a handicap than a help. Since Indians possessing civil rights were expected to defend themselves without special assistance from the government, California and New Mexico tribes immediately became a prey of selfish whites. The Mission Indians, quickly dispossessed of their holdings, soon became a particular concern of reformers and aroused the interest of Mrs. Jackson; while the Pueblos, held responsible by local courts for acts that could not have been charged against wards, were robbed of their property.[36] Yet United States action on behalf of the tribes was impossible because the

Indian Citizenship

Supreme Court ruled that government intervention was unconstitutional.[37] The advantages of citizenship, reformers learned, might be easily overemphasized.

As advocates of citizenship often revealed more of a desire to control than to benefit Indians, caution was still widely urged even after the ability of Indians to adjust themselves to new conditions was demonstrated by the educational experiments of the early eighties. Not only did Bishop Whipple write Schurz that citizenship would prove a "pitiable failure," but the Secretary himself announced that immediate extension of political rights would be no less cruel than extermination and rebuked a friend who felt death preferable to dependence.[38] Even the paper of the Carlisle Indian School, which might easily have demanded Indian equality, hailed the government's decision to insist upon education before citizenship and warned that Indians were "liable to be imposed on and cheated far more effectually under form of law than by any other means." [39] Until 1885 little evidence existed that reformers would favor Indian citizenship for many years.

The suddenness with which Americans reversed their opinions regarding the advisability of immediate Indian citizenship could hardly be believed, if proof did not exist in the periodical statements of prominent Indian organizations. As it is, records of both the Indian Rights Association and the Lake Mohonk conferences reveal a change which was not only sudden but complete. Henry S. Pancoast of the former organization, for instance, criticized advocates of immediate citizenship in 1883 for following a theory blindly in disregard of facts and urged the injustice of forcing strange laws upon an alien race. Yet the man who declared that a mistake of two hundred years could not be cancelled by a dozen lines upon a statute book was leading his organization in work for citizenship and law extension but two years later.[40] Even more remarkable was the desire for immediate citizenship expressed in 1885 by members of the Lake Mohonk conference, who had resolved two years previously that Indians should be admitted to United States citizenship as soon, and only as soon, as they were fitted for its responsibilities.[41] Any doubt of the permanency of this conversion was dispelled when the leading students of Indian affairs at the 1886 conference resolved:

> It is our conviction that the duties of citizenship are of such a nature that they can only be learned by example and practice, and we believe that quicker and surer progress in industry, education and morality will be secured by giving citizenship first, than by making citizenship depend upon the attainment of any standard of education and conduct; and we therefore urge upon Congress the necessity of ceasing to treat the Indians as incapable of responsibilities that we impose upon all other human beings competent to distinguish right from wrong.[42]

By upsetting contemporary theories of Indian citizenship, the Elk-Wilkins decision forced immediate consideration of the citizenship problem despite the previous reluctance of Americans to consider the issue.

The Campaign for Immediate Citizenship

Discussions of Indian citizenship, devoted to debating the advisability of suffrage extension before the Elk-Wilkins decision, were largely confined thereafter to arguments regarding the speed with which the change should be instituted. Whether citizenship would prove of advantage to the Indians concerned reformers of the mid-eighties very little. Feeling that the red man must ultimately become a citizen, reformers believed the sole problem was whether the process should be hurried or allowed to follow a more normal course. A gradual change had no appeal to crusaders who wished to emulate Luther and Garrison.[43] With characteristic impatience, such reformers insisted that the only way to prepare Indians for citizenship was to make them citizens.[44] Only ultraconservatives opposed action after 1884. Secretary of the Interior Lamar, it is true, warned in 1885 that citizenship would be "sad service to the Indian" and that few would survive if the change was made suddenly.[45] But only such men as Bland upheld the cautious Secretary by describing citizenship as "just such a policy as those who hang about the borders of Indian reservations, awaiting an opportunity to rob the Indians of their lands, would propose, if they dared."[46] Most Americans, for one reason or another, were convinced that Indians should be made citizens at once. With interest in extending civil rights at fever pitch, the only question to be decided was what safeguards should be provided.

Red men would have been denied any special protection if many reformers had had their way. Like a majority of fellow Americans, Indian workers over-rated the value of citizenship. While few advantages were to be gained by a surrender of tribal allegiance,[47] many intelligent people declared that all troubles would cease once Indians possessed the right to vote.[48] But even reformers who realized that the responsibilities might be too great urged that the race should prove its adaptability or die. If Indians could not learn to "paddle their own canoes," a surprising number of Americans believed no further sympathy should be wasted upon them.[49] Fortunately a few reformers distinguished themselves by insisting that Indian citizens should receive special consideration. Only because some advocates of citizenship demanded adequate safeguards was ruin averted.

No man among those who wished to protect Indian citizens worked more energetically than Senator Dawes. Although his daughter later declared that her father had considered liberty and law more important than protection,[50] the Senator was actually just as discreet in considering citizenship problems as he had been in accepting severalty. So persistent was his determination to demand preparation before citizenship that his conservatism was frequently criticized.[51] Legal responsibilities should not be imposed upon Indians, Dawes insisted, unless they were ready to bear them. As a result, he hoped to limit citizenship to Indians receiving allotments under the severalty act, for their land could not be taken from them for twenty-five years even though they were citizens. Any chance that political privileges would be confined to carefully selected Indians was defeated, however, when the House decided that all Indians holding land should be made citizens whether their plots had been obtained by treaty, by voluntary action, or under the protective provisions of the Dawes Act. Only in the case of reservation Indians was citizenship postponed.

Uncle Sam's Stepchildren

No part of the Dawes Act was of greater importance than that portion of section six which stated:

And every Indian born within the territorial limits of the United States to whom allotments shall have been made under the provisions of this act, or under any law or treaty, and every Indian born within the territorial limits of the United States who has voluntarily taken up, within said limits, his residence separate and apart from any tribe of Indians therein, and has adopted the habits of civilized life, is hereby declared to be a citizen of the United States, and is entitled to all the rights, privileges, and immunities of such citizens, whether said Indian has been or not, by birth or otherwise, a member of any tribe of Indians within the territorial limits of the United States without in any manner impairing or otherwise affecting the right of any such Indian to tribal or other property.[52]

For the first time in United States history, Indians could become American citizens. Yet few people were content with the measure. Senator Dawes, feeling too many Indians had been included, wrote a friend who complained of the speed with which newly created citizens were deprived of their holdings:

All the troubles under the severalty law, which I have been dreading . . . . have come upon Mr. Eells Indians sooner than I expected. This arises from the amendment to the citizenship clause inserted in the House making it apply to all allotments 'under any law or treaty,' so that all the Indians who had before under any tenure, taken up lands in severalty, became instanter citizens with all the consequences, and without the slightest preparation. There is less danger of these troubles among Indians who work it all out under the severalty law, because if wisely administered it will be applied only to Indians prepared for it, and only so fast as they are prepared for it beforehand.[53]

While the Senator criticized the provision for including Indians who were unprepared, however, advocates of immediate citizenship were disappointed because reservation Indians had been omitted. The privileges granted by the Dawes Act seemed only a minor victory to reformers who had hoped that every Indian would be made a citizen. As a compromise between champions of full racial equality and men who insisted that citizenship should be intro-

212

duced gradually, section six seemed to have the dubious distinction of satisfying no one. Yet acceptance of the principle of Indian citizenship was itself important. Just how widely it would be extended rested with the future. The campaign for immediate citizenship did not cease when the severalty act became law. Such organizations as the Indian Rights Association and the Boston Citizenship Association now fought with increased determination to obtain full rights for all Indians. Under the leadership of Professor James B. Thayer of the Harvard Law School, a large number of reformers not only insisted that even the most backward Indians should be instantly granted citizenship but demanded that all government control of Indian affairs should cease.[54] The race would never advance, such men agreed, if it continued to depend upon the government for assistance. Immediate and unqualified citizenship was regarded by many as the only possible solution of the Indian problem.[55] Yet even Professor Thayer's support of such radical action waned as he studied the problem more thoroughly. Although believing that certain privileges should be extended whether or not an Indian received land in severalty, he finally admitted that full citizenship would be dangerous.[56] For a time Thayer continued to urge an administration of Indian problems by the judiciary instead of politicians, but even this platform was surrendered in 1891 because of the great need for government protection.[57] The professor desired to acquaint the Indians with law, but unlike many of his colleagues he finally realized the necessity for continued Indian wardship. Luckily, enough others also recognized the value of government protection to prevent adoption of a general citizenship law for over a quarter of a century longer.

The Problem of Indian Wardship

Professor Thayer's desire to terminate the control of the United States government over Indian affairs was a fundamental part of the campaign for immediate citizenship. As long as a special agency existed for handling the problems of red men and protecting their lives, racial equality was impossible. The frequent scandals marking the administration of Indian affairs caused many Americans to advocate abolition of the Indian Bureau and obscured the advantages of government control. Autocratic decisions by government officials were equally obnoxious to frontiersmen who wished to be unmolested in their dealing with Indians and reformers who felt that the government was mistreating the tribes. Ultimate independence of government authority being accepted as desirable even by Indian officials, many Americans saw no reason why Indian dependence upon Washington should not be ended at once.[58]

While the federal government's administration of Indian affairs was responsible for many evils, the alternative of absolute freedom was even less promising. Judge Willard of the National Indian Defense Association, although admitting that the corruption characterizing political control of Indian problems made an end of wardship imperative, rightly warned that independence could not be achieved by presenting the Indian with responsibilities he was unprepared to carry.[59] Self-sufficiency would be encouraged by releasing tribes from the domination of Washington officials, but at the same time an important source of protection would no longer be available. Since too much freedom would expose the Indian to exploitation just as surely as full reliance upon the government had checked advancement, a balance was needed between absolute subservience and unlimited independence.[60] To destroy every possibility of aiding needy tribes was hardly the best way of insuring progress. Complete severance of all ties between Indians and the government promised few immediate benefits and many evils.

A major reason for the failure of legislators to reduce the power of American Indian officials was distrust in the ability of the American states to handle Indian relations judiciously. Although Senator Sherman recommended control by the states and territories as early as 1867,[61] local officers displayed little intention of treating their Indians justly. Instead of receiving co-operation from frontier officials, federal administrators constantly had to defend red men from local attacks. People living in the vicinity of important tribes were frequently more interested in Indian problems than national administrators; but only in Eastern states was there any certainty that such interest would result in the Indian's advantage. Where state control promised to relieve the government of burdensome duties without exposing Indians to unnecessary dangers, a change of administration was occasionally proposed. In 1875, for example, Commissioner Marble recommended that Indians should be placed under state control at the first possible moment and the Board of Indian Commissioners specifically advised surrendering jurisdiction over New York Indians.[62] No action was taken in line with these suggestions, but a measure authorizing negotiations with the governors of Michigan, New York, and North Carolina for transferring guardianship was presented to the House in 1877.[63] As the federal government lost all power once a state assumed responsibility for its Indians, most officials opposed state control and fought in case after case to uphold their authority before the Supreme Court.[64] Although ultimate assimilation was likely, Indians would profit by being treated as wards as long as the widespread hostility toward the race remained unabated.

While continued Indian wardship was frequently advised by men who wished to dictate to the Indians for selfish reasons,[65] the necessity for protecting the tribes justified the government in forcing its will upon the race. Until red men were ready to assume full responsibility, the government was able to render invaluable services.[66] Such help was of vital importance to the race, although the duties were sometimes of the peculiar nature requested by an Indian who wrote:

> Sir—I am a friend of the Great Father's and am going in the white man's ways. I have noticed white men cutting wood, and I thought I would be like a white man and chop some wood for my wife. A piece of wood flew up and put out my right eye, and now I would like the Great Father to send me another eye. I can have it put in here. I have always been a friend of the white man and am bringing my children up in the white man's way. I am getting old and wish my father would send me a cane. When you send the eye please send a brown one, as that is the color of my other eye. I hope the Great Father will do as I ask. I shake hands with a good heart. Your friend.[67]

The future welfare of the race did not rest upon maintaining a stock of glass eyes of whatever color, but prevention of raids upon

Indian property and prosecution of men who robbed and beat Indians were essential factors in racial preservation. For the time being, also, continued national jurisdiction was the only way in which a national policy could be shaped for the future. If reform was to be a reality, the full power of government officials over the Indians needed to be reasserted.[68] No danger was greater, Secretary Lamar warned Dawes, than efforts to remove Indians from federal supervision.[69] Recognition of the need to retain control over the tribes caused definite declarations of national authority to be included in the Dawes Act. New privileges were granted certain Indians, but choice of those who should be granted citizenship and control over land and financial matters left full responsibility in the hands of Indian officials. As the power to act rested with the government in every instance, cautious administration alone was necessary to insure that the new system was not employed to the Indian's disadvantage.

17. THE DEVELOPMENT OF
INDIAN LAND POLICIES

WHILE THE PORTIONS OF THE DAWES ACT DEALING WITH THE PROBlem of Indian citizenship were of the utmost importance, the primary purpose of the measure was to revolutionize the method of Indian land holding. The age-old practice of communal or tribal ownership was to be ended by dividing reservations into plots for distribution to individual Indians. The race would advance more rapidly, reformers held, if each Indian was encouraged by receiving personal title to the land he occupied. As a measure limited to abandoning communal for several ownership would not benefit the whites, however, more than a mere change in the method of land holding was necessary to win the favor of legislators. The Dawes Act was accepted by Congress only after its sponsors had made strange compromises between plans intended to aid the Indian and those meant to annex his land.

Two land holding provisions of the Dawes Act reveal unusually well the way in which Indian and white interests were balanced. Considerations of Indian welfare were uppermost when legislators provided that allotments should not be sold for twenty-five years. Yet self-interest was just as obviously the motive when Congress insisted that all unallotted land should immediately be opened to white settlement. Although funds from the sale of excess land were to be used for benefit of the Indians, the fact remained that undisputed title to a definite portion of land was to be gained only by surrendering any claim to the rest. Whether such a policy would prove of benefit to whites, to Indians, to both races, or to neither was far from certain.

The significance of the debates regarding land policy can be comprehended much more clearly after a brief summary of the arrangement which was ultimately approved. The process was to begin whenever the President believed that the members of a tribe would benefit from land distribution. An affirmative decision having been reached regarding the advisability of allotment, each head of a family was to receive one-quarter section (160 acres), each single person over eighteen as well as each orphan child was to have one-eighth section (80 acres), and all other single persons under eighteen born prior to an allotment order were to be assigned one-sixteenth section (40 acres). Where insufficient land existed, pro rata assignments were to be made in the same proportion; and where reservations were only of use for grazing, the amounts were to be doubled. In no case, however, was full title to an allotment to be granted for twenty-five years. Indians were to be prevented from disposing of their holdings during this time by patents declaring that the land was held in trust by the United States for the exclusive use of the allottee and his heirs. If still further protection proved desirable at the end of the period, government control might be extended indefinitely at presidential discretion. Once the patents had been issued to each Indian, or sooner if felt desirable by the President, unallotted areas were to be sold to white settlers. Sums realized from the disposal of such land were to be deposited in the United States Treasury and the annual interest accumulated by the funds was to be employed for the education and civilization of the tribe. Thus stated, the principles of the Dawes Act seem extremely simple. In reality, the system was pieced together only after extended debate as to what plan would aid whites the most while injuring Indians the least. Land provisions of the Dawes Act were not exclusively a product of sympathy for the Indian.

In stating that many supporters of the Dawes Act were moved by selfish motives, the impression should not be created that self-seeking legislators were from any particular part of the country. Motives were often so mixed even in the case of individual congressmen that no section's attitude can be characterized as either exclusively selfish or unselfish. The desire of frontiersmen to dispossess Indians was naturally strong; but interest in securing land was a powerful factor in winning the support of men from all sections. A conviction that no Indian land should be "a barrier against the swelling tide of American commerce" was universal.[1] Representatives of frontier states were more apt than their colleagues to

The Development of Indian Land Policies

emphasize the advantage of severalty legislation to whites, but arguments of Easterners explaining the gains to be made by Indians were almost always accompanied by others urging the necessity for commercial expansion. As Easterners had every reason to be more liberal, their emphasis upon the desirability of obtaining more Indian land was especially significant.

The interest of frontiersmen in opening Indian reservations to settlement was shared by both the individual reformers and the organizations of the East. Few Easterners believed that Indians should occupy land they could not use. Even a woman, who held that Indians as "Decedents of Father Abraham" were "within the covenant of mercy," wrote President Grant that if red men felt they had a right to their lands "it was high time they were better inform'd."[2] Undeniable as were the rights possessed by Indians, Senator Dawes believed that the advance of white civilization was as impossible to check as a river.[3] Members of the Indian Rights Association not only agreed, but announced that they would not resist a legitimate advance of civilization if they could.[4] So eager was their Washington representative to open reservations that he declared the purpose of filling the Indian Territory with settlers "ought never to sleep."[5] Similar interest in expansion led the Mohonk conference of 1884 to hail passage of a bill redistributing Sioux land as much because of the opening of a new highway as for any advantage gained by the Indians.[6] Even members of the Board of Indian Commissioners, who were particularly noted for their concern for the Indian, refused to uphold his land claims. Instead, they ably summarized the opinion of a large majority of Americans by writing in their 1879 *Report*:

We may moralize over the natural rights of the Indian as much as we please, but after all they have their limit. His right to the soil is only possessory. He has no title in fee. If he will cultivate it and use it as civilized men use their possessions, it will or should be well with him, but it is evident that no 12,000,000 acres of the public domain, whose hills are full of ores, and whose valleys are waiting for diligent hands to 'dress and keep them,' in obedience to the divine command, can long be kept simply as a park, in which wild beasts are hunted by wilder men. This Anglo-Saxon race will not allow the car of civilization to stop long at any line of latitude or longitude on our broad domain. If the Indian in his wildness plants himself on the track, he must inevitably be crushed by it.[7]

The white man's passion for possession was too great to protect Indian rights from invasion even by those known for their sympathy with the oppressed.

Railroad Expansion and American Indian Policy

No aspect of America's desire for internal expansion was pressed more strongly during the eighties than the demand that railroads should be allowed to cross Indian land. Although reservations threatened to prevent development of an adequate transportation system following the Civil War, the problem did not become acute for several years because the pressure for expansion was temporarily relieved when rights of way through the Indian Territory were given to a north-south and an east-west railroad in 1866. For some time objections arose almost entirely because the customary land grants to finance construction had been withheld in the Territory until Indian titles could be extinguished by voluntary cession as rapidly as "consistent with public policy and the welfare of the Indians."[8] Since the Indians had no intention of surrendering any of their land, and since the United States refused to force acceptance of the provisional grants, the officials of the roads spent much time agitating for an abolition of tribal titles. Yet despite this pressure, nothing was done to open the Territory. Even when tribal authority was challenged by the Dawes Act of 1887, any possibility that the roads might at last obtain their land grants was avoided by exempting the Indian Territory from its provisions. But while United States legislators refused to permit roads to annex large amounts of reservation lands, they already had decided that they would not deny rights of way to other lines.

National enthusiasm for railroad expansion mounted gradually. Railroads absorbed too much land to be regarded favorably by most frontiersmen. Both railroad owners and settlers wished to have the Indian reservations opened; but the effort of railroad companies to obtain large grants as a reward for providing access to the land disturbed individual citizens.[9] Most Westerners were especially critical of the reservation system because settlers were excluded from areas where large corporations were admitted.[10] Fear that railroads would absorb the best Indian land and demand exorbitant prices for its sale caused frontiersmen to oppose admitting any additional lines to reservations for several years. By degrees, their resolution weakened. A need for new connections, combined with hatred of the monopolistic practices of railroads already on the reservations, led Westerners to support the admission of other companies. As many friends of the Indians had long believed that railroad expansion would prove beneficial to the tribes, agitation for granting rights of way through reservations reached tremendous proportions.[11]

The question of whether Congress should permit more railroads to enter Indian reservations reached a climax in 1882 when the Saint Louis and San Francisco Railroad applied for consent to pass through a corner of the Choctaw reservation in Indian Territory. Since opponents of the measure challenged the validity of the tribe's consent and urged the right of neighboring Chickasaws to be consulted in regard to the cession, Congress had to decide not only whether the right of way should be allowed, but whether Indian consent should be required and had been legitimately obtained. With the issue clearly drawn between public need and Indian rights, few legislators were willing to admit that Indians might impede national development whatever their treaty rights might be. Under the principle of eminent domain, a majority argued, the United States government had as much right to seize the land of Indians upon just compensation as to take that of whites. Favorable votes of 31 to 13 and 116 to 43 following a thorough discussion of the railroad's application left no doubt that both the Senate and House desired expansion.[12]

An analysis of the Senate and House votes in favor of admitting the Saint Louis and San Francisco Railroad to Indian Territory in the face of Indian opposition shows that the decision was a result of sectional rather than partisan divisions. All but one senator from west of the Mississippi, all but one from the Middle Atlantic states, and all but two from the South voted for expansion, while but one of ten senators from New England and states north of the Ohio supported the railroad's request. Representatives from east of the Mississippi were more divided upon the subject than their Senate colleagues; but disagreement in the House was not on partisan lines (Republicans, 57-22; Democrats, 54-19; others, 5-2) and only a single member of twenty-eight from west of the river opposed the grant. Although Senator Ingalls of Kansas and Senator Jones of Florida deserted colleagues from their sections to oppose railroad expansion and plead for treaty observance, their fight was in vain.[13] Congress, the country learned, was no longer satisfied to let Indians stand in the way of progress.

The action of Congress in admitting railroads to Indian reservations was frequently repeated in the years following 1882. Thus in 1884 a provision affirming the right of Congress to grant rights of way upon just compensation was included in the Coke severalty bill and two acts presented land to railroads on condition that the managers would "neither aid, advise, nor assist in any effort looking toward the changing or extinguishing the . . . tenure of the Indians in their lands" nor request more land.[14] Congressmen frequently insisted that the legislation of 1882 in favor of the Saint Louis and San Francisco had established an unquestionable precedent.[15] Only when discussion centered upon such controversial regulatory features as taxation, rate regulation and the requirement of direct routes were votes forced which showed that opposition to the railroads still was concentrated in the North.[16] Even there opposition to expansion was becoming less common. When the New York *Herald* polled the Senate Indian Committee in 1884 on the advisability of a bill to open the Indian Territory to another railroad, not a single senator threatened to object if the Indians consented.[17] Not even the fact that agents were forced to apply for aid from the Army to prevent bawdy railroad camps entering reservations disillusioned Easterners who desired contact between the races.[18] Instead, the Indian Rights Association condemned opponents of railroad legislation as unprogressive, leaving the little criticism remaining to such extremists as Bland of the *Council Fire* and members of the Women's National Indian Association.[19]

The Development of Indian Land Policies

A few Easterners argued that Congress should cease destroying the Indians to make homes for foreigners,[20] but by far the larger number wished to push railroads into Indian reservations as rapidly as possible.

The coincidence of pressure for railroad legislation with passage of the Dawes Act inevitably arouses suspicion that the measure was passed to secure more land for railroads. The demand of Americans for commercial expansion had become so overwhelming that by 1886 twenty-three bills had been introduced requesting the admission of railroads to Indian reservations![21] Adoption of several of these measures immediately following passage of the Dawes Act provided excellent evidence that a desire for through routes had helped to popularize the severalty bill. Sharing Senator Dawes's belief that any encouragement of Indian resistance to white advancement would ignore "all that half a century of mistake and folly" had taught,[22] most Americans of the eighties sped the movement for utilizing Indian land.

Only a very few people successfully withstood the propaganda of men who sought to secure reservation land for railroads. President Cleveland, it is true, severely criticized the program in a series of vetoes;[23] but Congress refused to heed his warning that severalty measures could not be effectively administered as long as railroad grants continued to open reservations to white encroachment. The subsequent history of United States Indian policy might have been much less disastrous if Congress had listened when the President cautioned:

While maintaining their tribal condition they [the Indians] should not be easily subjected to the disturbance and the irritation of such encroachment. When they have advanced sufficiently for the allotment of their lands in severalty, they should be permitted, as a general rule, to enjoy and cultivate all the land set apart to them, and not discouraged by the forced surrender of part of it for railroad purposes. In the solution of the problem of their civilization by allotments of land they need the land itself, and not compensation for its appropriation by others. They can not be expected to understand this process in any other way than an indication that their tenure is uncertain and the assurance that they shall hold their allotted land for cultivation a delusion.[24]

Congressmen were so determined to use the Dawes Act for white advantage, however, that instead of profiting from the President's advice they continued to demolish the reservation system in many areas and forced Indians to live with whites long before they were prepared for such responsibilities.

The Selfishness of Early Reform Legislation

To declare that many provisions of the Dawes Act were inspired by selfish considerations is only to make a charge which is equally true of all Indian legislation of the period. Evidence exists that from the first many Americans wished to employ reform legislation for personal advantage. Even the most disinterested plans of the years preceding 1887 contained provisions intended to benefit whites rather than Indians. The low price paid for Osage lands in 1870 was frankly defended, for example, on the ground that the amount of such payments should be determined by the value of the property to Indians rather than to whites; while Senator Teller openly admitted during discussion of a Sioux bill over a decade later that the Indians were to be paid but twenty-five cents an acre for land that was worth from three to ten dollars an acre! [25] Similar self-seeking led representatives of the American Missionary Association to battle for a Santee severalty bill granting their organization exclusive missionary privileges which they had been denied by the tribe. As these reformers were willing to sanction the deletion of valuable guarantees of tribal welfare if passage of their clauses could be assured, and as they threatened to abandon the measure altogether if a knowledge of English was required for Indian citizenship, their enthusiasm for Santee rights was not notable for its sincerity.[26] White advantage was unquestionably accepted by many supposedly disinterested reformers as a proper standard for evaluating Indian legislation.

Although self-interest was responsible for much Indian legislation of the seventies and eighties, the motives of legislators were

The Development of Indian Land Policies

often less reprehensible than those of administrators. The ease with which measures intended for the benefit of Indians might be employed to their detriment was revealed with unusual clarity by the difficulties which the government encountered in attempting to insure honest enforcement of the Ute agreement of 1880. Only the presence on the Ute Commission of such well-known reformers as ex-Indian Commissioner Manypenny and A. B. Meacham prevented Commissioners Bowman and Mears from using allotment for personal advantage. The attempt of these men to profit from their appointment not only caused Chairman Manypenny to send frequent complaints to Secretary Schurz,[27] but impelled a fellow commissioner to write:

I have never witnessed an act or word on the part of either Bowman or Mears that evinced the least interest in the trust which they have accepted. They have no appreciation of this Indian problem, in any of its relations, and apparently care as little for the welfare of the Indian as they do for the barking Coyotes . . . Their only interest in the Commission is the hope that it may give them *earlier* opportunity than the outside world for pushing this or that speculation.[28]

The justice of this amazing charge became evident as Bowman and Mears, unable to use the Commission for their personal ends, joined Colorado politicians in an attempt to discredit the commissioners for their refusal to surrender to local demands for rapid allotment. Every possible obstacle was placed in the way of the unfortunate commissioners—politicians pressed for Meacham's replacement by a Coloradoan, the co-operation of local authorities was refused, Meacham was arrested for murder while carrying out his duties.[29] In the face of such difficulties, only energetic support of the Commission by Secretary Schurz prevented administration of the agreement from becoming a national scandal. Later officials were not so successful in avoiding public criticism.

Two instances of corrupt administration between 1883 and 1885 aroused reformers to the necessity for constant care in examining the actions of Indian officials. Many friends of the race were eager to diminish tribal holdings, but they objected vociferously when an agreement of 1883 reduced the Sioux Reservation

225

without other compensation than payment of a long-standing debt. Once investigation revealed that negotiators had secured Indian consent only by signing children, making false promises and threatening force, ratification of the arrangement became impossible and a new and less objectionable plan was concluded the following year.[30] An equally obnoxious plot was exposed just in time to prevent its fulfillment early in 1885. Reformers were taken by surprise when President Arthur opened the Crow Creek Reservation in Dakota Territory less than a week before the end of his administration. Even if existing treaties bestowed no title on the tribe as Secretary of the Interior Teller assured the President, such hasty action was inexcusable. The move seemed so indefensible that the Indian Rights Association rushed to defend the Indians. As President Cleveland also sympathized with the tribe, the order opening the reservation was officially suspended until proof of the validity of the Indians's title enabled its revocation.[31] For a second time in three years reformers had succeeded in preventing administrators from abusing important tribes. Yet neither experience provided any reason for future confidence. Unless reformers remained constantly on guard, similar conspiracies might proceed without interruption and the good intentions of reform legislation be disregarded.

Early reform bills had been so uniformly employed for selfish gain that friends of the Indians were justly suspicious of all legislation. Representatives who opposed Coke's severalty bill in 1882 had good reason to declare, "The main purpose of this bill is not to help the Indian, or solve the Indian problem or provide a method for getting out of our Indian troubles, so much as it is to provide a method for getting at the valuable Indian lands and opening them up to white settlement." [32] Aid to the Indians was definitely a secondary object of reform in most instances. What friends of the Indian demanded was that benefits to the white race should be balanced by benefits to the red. But even after the most objectionable features of the first severalty bills were removed, Indian welfare was not allowed to interfere with important interests of the white race.

The Development of Indian Land Policies

The Final Compromise

The nature of the compromise which enabled passage of the land provisions of the Dawes Act has already been described. No measure could have been successful without provision for the sale of large portions of the reservations. Yet reformers were strong enough to insist that no Indian land should be taken without compensation. As a result, the sale of surplus land was balanced by granting a secure title to the remainder and setting aside all profits to be used for racial advancement. Whether or not such a policy would prove fair to the Indians and whether or not it could be successfully administered remained to be discovered. But as far as most contemporaries were concerned, a plan for remodeling Indian policy had been found which would prove equally advantageous to the members of both races.

The forced sale of surplus land was naturally the most popular administrative provision of the Dawes Act. As early as 1870, Quakers had officially proposed that superfluous Indian land should be sold to secure money for education and the establishment of tribal members upon individual allotments.[33] Since many students of Indian affairs believed advancement would be impossible as long as tribes were permitted to roam over large areas, plans for reducing reservations by the sale of land received wide support and were occasionally adopted for restricted use.[34] Government officials were not enthusiastic about applying the idea generally as they realized the difficulty of securing a satisfactory administration of land sales and tribal funds.[35] Westerners likewise opposed plans for the acquisition of surplus land as long as hope remained that Indians might be completely removed from a reservation instead of being presented with a clear title to any portion of it. But as the impossibility of further removals became apparent, frontiersmen displayed an increasing willingness to grant land to individual Indians in return for admission to areas which were not needed. Enthusiasm for such an arrangement mounted irresistibly when legislators proposed that claims for damages pending against a tribe should be paid from funds obtained from sale of its land! Even though reformers insisted that money derived from land sales should be used exclusively for purposes of civilization, frontiersmen hoped to divert purchase money into the hands of border communities so that the land of the Indians might be secured without expense. This purpose was ultimately defeated; but in the meantime Western support insured success for the proposal to sell surplus land. Action was delayed until 1887 only because details had to be worked out which would facilitate administration and provide adequate compensation for the Indians.

Problems to be decided before the sale of surplus land could be successfully instituted were far more complicated than the apparent simplicity of the process would indicate. Success or failure might well depend upon whether allotments were selected by the Indians or by government administrators. Yet the superiority of neither method was clear. If complete freedom of choice was permitted, unintelligent selections could not be prevented and land necessary for commercial expansion might be absorbed. But if plots were assigned by the government, Indian antagonism would be aroused and opportunity provided for the intrigues of selfish officials. Even though a decision might be avoided on this controversial point, the question remained whether allotments should be compact or scattered throughout a reservation. While Senator Teller of Colorado was so convinced of the need for racial contact that he endeavored to limit severalty assignments to alternate quarter sections,[36] most legislators wished to confine Indian settlements within as restricted an area as possible. Thus all plans for mixing the races were thwarted in spite of Senator Dawes's interest in encouraging contact; and gaps in assignments were not even permitted either for communal use or to supply the future needs of a tribe.[37] Decisions of equal importance also had to be reached concerning the funds obtained from land sales. Congress debated at length whether every cent should be made available for tribal use at presidential discretion. Senator Dawes was willing to allow the executive department to control the entire fund, but fellow senators successfully insisted that only the interest might be spent without specific congressional authorization.[38] While such problems were only a few of those which arose during discussion of the sale of surplus land, agreement regarding the Dawes Act was even more seriously delayed by the necessity of deciding what protection should be offered Indian allottees.

The portion of the severalty act which made Indian allotments inalienable for twenty-five years was adopted in spite of violent protests against withholding any areas from prospective buyers. Although the speed with which red men had lost their land under early allotment measures emphasized the importance of prohibiting the sale of all land assigned to Indians, a powerful group fought every effort to protect the race. Yet no doubt regarding the validity of such inalienation provisions was possible in the light of Supreme Court decisions. When purchasers endeavored to retain land sold by a Kansas Indian without government consent, the justices refused the claim and discouraged further suits by declaring:

It was considered by Congress to be necessary, in case the reservees should be desirous of relinquishing their occupation of their lands, that some method of disposing of them should be adopted which would be a safeguard against their own improvidence; and the power of Congress to impose a restriction on the right of alienation, in order to accomplish this object, cannot be questioned. Without this power, it is easy to see, there would be no way of preventing the Indians from being wronged in contracts for the sale of their lands, and the history of our country affords abundant proof that it is at all times difficult, by the most careful legislation, to protect their interests against the superior capacity and adroitness of their more civilized neighbors.[39]

In cases where Congress failed to forbid sale, the Court subsequently held that Indians might dispose of their title even before a patent had been issued.[40] But the Court made clear that whenever Congress banned alienation of Indian allotments such restrictions were entirely legal.

Although the legality of prohibitions against the sale of Indian land could not be questioned, many Americans refused to admit the justice of providing Indian land holders with special protection. If red men were sufficiently advanced to be granted citizenship, opponents of inalienation insisted that they should be required to take care of themselves.[41] True freedom would be impossible, they pointed out, as long as Indians were prevented from disposing of their allotments. In most cases, this hatred of inalienation was due to hope of obtaining land from Indian owners. Yet some friends of the race also criticized prohibitions against the sale of allotments on the ground that Indian independence should not be jeopardized in any way. Ill-considered insistence that red men must stand upon their own feet was evident, for example, in the remarks of a Baptist reformer who declared:

> The land belongs to them or it does not. If it does belong to them, give it to them; but we give it to them as I give anything to my little son. I say, 'That is yours, but don't you sell it, my boy.' Well then it is not his. The Indians are simply playing that it is theirs, while we have everything in our power to do as we please. . . . The time is coming when we should step forth and recognize the rights of these Indians to citizenship and property. If they lose their property, they are doing no more than we have done before them. More than one-half of us are losing ours, but we go to work and get more . . . 'Root hog or die' is a principle; and let us put them in a position to 'root.' [42]

Fortunately such an extreme view of the necessity for independence was exceptional among reformers. Most leaders of the Indian movement were too well informed to disregard the fact that allotment measures must prove ineffective unless provisions were included protecting Indian titles.

Inclusion of an inalienation provision in the Dawes Act did much to counteract portions of the bill which were less favorable to the Indians.[43] Yet some reformers considered the twenty-five year prohibition inadequate even after a clause had been added allowing an indefinite extension of the period by presidential action.[44] Senator Miller of California believed that Indians would not be ready to forego United States protection in less than fifty years.[45] But even if government control had been made perpetual, officials rarely displayed sufficient interest in protecting Indian land to justify confidence that any prohibition against sale would be of value. In many cases, the United States had been unnecessarily slow in issuing patents. Puyallup Indians were forced to wait thirty years because their land was desired by the Northern Pacific;[46] while delay in granting inalienable patents to the Crows led their disgruntled agent to expose the folly of inconsistent Washington land administration by writing:

It would be better to maintain the reservations forever (reducing them to reasonable size) than to patent lands to Indians without making them inalienable.

The government is altogether too slow in these matters.

It is too slow in doing what is right, and after going slow for a few years it wakes up and litterally 'makes a break' and then is too fast in doing what is wrong (as for instance in patenting lands to Indians in Kansas and other places without making them inalienable).

It is provided by treaty with these Indians—the Crows—that their homesteads shall be inalienable, and there is no reason in this world why with this proviso every patent should have been issued by this date . . . The only reason it has not been done is that the people at Washington dont know anything about this work.

It sometimes seems as if they were incapable of learning or else that they dont care.[47]

Whatever protection was provided at the moment, the safety of the Indians depended upon future legislators and administrators. The very fact that many Americans wished to force severalty upon the Indians regardless of treaty obligations raised the question whether inalienation clauses might not be similarly abrogated if Congress so desired.[48] Yet as long as people feared that Indians would become paupers and vagabonds if freed from government control, special protection was certain to be widely advocated. Even if the effectiveness of inalienation provisions had been indisputable, however, there would still have been reason to question whether the increased protection was worth the price demanded.

An Appraisal of the Land Provisions of the Dawes Act

In attempting to determine whether the Dawes Act adequately defended Indian interests, the aims of its supporters must be distinguished from its results. The measure would certainly never have been adopted if its provisions had been considered exceptionally unjust to the Indians. Too many Americans were interested in Indian welfare at the time to permit acceptance of plans intended to destroy the race. But advocates of the Dawes Act did not deny that Indians would lose land. Pressure upon reservations was so strong that a realistic outlook forced recognition of the necessity for surrender of some Indian land in return for an undisputed title to the rest. If legislators could have insured that secure title to good land would be granted, encouragement of individual initiative by limitation of Indian holdings might have proved possible.[49] Since the success of the compromise depended upon future administration, criticisms of the measure were justified.

Like many other Indian measures, the Dawes Act failed to achieve a just balance between white and tribal interests. In 1880 General Armstrong had complained, "The Indian question has been put wrong end first. It points to us not to them." [50] A similar criticism could have been made of the Severalty Act of 1887. Most friends of the measure were more interested in securing Indian land than in establishing a just policy for the control of Indian affairs. Contemporary critics were able to point out that if legislators were really interested in Indian advancement they might teach them to use their land instead of taking it from them on the ground of idleness.[51] As funds obtained from the sale of Indian land would only tend to strengthen racial indolence, some commentators announced that the red men would be "better off with the land than the proceeds." [52] Certainly national progress did not have to be made at the expense of the Indians. Reformers who feared that allotment would prove a means for robbing the tribes were much more realistic than those who held that whites would respect the property of industrious Indians.[53] With Senator Dawes hesitating to push the measure for fear that the Indians *would* not receive good land, and with evidence existing that many settlers were determined that Indians *should* not receive good land, Bland wisely suggested that the reform should at first be limited to experiments undertaken on a small scale among advanced tribes, and that in even these instances the sale of surplus land should be postponed until a more adequate idea of the amount of land needed by the Indians was obtained.[54] But instead of agreeing to apply the severalty program gradually, impatient legislators exerted every effort to speed application of the new policy.

18. THE DECISION TO USE FORCE

AGREEMENT CONCERNING ADMINISTRATIVE FEATURES OF THE DAWES Act did not solve the important question of how rapidly the new policies should be applied. While a large number of reformers wished legislators to force immediate allotment upon the tribes, many opposed action without Indian consent. As in the case of other parts of the measure, therefore, sections dealing with enforcement were the result of compromise. The attempt of legislators to avoid antagonizing either of two widely divergent groups played a part in the decision that selection of tribes to which the Act was to be applied should be left to the President. Advocates of rapid allotment were more critical of this method than their opponents, but even the most enthusiastic champions of the cause supported presidential discretion in the end because of confidence in their ability to exert pressure upon the Chief Executive. A definite decision as to whether tribes selected by the President should be allowed to reject the change, however, could not be similarly avoided.

While legislators tried to satisfy both the friends and enemies of force, the ultimate effect of the Dawes Act was to require submission to government policies. The measure left no question about the authority of federal officials in the matter of allotment, section two declaring:

> . . . if any one entitled to an allotment shall fail to make a selection within four years after the President shall direct that allotments may be made on a particular reservation, the Secretary of the Interior may direct the agent of such tribe or band . . . to make a selection for such Indian, which selection shall be allotted as in cases where selections are made by the Indians.[1]

Even the four years thus allowed for the choice of allotments seemed too long to many congressmen. Six months had been considered adequate by Representative Scales in 1879 and the House of Representatives fought for only a two-year limit until the conference committee capitulated to Senate pressure just before final passage of the Act.² If senators and members of the Board of Indian Commissioners had not striven to obtain a period of at least five years, Congress might even have demanded immediate acceptance of allotments. The only important concession to Indian opinion was the provision that unallotted land should not be sold without tribal consent.³ As surplus land would be of no value after a tribe had been forced to accept individual allotments, however, there was little reason to fear that opposition to white occupancy would overcome a desire to profit from the sale of property which was no longer of use. A forced surrender of land could hardly have been demanded by reformers who were interested in just treatment of Indians. But failure to require abandonment of unallotted areas specifically did not mean that Indians could avoid the outcome. Despite frequent denials, passage of the Dawes Act marked official acceptance of the view of those Americans who had believed that Indian progress would prove impossible without coercion.

The decision of American legislators to effect vital changes in Indian society by forceful methods was perhaps inevitable. The distaste of reformers for gradual advancement has always been a subject of comment, while measures of unquestionable merit have frequently failed because their advocates lacked sufficient patience to prepare the ground for their success. Yet American Indian reformers had been constantly warned that civilization was a matter of gradual growth and not of sudden conversion.⁴ For many years, indeed, most Indian friends had followed the advice of the agent who declared that in elevating barbarous nations to a state of civilized life work must proceed upon the principle of "making haste slowly." ⁵ Such warnings were heeded less often as the movement advanced; and once Indian organizations were formed in the early eighties all pretense of caution disappeared.

While the decision to employ force in the reformation of Indian affairs has been frequently condemned, the number of able men recommending coercion testified to the strength of arguments advanced in its favor in the eighties. Secretary Schurz believed that compelling unprepared Utes to accept individual ownership would

The Decision to Use Force

be preferable to allowing their entire reservation to be seized by angry whites; while young Teddy Roosevelt held that Indians were bound to perish as they were and should, therefore, be required to adjust themselves to white life even though all but the best would die.[6] Innumerable other Americans urged speedy allotments among backward tribes in the spirit of an agent who wrote, "Of course in many ways the Indians will be wronged and cheated, but such a condition has got to be met sometime, and why not commence at once, instead of putting off the evil day?" [7] Reformers, who refused to believe that allotment would endanger the welfare of any Indian, naturally urged its adoption even more heartily. Lyman Abbott of the *Christian Union* supported the severalty movement so enthusiastically that he declared any means could be defended that would help attain the goal.[8] The refusal of Congress to tolerate opposition made force an indispensable part of any reform program. But before the effect of this decision can be fully understood, the battle between the advocates and opponents of force must be described.

Indian Opposition to Reform

As force would have been unnecessary if land allotment had been welcomed by the tribes, Indian opposition may be held primarily responsible for the coercive character of the Severalty Act. Some of the more advanced tribes supported the measure in hope that they might prepare for contact with the whites more easily; but in most cases the principle of severalty required too great a revolution in tribal customs to justify the Board of Indian Commissioners' belief that "no single measure of legislation would give such general satisfaction to the Indians." [9] Petitions requesting the division of a reservation among its residents were more often due to a desire to escape government control or to profit at the expense of fellow Indians than to sincere interest in the merits of allotment.[10] The average red man resisted the change so strongly that there was little hope of success if Americans insisted upon waiting for Indian consent.[11]

The opposition of American Indians to land allotment can not be regarded as mere obstructionism. Although chiefs were un-reasoning in their opposition to abolition of a system upon which their influence depended, and although young warriors were unduly resentful of outside interference, there was no question that the race was more securely protected under tribal rule than it ever would be with individual ownership.[12] Maintenance of a tribe's authority not only guaranteed the continuance of long-established customs, but was a vital factor in the conduct of satisfactory inter-racial relationships. Opportunities for robbery, numerous enough under existing conditions, would only increase once united resist-ance was no longer possible,[13] while all pretense of racial inde-pendence would have to be surrendered once tribes were destroyed. Fear of white settlers, distrust of government officials, racial pride and a spirit of freedom were fully as responsible for the unpopu-larity of severalty as unreasonable opposition to change.

The wisdom of Indian opposition to severalty was never more effectively confirmed than in the answers of forty-nine Indian agents to a Board questionnaire of November, 1885, asking whether individual ownership would prove of benefit to their Indians.[14] To reformers hoping to secure assistance in their fight for allot-ment, the replies could hardly have been more disappointing. Not only did nine agents question the ability of their Indians to assume the responsibilities of land holders, but nineteen stated that there was not the remotest possibility of success. The refusal of a majority of field officials to support the severalty program is especially sig-nificant when the attitude of the tribes under their direction is considered. Strange as it seems in face of the widespread convic-tion of contemporaries that Indian opposition to severalty was unjustified, not a single agent whose charges resisted allotment believed his Indians prepared for radical social adjustments! Wher-ever a tribe opposed severalty, an agent was ready to uphold the wisdom of his Indians. Yet in spite of this astonishing circum-stance, the enthusiasm of reformers for allotment did not abate. Opposition to the use of force was successful only in cases where unusual conditions rendered allotment extremely dangerous.

Section eight of the Dawes Act, which stated "the provisions of this act shall not extend to . . . the Indian Territory, nor to any of the reservations of the Seneca Nation of New York Indians in the State of New York," was the result of peculiar conditions and not of any desire to extend special favors.[15] If reformers had had a free hand, the Five Civilized Tribes of Indian Territory would have been the first required to select allotments. But while no Indians were better prepared to assume the responsibilities of individual ownership than those of New York and the eastern Indian Territory, allotment was inadvisable because of the existence of large provisional land grants which permitted private corporations to claim possession once tribal title was extinguished. Immediate occupancy of the Seneca reservations in New York had been promised to the Ogden Land Company of Buffalo, in case tribal ownership was abandoned. Soon after the Revolution, investigation revealed, dispute over Massachusetts's right to land occupied by the Indians of western New York had resulted in sovereignty being ceded to New York and a pre-emptive right of purchase to Massachusetts. This right, ultimately obtained by the Ogden Land Company, had been recognized by the United States in the Seneca treaty of 1794. The abolition of tribal title contemplated by the Dawes Act, therefore, would open Seneca land to preferred white buyers before allotments could be made to individual Indians.[16] As title to much of the Indian Territory had been similarly promised to the Atlantic and Pacific Railroad, fear of dispossessing New York and Indian Territory Indians forced introduction of the exemption provision. Popular pressure might easily have caused Congress to force severalty upon all tribes, however, if Indians of the Territory had not strongly resisted the change.

By far the most effective Indian opposition to the Dawes Act was conducted by the Five Civilized Tribes.[17] Believing that their future would prove a determining factor in the fate of other tribes, the five nations hoped to forward the cause of all Indians by advancing their own. Their struggle to preserve their right of self-government, therefore, rested upon arguments of more than local significance. Their frequently expressed apprehension that severalty would result in robbery and subjection was especially convincing when applied to tribes less prepared for responsibilities than themselves. Such a defense of Indian independence was absolutely essential if Indian rights were to be respected, for there was no end to the inroads that might be made once the power of Washington officials over tribal affairs was accepted. As it was, the intelligent arguments of delegates of the Five Civilized Tribes and their ability to cite definite treaty provisions won sufficient sympathy to secure temporary exemption for themselves. In resisting severalty for others, they convinced only a few that force should be avoided.

The Opposition to Force

The decision of reformers to demand acceptance of land allotments was reached only after the implications of such action had been fully considered. Whenever Indian policy was debated, opponents of coercion urged the inadvisability of proceeding without tribal consent. Impatience with Indian backwardness and a conviction that a rapid change was necessary caused reformers to disregard all criticism of compulsion. The failure of the case against force to make an impression provides excellent evidence of the extremes to which advocates of severalty were willing to go to insure adoption of their plan. Even a brief examination of the frequent clashes over the use of force reveals that reformers were fully warned of the danger of acting without Indian consent.

Most opponents of coercion were not fanatics. In nearly every instance, their arguments were exceptionally reasonable. There was nothing irrational in criticizing the inconsistency of reformers who had opposed compulsory removal only to champion forcible allotment, while there was similar logic in sarcastic comments regarding the supernatural insight assumed by advocates of any policy of force.[18] Enemies of coercion were determined that compulsion should not be adopted until every possible means of securing Indian consent had been tried. If severalty supporters argued that immediate allotment was necessary to prepare the Indians for contact with whites, opponents of force replied that successful introduction of any reform would depend upon Indian co-operation. Unless a tribe was convinced of the necessity for change, reformers could hope to accomplish little.[19] Real progress, if ever achieved, must rest on persuasion and conversion, not on compulsion and force.

Although there were but few opponents of force, both their influence and activity helped to compensate for their lack of numbers. No one was more determined to consult Indian wishes than President Cleveland. When a Mohonk delegation demanded immediate action of the newly elected President, Cleveland insisted that justice was more important than speed.[20] This caution was shared, if not inspired, by Secretary of the Interior Lamar, who announced in his first report that changes of Indian policy must be both gradual and tentative.[21] But while the President and his Secretary were often able to resist the demands of impatient reformers, the most active critics of force were Meacham and Bland of the *Council Fire*. Every issue of the Indian magazine stressed the desire of its editors to protect tribes from outside interference. While both men professed to believe that severalty would prove the ultimate solution of the Indian problem, neither wished to have the change instituted without consent.[22] No Americans saw the evils of force more clearly nor publicized their respect for Indian opinion more persistently than Meacham and Bland. If legislators had decided to consult the Indians instead of insisting upon allotment, chief credit for the success would have been due to the *Council Fire* and its editors.

In spite of the failure of the men who opposed the coercive clauses of the Dawes Act, the tactics employed in attempting to prevent passage of the measure are of exceptional interest. Realizing the strength of sentiment in favor of allotment, enemies of force concentrated their energy upon securing as much delay as possible in consideration of the bill. They heartily welcomed, therefore, the interest in establishing a commission to study proposed reforms expressed by President Cleveland in his first annual message.[23] Since transfer of the Indian Bureau to the War Department had been defeated by an investigation less than a decade before, the possibility of delaying severalty by the same process seemed especially promising. The success of the reform program was seriously threatened when Representative Holman climaxed the trip of a special investigating committee of the House in 1886 by recommending appointment of a commission of three Army officers and three civilians to provide for readjustment of the Indian question on a permanent basis.[24] Although President Cleveland and Secretary Lamar displayed unusual interest in the suggestion, and although Bland did everything in his power to win support for the plan, the proposal failed by a vote of 68-48.[25] Men interested in speeding reform were not willing to accept a bill which might be used to delay legislation indefinitely. As the Woman's National Indian Association declared:

> The practical effect of the bill would have been, to postpone indefinitely any great and radical legislative action on behalf of Indians, for the authority of such a Commission would be, of course, referred to as a standard, and even its warmest promoters could see no end of its proposed investigations, certainly not for ten or twenty years, it might be for generations, and it might even be a Commission in *perpetuo*.[26]

Such postponement having been defeated, the only path remaining to critics of force was modification of a bill they could not delay.

Attempts to revise the enforcement provisions of the Dawes Act were no more successful than efforts to postpone it. Addition of a clause providing for Indian consent would have been enough to satisfy most critics. Even Bland promised more than once to support a severalty act which outlawed force. Thus an 1884 version of the Coke bill which provided for land allotment only upon request was lauded by the *Council Fire*; and when the House added an amendment requiring Indian consent to the Senate severalty bill of early 1886, Bland hailed the improvement resulting from delay.[27] Pressure for consultation of the Indians nearly succeeded, in fact, during the final months before the Act was passed. In December, 1886, the National Indian Defense Association secured a House amendment to the severalty bill stating that nothing in the act should be construed as authorizing the Secretary of the Interior to abolish any reservation until the consent of a majority of the male members over twenty-one years of age should have been obtained.[28] The Dawes Act would have been acceptable to Bland in this form, as he wrote the New York *Herald* that the action of the House had rendered the bill comparatively harmless.[29]

The Decision to Use Force

He was exceedingly surprised and disappointed, therefore, when Dawes successfully persuaded the conference committee to omit the Association's amendment.[30] With the bill reported for adoption with its coercive clauses intact, forceful reform seemed unavoidable.

The possibility that sections providing for compulsory allotment might be dropped from the bill still remained even after the conference committee had agreed upon their inclusion. Charges that severalty advocates intended to place Indians at the mercy of unscrupulous whites seriously endangered passage of the conference report. Although a resolution to strike out coercive features of the bill was defeated by 47-13 at the Church-Board meeting of January, 1887,[31] friends of the measure felt it necessary to disclaim any desire to dictate to the Indians. Senator Dawes, in fact, stated both before and after passage of his bill that civilization was "a work of time" which could not "triumph by force." [32] Yet despite his frequently professed dislike for compulsory tactics, Dawes could not deny that forceful methods were possible under his Act only because he had defeated introduction of a specific prohibition. A majority of reformers undoubtedly opposed coercion as a regular practice; but because they felt a show of strength necessary in initiating the severalty program, they opened the way to serious abuse of Indian rights.

The Decision to Use Force

Advocacy of force as a method of solving the Indian problem was not a monopoly of reformers of the eighties. Bishop Whipple, whose interest in the Indian could not be denied, had recommended the adoption of stringent laws a quarter of a century before the Dawes Act.[33] As long as hostile tribes continued to defy the government, interest in requiring obedience was natural. The outstanding feature of the new movement was a desire to coerce the peaceful as well as the warlike. Yet even during the seventies Commissioner Walker, Colonel Otis and other prominent students of Indian relations insisted that progress would be impossible unless all red men were made to obey the wishes of the government.[34] As there was no use in enacting legislation if the power necessary for successful administration was omitted, more and more Americans were becoming convinced of the necessity for force as the decade ended. The effect of this growing impatience with Indian opposition was clearly revealed when George E. Ellis concluded a history of American Indian affairs in 1882 by announcing:

> We have a full right, by our own best wisdom, and then even by compulsion, to dictate terms and conditions to them; to use constraint and force; to say what we intend to do, and what they must and shall do . . . This rightful power of ours will relieve us from conforming to, or even consulting to any troublesome extent, the views and inclinations of the Indians whom we are to manage. A vast deal of folly and mischief has come of our attempts to accommodate ourselves to them, to humor their whims and caprices, to indulge them in their barbarous ways and their inveterate obstinacy. Henceforward they must conform to our best views of what is for their good. The Indian must be made to feel he is in the grasp of a superior.[35]

With this uncompromising statement, a majority of the public was in accord. Americans of the eighties were determined to brook no further opposition to Indian reform.

Among the most active champions of force were many Indian agents. Although numerous field officials opposed the severalty program, a large number of others insisted that it was "the duty of the Gov't to push the Indians on to civilization, not lead and expect them to follow."[36] Several of the men most closely connected with the tribes, in fact, sprang into prominence because of the vigor of their reports. Thus Agent McGillycuddy of Pine Ridge attracted national attention because of his attacks on Indian independence; while Agent Milroy, who never failed to send a detailed report of the Yakimas, believed that "the whims and wishes of ignorant Indians should not be consulted or permitted to interfere" once proper methods for reform had been decided.[37] Agent Armstrong of the Crows, who had so strongly insisted upon the inalienability of allotments, was equally determined that Indians should not reject severalty. He well expressed the disgust of many

The Decision to Use Force

Indian workers with any policy of temporizing when he complained:

> I believe the Government should adopt a more vigorous policy with the Indian people. I can see no reason why a strong Government like ours should not govern and control them and compel each one to settle down and stay in one place, his own homestead, wear the white man's clothing, labor for this own support, and send his children to school. I can see no reason why . . . good and true men and women should come to an Indian agency and labor honestly and earnestly for three or four or a dozen years trying to coax or persuade the Indians to forsake their heathenish life and adopt the white man's manner of living, and then go away feeling they have thrown away, almost, the best years of their lives. The truth is the Indians hate the white man's life in their hearts, and will not adopt it until driven by necessity.[38]

As several other agents were only slightly less outspoken, wholehearted co-operation in a policy of force could be expected from many field workers.

The hatred of caution, which led Armstrong to condemn American Indian policy, was shared by a group of United States senators who became noted for the bitterness of their attacks upon Indian autonomy. No doubt concerning the value of coercion was entertained at least by Senator Ingalls of Kansas when he remarked:

> Some races are plastic and can be molded; some races are elastic and can be bent; but the Indian is neither; he is formed out of rock, and when you change his form you annihilate his substance . . . Civilization destroys the Indian . . . and the sooner the country understands that all these efforts are valueless unless they are based upon force supplemented by force and continued by force, the less money we shall waste and the less difficulty we shall have.[39]

Senator Morgan of Alabama and Senator Teller of Colorado were especially active in demanding the exercise of congressional authority over all Indians.[40] Whatever policy was adopted such senators insisted that it must be solely the product of white deliberation. Concessions to Indian prejudices should not be permitted to stand in the way of wise legislation. Certain features of the Dawes Act were the result of sympathy for the red man's interests; but the measure as a whole gave the United States more power over Indian affairs than any previous enactment mainly because a number of legislators had at last decided that the whims of a minority race should dictate American Indian policy no longer.

While the interest of Indian agents and congressmen in strengthening their control over the Indians was not surprising, the enthusiasm of reformers for a drastic assertion of national authority is less easy to explain. Whereas concern for Indian rights might have been expected to cause opposition to the use of force, many leading friends of the race recommended coercion. Lyman Abbott, who exercised a wide influence among American intellectuals as editor of the *Christian Union*, urged Senator Dawes to make allotment both immediate and compulsory.[41] The second conference of Indian friends at Lake Mohonk criticized a Coke bill clause requiring two-thirds consent as an outrageous impediment to freedom of action.[42] Captain Pratt of Carlisle advised that Indians be "so thoroughly conquered as to be convinced of the futility of further resistance."[43] In each case, reformers hoped that the race would benefit from the forceful action of whites who had studied the Indian problem and believed that they had found a way to avoid ultimate racial conflict. Only if all Indians surrendered their right of self-determination did such men feel that annihilation could be averted. No better proof of the strength of this conviction exists than the eagerness with which reformers urged violation of Indian treaties whenever attainment of their end seemed impossible by other means.

Indian treaties had been condemned as obstacles to an effective Indian policy long before the eighties. When the act of 1871 prohibited further negotiations with Indian tribes, abrogation of previous treaties was prevented only because the Senate insisted that nothing should be interpreted as invalidating any arrangement already concluded. As provisions of outmoded agreements rapidly grew more and more embarrassing to the government, the treaty problem attracted increasing attention. A surrender of established rights in return for new privileges was frequently suggested as a solution of the difficulty;[44] but actual abrogation under a higher law appealed much more strongly to the realistic men in charge of Indian relations. Thus Commissioner E. P. Smith asked in 1874 whether the government should hold itself bound forever by bargains which damaged both the nation and its wards; and his successor urged that public necessity demanded the adoption of enforced allotment and sale of surplus land as the supreme law of the land.[45] For a time, this official attitude was reflected only in abrogation of such out-moded provisions as the right to hunt.[46] But the idea spread rapidly that Congress should modify all treaty provisions for Indian benefit. Since legislators had not hesitated to violate treaties for selfish gain, reformers argued, there was no reason why they should not also be disregarded when the future of the Indian was at stake.[47]

In recommending treaty violation, reformers were treading on dangerous ground. Although previous treaties now seemed "absurd" in many instances,[48] there was a strong possibility that the chaos resulting from their abrogation might make matters considerably worse. Legislators could not "make the bargain upon both sides," as a House committee proposed, without exposing American Indian policy to change at the whim of each succeeding Congress.[49] Yet many reformers condemned all who insisted that Indian treaties should be observed. Lyman Abbott, in particular, used his influence as editor of the *Christian Union* to demand that no agreement should be allowed to prevent immediate land allotment.[50] So seriously did Abbott's position threaten the sanctity of Indian treaties that men interested in upholding the honor of the United States became greatly alarmed. Senator Dawes and Secretary Welsh of the Indian Rights Association occasionally displayed an interest in forceful reform; but a report in which the latter described an unsuccessful effort to battle Abbott's views reveals the earnestness with which both men fought treaty violation. Welsh left no doubt that abrogation of Indian agreements was obnoxious to many supporters of severalty when he wrote Dawes:

I am well aware of the views held by Dr. Abbott. I do not think that he has long studied the Indian question or has seen the Indian in his home. I believe that the radical nature of his views as to how

245

the Indian problem may and should be solved would be greatly modified by close contact with the cold facts of the question, which at present do not come within his range of vision. I think he is disposed to look with impatience upon Indian Treaties, and to believe that *they*, rather than *their violation*, have heretofore prevented the solution of the question. I believe he is inclined to give more credit to Western men for honest and just intentions toward the Indian than my short experience makes me think they are entitled to. The more I reflect upon it the more I regret your absence from the meeting recently held at the office of the Christian Union. I of course fully understand that it was unavoidable. The burden rested upon my shoulders of opposing the crude and radical views expressed by Dr. Abbott. Dr. Rhoads who previous to our meeting had spoken to me with extreme dissatisfaction of these views as already set forth in the columns of the Christian Union, remained perfectly silent when the same opinions were expressed by word of mouth. I did my best to show that it was only by an appeal to treaties which were the groundwork of our relations to the Indians that we had so far succeeded in protecting him from fraud and spoliation, and that in cases where a modification of the treaties was necessary a fair appeal to the Indians in the matter would secure the needed change without a lawless violation of our faith. I do not know how far my views had the sympathy of those present. I felt as though I were very much alone.[51]

Welsh's despair was justified. With many reformers becoming so radical that the movement threatened to exceed proper bounds, advocates of severalty had a harder task defeating dangerous proposals than they had winning votes for reform.

While Senator Dawes denied that his act interfered with the fulfillment of treaty obligations,[52] the measure gravely menaced racial independence. Stimulation of a respect for Indian agreements could hardly be expected of legislation obviously constructed on the theory that tribes should be destroyed by being ignored. The continued effectiveness of treaty provisions depended upon preservation of the tribal units which had concluded the agreements. Such a destruction of Indian government could hardly be achieved by voluntary action. "The idea," Senator Dawes explained, "is to take the Indians out one by one from under the tribe, place him in a position to become an independent American citizen, and then before the tribe is aware of it its existence as a tribe is gone." [53] Although responsibility for outright treaty violation was avoided by such indirection, the ultimate effect on established Indian rights was the same. Attempts to under-estimate the coercive nature of the Act by pointing out that ninety of 159 reservations were already subject to executive order were beside the point.[54] The significant accomplishment of the Dawes Act, as realistic students of Indian affairs recognized at the time, was the portion of the measure which brought an end to tribal authority by forcing tribes to allow allotment upon the request of individual members.[55] Thereafter privileges based upon racial dissimilarity were no longer of importance.

Passage of the Dawes Act was a victory for the champions of force. Most reformers only regretted that President Cleveland might not demand immediate allotment.[56] But while presidential discretion could protect the tribes temporarily, ultimate Indian submission was certain to prove only a matter of time. Little chance of delay in forceful application of the Dawes Act remained after such a strong and influential conservative as Secretary Lamar reported in 1887 that the government should no longer rely solely upon the attractive aspects of civilized life to convince Indians of the value of reform.[57] Executive judgment was the sole obstacle to coercive action and popular pressure immediately gave indications of weakening the caution of even Cleveland and Lamar. A new day for the Indians was clearly at hand. Whether it was to be bright or stormy rested with the future.

19. THE DAWES ACT

AND INDIAN REFORM

PASSAGE OF THE DAWES SEVERALTY ACT WAS WIDELY ACCLAIMED AS the culmination of years of labor. Having successfully united to force adoption of their favorite plan, Indian friends looked to the future optimistically.[1] Although many concessions had been necessary to achieve victory, the prospect that red men would ultimately be recognized as equal was not to be disparaged. Indian ability and wise administration were still just as essential to racial advancement; but the worst evils of the old system no longer stood in the way of reform and further changes seemed certain to follow. Captain Pratt expressed the attitude of most fellow reformers toward the Act when he told Dawes, "You have opened a way for us. I congratulate you on the passage of the Severalty Bill & the first enactment of any law looking to the divorcement of the Indian from the worse than slavery of his old Communistic systems. I am filled with new courage and hope. Of course there is yet much to be done, but the ice being broken the way will open up and all thereafter come easier." [2] Whatever the future held, Indian work seemed less hopeless than it had for many years.

In spite of the optimism awakened by passage of the Dawes Act, hard work was still necessary. As President Cleveland's first biographer remarked, "The law had enacted an opportunity and nothing more." [3] The solution of old problems had proved possible only by creating others of equal difficulty. No measure could have established a detailed course of action, but the Severalty Act was especially deficient in this respect. Complex administrative problems were left for future determination and many wise provisions were omitted in the final rush.[4] The completed measure left so much to the judgment of Indian officials that Senator Dawes himself was alarmed at the possibilities of abuse. Success depended so largely upon the character of governmental officers that only a month before President Cleveland signed the measure the Senator declared:

If my land-in-severalty bill should become a law, it will depend entirely on the character of the government agents, who execute its provisions whether it is a success or a failure. If it be entrusted to men of unflinching honesty and broad views, the Indian will be secure in the possession of homes on the best lands of the reservations; but if it is entrusted to dishonest men, the Indians will be cheated out of their lands.[5]

The Senator again voiced his fear of maladministration just a few days before the Act was passed by confessing:

Almost at the last moment, when I see this bill so near the end, I begin to fall back and ask myself seriously, whether, after all, too much risk is not being taken with him, because if the bill become a law, and is administered in bad faith, and by bad men, it first wipes out all of the heritage of the Indian, and then it scatters him among our people without preparation for citizenship, and without the capability of maintaining himself, really in a worse condition than he can be in now.[6]

The danger inseparable from a severalty program could not have been more concisely presented. Dawes, at least, realized that unless reformers remained active there was great danger of the measure doing more harm than good.

No development of late nineteenth century Indian history was more discouraging to those who hoped for racial advancement than a decline in the membership of Indian organizations. Just as public co-operation was especially necessary to assist the red man's adjustment to new conditions, most Americans lost interest in his problems. Instead of realizing that the Dawes Act added to their responsibilities, most members of Indian associations considered their work was ended. In an attempt to prevent resignations following passage of the Severalty Act, the Indian Rights Association announced:

The mere enactment of such a law is only the enlargement of opportunity. It does not, in itself, change the condition of a single Indian . . . As this new measure . . . has been pressed to adoption by the

Indian Rights Association in the face of opposition . . . from white men who think themselves better friends of the Indian than we are, we accept a large measure of the responsibility of its enactment, and recognize a solemn obligation to aid in every way in our power in the practical work of carrying its provisions into effect, and of organizing and shaping the new conditions under which the Indians affected by it are henceforth to live.[7]

But in spite of this pledge and in spite of appeals by other Indian organizations, both the contributions and memberships of such groups began to decrease in the nineties as if the danger of public indifference had not been pointed out. Thus, although the Indian Rights Association was able to continue its work, the peak in contributions was reached in 1889 ($10,168.76) and in membership in 1893 (951). Indian organizations continued to urge the necessity of securing further protective measures before Indian workers could feel their task completed,[8] but the average citizen insisted that the time had come for Indians to help themselves. This attitude was reflected in Congress where legislators objected so strenuously to requests for aid that they threatened to abolish appropriations for education altogether in 1891 instead of encouraging Indian advancement by increasing the funds! [9] With the nation determined to resist special concessions to the red men, the failure of the Dawes Act to revolutionize the condition of the race is hardly surprising.

After Fifty Years

In judging the Dawes Act half a century after its passage, no one can deny that the expectations of its sponsors were never realized. Senator Dawes himself confessed only a few years after the Act had passed that the measure would never have been placed on the statute books if the radical character of the resulting changes had been realized.[10] As his daughter testified in later years, Dawes expected aid from churches, philanthropic societies and advanced Indians which never materialized.[11] Lacking such assistance, President Cleveland and Secretary Lamar were frequently unable to resist pressure for immediate allotment.[12] Their less cautious Republican successors not only refused to struggle against the tide, but boasted that Secretary of the Interior Noble had "opened to settlement more Indian reservations than all of his predecessors combined." [13] With administrators anxious to seize Indian land as rapidly as possible, Dawes was soon forced to complain that only an eye witness could understand how vain and cruel the policy of forcing was proving.[14] Before half a decade had passed, United States officials had clearly demonstrated that they were either unable or unwilling to use the Dawes Act for Indian benefit.

No important changes were made in the Dawes Act for several years in spite of the abuses which immediately appeared. Reformers who believed the administration of the Act rather than its principles at fault, finally succeeded in securing fundamental modifications in the Burke acts of 1906.[15] Thus the right of citizenship was withdrawn from allottees because of the number of incompetent tribes granted land in severalty, and the inalienation period was extended because few Indians showed any indication of ability to meet white competition despite years of individual land holding. Such moves were the result of serious dissatisfaction with administration of the Dawes Act. Until the presidency of Franklin Roosevelt, however, there was little suggestion that land allotment itself was undesirable. Yet today the Act, which was compared by contemporaries with Magna Charta and the Declaration of Independence,[16] is officially regarded as merely the latest and most contemptible feature of America's long abuse of the Indian race.

A study of the background of the Dawes Act can not close without a brief appraisal of the contemporary Indian policy of the United States. Although allotment was the outgrowth of a desire for expansion, it was also the product of a sincere conviction that emulation of the whites was essential. In prohibiting individual ownership of land, Washington officials of the present day must confess either that Indians can not or that they should not live like other citizens. The current Indian program clearly abandons all effort to establish individual independence.[17] Some change was necessary, one must admit, as previous attempts to make a place for the Indian in American society had failed. Whether an absolute reversal was wise is another question, for failure to pursue one goal persistently has always been a major fault of American Indian policy. It is unfortunate, for instance, that under the current program Indians who have shown their ability to adapt themselves to modern conditions are faced with the unenviable choice of returning to tribal life or breaking from their race. If individual ownership of land could be made compatible with racial preservation by careful government administration, the excesses of both past and present might be avoided. If not, the return to a policy of isolation will mean the defeat of fifty years of effort to solve the Indian problem. In either case, modern sympathy for the Indian must prove more lasting than that of the eighties if future Indian policy is to escape the pitfalls of indifference.

In spite of the failure of the Dawes Act, the sponsors of Indian reform in the years following the Civil War deserve praise for their work. The first attempt to solve the problem permanently was the most significant step taken to aid the red man since the formation of the Republic. Superficial efforts at reform proving insufficient. a small group undertook the introduction of vital changes. By organization and pressure combined with clever compromises, success was finally achieved and the old, out-moded system replaced by a new. Unfortunately these Indian workers, as reformers both before and since, viewed their plans too optimistically, and pushed rapidly ahead without realizing that caution was desirable or that even citizenship itself might prove disastrous. Subsequent generations may well wish the advance had been less hasty; yet they can hardly regret that for the first time in the history of the country sympathy for the Indian received concrete expression. Like most measures, the Dawes Act was a mixture of selfishness and idealism. But although self-seeking was not absent, legislators made the measure memorable by providing a definite plan for the Indian's future. The failure resulting was unfortunate; but misapplication by administrators rather than the evil intent of legislators was responsible for the disastrous history of America's first systematic effort to provide for Indian welfare.

NOTES

Key to Abbreviations in Footnotes

In addition to standard footnote abbreviations, the following have been used:

B.C.   United States—Board of Indian Commissioners, *Correspondence.*

B.C.M.   United States—Board of Indian Commissioners, *Miscellaneous Correspondence.*

B.L.S.   United States—Board of Indian Commissioners, *Letters Sent.*
                    (Note: There are two series, the first Roman numeral in each citation referring to the series number.)

Board   United States—Board of Indian Commissioners.

Board Scrap Book   United States—Board of Indian Commissioners, *Scrap Book.*

Com. Rep.   United States—Indian Office, *Annual Report of the Commissioner of Indian Affairs.*

Cong. Globe   United States Congress, *Congressional Globe.*

Cong. Rec.   United States Congress, *Congressional Record.*

House Exec. Doc.   United States—House of Representatives, *Executive Document.*

House Misc. Doc.   United States—House of Representatives, *Miscellaneous Document.*

I.D.L.S.   United States—Interior Department, *Letters Sent, Indian Division.*

I.O.   United States—Indian Office.

I.O.Civ.   United States—Indian Office, *Correspondence, Civilization Division.*

I.O.Land   United States—Indian Office, *Correspondence, Land Division.*

I.O.Misc.   United States—Indian Office, *Miscellaneous Correspondence.*
                    (Note: If a letter is filed in a year other than that in which it is dated, the year is included in the reference.)

I.R.A.	Indian Rights Association.
Lake Mohonk Proceedings	Lake Mohonk Conference on the Indian and other dependent People, *Proceedings.*
Opinions	United States—Department of Justice, *Opinions of the Attorney General.*
Sec. Rep.	United States—Interior Department, *Annual Report of the Secretary of the Interior.*
Sen. Exec. Doc.	United States—Senate, *Executive Document.*
Sen. Misc. Doc.	United States—Senate, *Miscellaneous Document.*
U.S.Rep.	United States—Supreme Court, *United States Reports.*
U.S.Stat.	United States Congress, *The Statutes at Large of the United States.*
W.N.I.A.	Women's National Indian Association.

Note: Legal cases have been cited in the usual abbreviated form— volume number, name of reporter or series, page. References to James D. Richardson's *A Compilation of the Messages and Papers of the Presidents 1789-1897* (Washington, 1898) are also abbreviated. The *Dawes Papers* and *Schurz Papers* are located in the Manuscript Division of the Library of Congress. The Library also has the most complete collection of the *Council Fire* and the pamphlets of Indian organizations. Board material is in the Indian Office Library.

Chapter One

1. Statistics regarding the extensive land sales which characterized the years covered by this study may be found in the *Annual Reports* issued by the Land Commissioner.
2. For such treaties, see *U.S.Stat.*, XIV, pp. 803-804; XV, p. 636.
3. *Sec. Rep.*, 1871, p. 7.
4. *Cong. Globe*, 40th Cong., 1st Sess., pp. 374, 460-461.
5. Details of this dispute are discussed a few pages later.
6. For their arguments, see *Cong. Globe*, 40th Cong., 1st Sess., pp. 669ff., 709ff.
7. Henry Benjamin Whipple, *Lights and Shadows of a Long Episcopate*, New York, 1899, p. 516.
8. *Cong. Globe*, 40th Cong., 1st Sess., p. 670.

Notes

9. *Cong. Globe,* 41st Cong., 2nd Sess., pp. 4160ff.
10. *Cong. Globe,* 42nd Cong., 2nd Sess., p. 2200.
11. *Cong. Globe,* 42nd Cong., 3rd Sess., p. 439.
12. *Cong. Rec.,* V, p. 1057.
13. Mills's original failure and ultimate victory may be followed in *ibid.,* pp. 1349-1350, 1357, 1615-1617.
14. Of twenty-one opposition votes, six were from New England and seven from the plains states. Only three senators from these sections voted with the twenty-seven supporting removal (*Cong. Rec.,* VII, p. 3266).
15. Senator Ingalls of Kansas in *Cong. Rec.,* VII, p. 3237, e.g.
16. *Cong. Rec.,* VIII, p. 403.
17. *Ibid.,* p. 325.
18. *Ibid.,* pp. 314-317. It is interesting to note that divisions over Indian removal were not always confined to inter-state rivalry. For disagreements splitting Colorado into hostile sections, see *Cong. Rec.,* X, pp. 2061-2064; XVIII, pp. 1048, 1892, 1933, 3375, 4446, 5743.
19. *Cong. Rec.,* VIII, p. 403.
20. *House Report 474,* 46th Cong., 2nd Sess. and *Cong. Rec.,* XVII, pp. 4553-4560, 8028.
21. For a detailed discussion of the Ponca incident and the prominent part it played in arousing interest in Indian reform, refer to the final portions of Chapter VI. Recent descriptions of the other episodes may be found in Chester A. Fee, *Chief Joseph,* New York, 1936; and Howard Fast, *The Last Frontier,* New York, 1941, an able account in fictional form of the Cheyenne escape. See also the articles by General Miles and Chief Joseph in the March and April issues of the *North American Review* for 1879. A less important outbreak of these years is described in George F. Brimlow, *The Bannock Indian War of 1878,* Caldwell, Ida., 1938.
22. The Board's position against removal is clearly stated in *Board Report,* 1879, pp. 6-7; and Barstow to Schurz, Feb. 6, 1879 (*Schurz Papers*). Scales's bill may be found in *Cong. Rec.,* X, p. 618.
23. Statements by reform groups may be found in *Board Report,* 1878, pp. 60-64, 113-114; *Lake Mohonk Proceedings,* 1883, p. 16; and C. C. Painter, *Proposed Removal of Indians to Oklahoma,* Philadelphia, 1887.
24. Annie H. Abel, "Proposals for an Indian State," in *American Historical Association Annual Report,* 1907, pp. 87-104; and Elsie

Mitchell Rushmore, *The Indian Policy during Grant's Administration*, Jamaica, N. Y., 1914, pp. 48-52.
25. *Sec. Rep.*, 1880, p. 4; 1881, p. VI.
26. *U.S.Stat.*, XXII, p. 449.
27. *Com. Rep.*, 1885, pp. IX-XII; *Board Report*, 1885, p. 114.

Chapter Two

1. This period of Indian history is excellently treated in Annie H. Abel, *The American Indian as Slaveholder and Secessionist*, Cleveland, 1915, and *The American Indian as a Participant in the Civil War*, Cleveland, 1919.
2. Harlan to General Pope, July 6, 1865 (*I.O.Misc.* I1133); and Harlan to Commissioner Cooley, July 11, 1865 (*I.O.Misc.* I1130). See also Fairfax Downey, *Indian-Fighting Army*, New York, 1941.
3. John T. Morse, ed., *Diary of Gideon Welles*, III, Boston, 1911, pp. 30, 74, 98-100.
4. General Sherman to Senator Sherman, March 18, 1875, in R. S. Thorndike, ed., *The Sherman Letters*, New York, 1894, p. 344.
5. A. G. Bradley, "The Red Man and the White," in *Macmillan's Magazine*, LXIII, p. 384. Compare this point of view with Pope to Grant, Jan. 25, 1867; and Dodge to Pope, June 17, 1865 (*I.O.Misc.* P14, 1867).
6. C. A. Huntington to Senator Harlan, Nov. 22, 1869 (*I.O.Misc.* S544, 1870); and *Com. Rep.*, 1871, p. 271.
7. *Cong. Rec.*, IV, p. 2666.
8. Compare *Council Fire*, I, p. 178 with *Com. Rep.*, 1875, pp. 303, 331-332, e.g.
9. Hammond to Commissioner Hayt, Jan. 24, 1878 (*I.O.Misc.* H565½, 1879); and *Com. Rep.*, 1875, p. 19.
10. *Board Report*, 1875, pp. 64-103.
11. *Cong. Globe*, 39th Cong., 2nd Sess., p. 898. For the report, see *Senate Report 156*, 39th Cong., 2nd Sess.
12. *Cong. Globe*, 39th Cong., 2nd Sess., pp. 1720, 1988.
13. *House Exec. Doc.* 97, 40th Cong., 2nd Sess., p. 20.
14. Both statements and the reaction of Indian friends to the change may be found in *Com. Rep.*, 1868, pp. 7-15, 26-50, 371-376.
15. *Cong. Globe*, 40th Cong., 3rd Sess., p. 21.
16. For this debate, see *ibid.*, pp. 39-43.

Notes

17. *Ibid.*, pp. 880-883, 1376-1378.
18. *Cong. Rec.*, IV, p. 2673.
19. *Ibid.*, p. 2686.
20. *Ibid.*, p. 3964.
21. *Ibid.*, p. 5602.
22. *Cong. Rec.*, VII, pp. 3876-3877. Transfer had been supported by the House Indian Committee earlier in the session (*House Report 241*, 45th Cong., 2nd Sess.).
23. *Cong. Rec.*, VII, pp. 4192-4200, 4234-4239, 4684-4686.
24. *Sen. Misc. Doc. 53*, 45th Cong., 3rd Sess.
25. *Cong. Rec.*, VIII, p. 1142.
26. *Ibid.*, p. 1142.
27. *Ibid.*, pp. 1221-1226.
28. *Cong. Rec.*, X, pp. 2491-2493, 2497-2498; XI, pp. 538-541.
29. The course of Throckmorton's proposal may be followed in *Cong. Rec.*, XV, pp. 2522-2532, 2559-2567, 5803.
30. Representative Wood of New York and Senator Morrill of Maine. The votes considered are those referred to in notes 11, 15, 19, and 22. Wood supported transfer on the last three occasions, while Morrill opposed it on the first three.
31. Sheridan to Sherman, undated (*I.O.Misc.* W68, 1879). The *Schurz Papers* contain much information regarding this dispute. For criticism of civilian administration by other officers, see Sherman to Schurz, Jan. 25, 1878 (*Schurz Papers*); Terry to Schurz, Dec. 26, 1878 (*Schurz Papers*); and Miles to Schurz, Jan. 16, 1879 (*I.O.Misc.* M196).
32. Hazen to Schurz, Confidential, Dec. 14, 1878 (*Schurz Papers*).
33. *Cong. Rec.*, IV, pp. 2617, 2630.
34. *The Nation*, VII, p. 544; X, p. 389; XXVIII, p. 7.
35. An attempt to prevent this action led Chairman Brunot of the Board of Indian Commissioners to issue his first public statement in opposition to transfer (Charles Lewis Slattery, *Felix Reville Brunot, 1820-1898*, New York, 1901, p. 236).
36. See *Wowapi: A Magazine Devoted to the Cause of the Indians*, Boston, November 7, 1883, p. 16; and Herbert Welsh, *The Apache Prisoners*, Philadelphia, 1887, p. 8.
37. The situation in Kansas, which was typical of conditions throughout the west in the late sixties, is excellently described in Marvin H. Garfield, "The Indian Question in Congress and in Kansas," in *The Kansas Historical Quarterly*, II, pp. 29-44.

38. *Cong. Rec.*, IV, p. 2674.
39. See, for example, *Indians, Soldiers and Civilization*, an anonymous pamphlet of Feb. 29, 1872; Society of Friends, *Minutes*, 1876, p. 16; and Cutting to Hayt, May 27, 1878 (*I.O.Misc.* C357).
40. Ewing to Delano, July 2, 1875 (*I.O.Misc.* E106).
41. Capt. Edward Butler, *An Essay on 'Our Indian Question,'* New York, 1882.
42. George W. Manypenny, *Our Indian Wards*, Cincinnati, 1880, p. 391.
43. *Council Fire*, I, p. 72.
44. *Ibid.*, I, p. 189; II, pp. 5-6, 36, 60-61. For severe statements against the Army in later issues, see IV, p. 9; VI, p. 95; VII, p. 103.
45. De Smet to Gerard, Feb. 25, 1868, in Hiram Martin Chittenden and Alfred Talbot Richardson, *Life, Letters and Travels of Father Pierre Jean de Smet, S.J.*, New York, 1905, p. 895.
46. Slattery, *op.cit.*, p. 237; Morgan to Hayes, Aug. 6, 1877 (*I.O. Misc.* P356).
47. Col. Ihrie to Schurz, Sept. 11, 1877 (*Schurz Papers*).
48. *Cong. Rec.*, VIII, p. 1142; IV, pp. 2658, 2663.
49. Frederic Logan Paxson, *The Last American Frontier*, New York, 1910, p. 344.
50. From the Arizona *Citizen* (*Schurz Papers* 9237). See also Kautz to Schurz, Feb. 11 and 13, 1878 (*Schurz Papers*).
51. *Grand Army Journal*, Dec. 9, 1871.
52. Manypenny, *op.cit.*, p. 284.
53. E. B. Tuttle to "Collyer," May 25, 1870 (*B.C.* I 50). Both Miles and Howard wrote of their experiences with the Indians in reminiscences (Nelson A. Miles, *Personal Recollections and Observations*, Chicago, 1896, *passim*; and O. O. Howard, *My Life and Experiences among Our Hostile Indians*, Hartford, 1907).
54. *Cong. Rec.*, X, pp. 2194, 2224-2226.

Chapter Three

1. *Cong. Globe*, 39th Cong., 2nd Sess., p. 1714.
2. Society of Friends, *Address of Sixth Yearly Meeting*, Baltimore, 1869, p. 2.
3. *U.S.Stat.*, XVI, p. 319.
4. Butler to Taylor, March 14, 1869 (*I.O.Misc.* B109).

Notes

5. William Welsh to Schurz, March 14, 1877 (*Schurz Papers*).
6. Bishop to Colyer, June 28, 1870 (*B.C.* I 70).
7. For the problem of one church, see Francis Moore, *A Brief History of . . . Work in the Indian Territory*, Muskogee, 1899.
8. J. W. Goodlin of the Board of Home Missions to Brother Derr, June 17, 1875 (*I.O.Misc.* D293).
9. Criticism of church indifference was frequent (Kemble to J. Q. Smith, March 2, 1876 *I.O.Misc.* K70; and *Board Report*, 1874, pp. 147ff.).
10. *Board Report*, 1874, p. 152.
11. Board, *Journal of the Second Annual Conference with Religious Societies*, Washington, 1873, p. 29.
12. Stanley Pumphrey, *Indian Civilization*, Philadelphia, 1877, p. 31; and correspondence regarding pressure on the Congregational Church (*I.O.Misc.* S145, 1879), e.g.
13. Zadok Street to E. P. Smith, Nov. 4, 1875 (*I.O.Misc.* S1724).
14. For a marshaling of Protestant testimonials regarding the success of Catholic work, see *The Pilot*, Boston Catholic publication, Jan. 16, 1875. The most successful Protestant churches were those resting on external forms rather than individual participation—Episcopal and Presbyterian rather than Methodist or Congregationalist.
15. For official suspicion of Mormon activities, see Cram to Delano, July 1, 1875 (*I.O.Misc.* C900); and Price to Wheeler, Jan. 20, 1882 (*I.O.Letter Book*, 164, p. 45).
16. J. A. Cohen to Cree, July 8, 1872 (*B.C.* IV 240).
17. J. G. Brown to Cree, Dec. 2, 1872 (*B.C.* IV 49); also D. K. Flickinger to "Shurz," April 4, 1879 (*I.O.Misc.* F80)—United Presbyterians and United Brethren respectively.
18. F. M. Green to "Shurtz," July 11, 1878 (*I.O.Misc.* G366); Garfield to Hayes, June 12, 1879 (*I.O.Misc.* G284); and J. B. Mitchell to Garfield, April 10, 1880 (*I.O.Misc.* G244).
19. H. C. Derr to E. P. Smith, June 28, 1875 (*I.O.Misc.* D297).
20. A. L. Riggs, "The New Departure," in *The Congregationalist*, Sept. 7, 1871.
21. R. W. Hayt to "Dear Father," April 27, 1877 (*Schurz Papers*).
22. Riggs et al. to Schurz, Feb. 11, 1880 (*I.O.Nebraska* R163).
23. Intimate personal correspondence regarding this quarrel may be found in Herbert Welsh to Dawes, Aug. 8 and Oct. 16 and 23, 1884 (*Dawes Papers*).
24. Swan to Trowbridge, March 19, 1881 (*I.O.Civ.* 5721).

25. W. F. Harvey to Grant, May 3, 1869 (*I.O.Misc.* H181).
26. Thomas J. Morgan, *The Present Phase of the Indian Question*, Boston, 1891, p. 21.
27. T. W. Eddy to E. P. Smith, June 10, 1873 (*I.O.Misc.* E31).
28. Charles Ewing, *Circular to the Catholics of the United States*, Baltimore, 1874, p. 5.
29. For some of the criticism of the government from Catholic sources, see *Catholic Sentinel* of Oregon (*Board Scrap Book*, II, pp. 21-23); *The Pilot*, Jan. 16, 1875; Anon., *Memorial relative to Removals and Appointments in the Indian School Service*, Washington, 1890.
30. Blanchet to Parker, July 8, 1871 (*B.C.M.*); and Delano to Blanchet, July 25, 1871 (*ibid.*).
31. See *The Washington Catholic*, Aug. 4, 1883 and Ewing's excellent instructions for cautious action quoted in the *Council Fire*, III, pp. 36-37.
32. The customary position of the government is well expressed in Price to Agent Montieth of the Nez Percé, June 21, 1883 (*I.O. Letter Book*, 173, p. 477).
33. Stickney to Grant, March 30, 1876 (*B.L.S.* I-VI 527).
34. Hayt to Schurz, Personal, May 3, 1879 (*Schurz Papers*). Hayt had already told the Joint Transfer Committee that he accepted preachers only if they had had commercial experience (*Sen. Misc. Doc.* 53, 45th Cong., 3rd Sess., pp. 321, 325).
35. Garfield to Schurz, Feb. 2, 1881 (*Schurz Papers*).
36. G. T. Bedell to Hayes, Nov. 14, 1878 (*I.O.Misc.* B574, 1879).
37. Tatham to Hayt, April 20, 1878 (*I.O.Misc.* T411, 1880).
38. See Ferris to Acting Commissioner, Feb. 10, 1880 (*I.O.Misc.* F19) expressing the views of the Reformed Church, e.g.
39. *Board Report*, 1881, pp. 84-87; 1882, pp. 52-54.
40. John Pope, *The Indian Question*, n.p., n.d., p. 14; Col. Richard Irving Dodge, *A Living Issue*, Washington, 1882, p. 21.
41. See especially G. C. Elliott to Secretary of War Belknap, Jan. 21, 1875 (*I.O.Misc.* W119); W. F. Wheeler to Hayes, June 20, 1877 (*Schurz Papers*); and Henry Butterfield to Hayes, Aug. 2, 1878 (*I.O.Misc.* P724). The Indian agents and their problems during these years deserve the special treatment that is given them over a longer period in Flora Warren Seymour, *Indian Agents of the Old Frontier*, New York, 1941.
42. William H. Hare, *Reminiscenses*, Philadelphia, 1888, p. 11.
43. *Council Fire*, I, p. 105. See also Representative Garfield's recom-

Notes

mendation for a gospel of food and clothing which should precede the theology of the pulpit (*Board Scrap Book I*, p. 46).

44. J. R. Thompson in the Puget Sound *Weekly Courier*, Jan. 30, 1880.
45. J. B. Harrison, *The Latest Studies on Indian Reservations*, Philadelphia, 1887, p. 136.
46. Significant material on the reluctance of the churches to exert political pressure includes *Board Report*, 1873, pp. 201ff.; Cree to Ferris, Feb. 5, 1874 (*B.L.S.* I-V 463); and reports of the General Episcopal Convention of 1880 in the *New York World* and *New York Tribune* of October 20.
47. See the discouraging reports of Thomas C. Battey in *The Life and Adventures of a Quaker among the Indians* (Boston, 1875); and Lawrie Tatum in *Our Red Brothers* (Philadelphia, 1899).
48. Miles's work, which may be followed in detail in his annual agency reports, was frequently the subject of favorable comment.
49. Contemporary and more recent critics agree that a decided improvement in the type of Indian agent was brought about by church appointments (Long Committee, *Report on the Indian Question*, Boston, 1880, p. 4; and Paxson, *op. cit.*, pp. 345-346).

Chapter Four

1. Henry Benjamin Whipple, *Lights and Shadows of a Long Episcopate*, New York, 1899, p. 513.
2. William Welsh, comp., *Taopi and His Friends*, Philadelphia, 1869, p. 77.
3. *U.S.Stat.*, XVI, p. 40.
4. *Cong. Globe*, 41st Cong., 1st Sess., p. 451. The original wording had said that the Board should "supervise and control" Indian affairs (*ibid.*, p. 448)!
5. *U.S.Stat.*, XVI, p. 360.
6. *Ibid.*, p. 568; and *Cong. Globe*, 41st Cong., 3rd Sess., pp. 768, 1480, 1810.
7. *Board Scrap Book*, I, p. 5. For Parker's recommendation of a Board, see Parker to Grant, Jan. 24, 1867 (*I.O.Misc.* W111).
8. William Welsh to Parker, June 27, 1869 (*I.O.Misc.* W339½).
9. Brunot to Welsh, June 24 and July 1, 1869 (*I.O.Misc.* B278); and Cox to Brunot, July 5, 1869 (*B.C.M.*).
10. Welsh to Colyer, Feb. 19, 1870 (*B.C.* I 5).

11. Brunot to Colyer, April 13, 1870 (*B.C.* I 39).
12. Bishop to Colyer, Jan. 26, 1871 (*B.C.* I 116).
13. The defensive position to which Parker's counsel was forced is revealed in N. P. Chipman, *Argument on Behalf of Hon. E. S. Parker*, Washington, 1871.
14. Campbell to Colyer, July 18, 1871 (*B.C.* II 51).
15. Bishop to Cree, Dec. 22, 1872 (*B.C.* IV 56).
16. Brunot to Colyer, April 1, 1871 (*B.C.* I 156).
17. Delano to Brunot, Jan. 12, 1872 (*D.I.L.S.*, X, p. 371); Brunot to Delano, Jan. 13, 1872 (*B.C.M.*); and Brunot to Colyer, Jan. 19, 1872 (*B.C.M.*).
18. Brunot to Cree, April 8, 1872 (*B.C.* IV 181).
19. *Board Report*, 1876, p. 11; see also *ibid.*, 1872, pp. 60-61.
20. *Board Report*, 1870, pp. 60-72; Brunot to Colyer, June 25, 1871 (*B.C.* II 6); and Long to Colyer, April 11, 1871 (*B.C.* II 103).
21. *U.S.Stat.*, XVII, p. 186. The task of examining accounts, which Congress thus rendered futile, was not discontinued until 1881. In the meantime, over nine-tenths of the Board's correspondence was composed of routine letters dealing with accounts and contracts (*B.L.S.*).
22. *Board Report*, 1873, pp. 9-11.
23. Documentary evidence indicates that several factors played a part in the conclusion that the possibility of service was at an end (D. Stuart Dodge, *Memorials of William E. Dodge*, New York, 1887, pp. 177-178; Charles Lewis Slattery, *Felix Reville Brunot*, New York, 1901, p. 211; Brunot to Delano, Nov. 21, 1873 *I.O.Misc.* B1034; and Bishop to Cree, May 11, 1872 *B.C.* IV 73).
24. Brunot to Cree, March 2, 1872 (*B.C.* IV 162).
25. Contrast the views of Representatives Sargent and Garfield with the attitude of Representative Beck, for example (*Cong. Globe*, 42nd Cong., 2nd Sess., pp. 3155-3156; and *Cong. Rec.*, II, pp. 3740-3745).
26. *Cong. Rec.*, III, pp. 1989-1990.
27. *Cong. Rec.*, V, p. 1062.
28. *Cong. Rec.*, X, pp. 2484-2487, 2499, 2823-2829, 3076. For the vote a year later, see *ibid.*, XI, pp. 541-542.
29. *Cong. Rec.*, X, pp. 2823-2826.
30. *Cong. Rec.*, X, p. 2824; XIII, p. 1533.
31. For reports praising the Board, see Bell to Schurz, May 9, 1877; and Lockwood to Schurz, June 8, 1880 (*Schurz Papers*).

Notes

32. Hawley to Schurz, Jan. 8, 1881 (*Schurz Papers*).
33. The various phases of this dispute may be followed in *Cong. Rec.*, X, pp. 3075-3076, 3103-3107, 4317; XI, pp. 532-533, 541-542, 2207.
34. Brunot to Cree, March 5, 1872 (*B.C.* IV 154-156); Brunot to Cree, Dec. 10, 1872 (*B.C.* IV 20); Charles Ewing quoting Brunot in *Petition of the Catholic Church for the Agency of the Chippewas*, Washington, 1873, p. 8; and note in Brunot's handwriting, no addressee and no date (*B.C.* III 29).
35. Criticism of Fisk may be found in the New York *Tribune* during late January and early February, 1875 and on April 29 and May 6 of the same year. See also Samuel Hays to Schurz, Jan. 17, 1878 (*Schurz Papers*); and *Board Scrap Book*, II, pp. 68, 113-114. The Board endeavored to explain its stand in Hammond to Averill, Jan. 16, 1875 (*B.L.S.* I-VI 110).
36. Riggs to Whittlesey, Nov. 29, 1877 (*B.C.M.*).
37. New York *Herald*, March 2, 1882.
38. Lang to Cree, Dec. 16, 1872 (*B.C.* V 74).
39. Walker to Cree, Dec. 29, 1873 (*B.L.S.* I-V 260).
40. Kingsley to Schurz, June 19, 1880 (*Schurz Papers*); and Barstow to Dawes, Feb. 13, 1881 (*Dawes Papers*).

Chapter Five

1. Comments on public indifference punctuate all reform literature of the period.
2. Leading criticisms of the sensationalism inseparable from descriptions of Indian affairs include Austin to Cooley, March 1, 1866 (*I.O.Misc.* A71); *Board Report*, 1872, p. 20; Richard Irving Dodge, *Our Wild Indians*, Hartford, 1882, p. 641; and *Council Fire*, VII, p. 161.
3. A discussion of the possibilities of accurate news reporting may be found in Walker to Lockley, Sept. 26, 1872 (*I.O.Letter Book* 108, p. 523). Both *The Republic* and *Harper's* requested information following Schurz's first annual report (James B. Walker to Schurz, Dec. 11, 1877 *Schurz Papers*; and H. M. Alden to Hayt, Dec. 20, 1877 *I.O.Misc.* A2, 1878).
4. Bishop Seabury Mission, *Missionary Papers No. 30*, Fairbault, Minn., 1864, pp. 4, 13.
5. For an account of the debate regarding Indian citizenship during

Uncle Sam's Stepchildren

consideration of the Fourteenth Amendment, see G. M. Lambertson, "Indian Citizenship," in *The American Law Review*, XX, pp. 183-184.

6. L. Maria Child, *An Appeal for the Indians*, New York, 1868; Ellen Terry Johnson, *Historical Sketch of the Connecticut Indian Association*, Hartford, 1888, p. 3; and introduction to Stanley Pumphrey, *Indian Civilization*, Philadelphia, 1877.

7. Phillips's work may be followed in *Board Scrap Book*, I, p. 9; Zylyff, pseud., *The Ponca Chiefs*, Boston, 1880, p. iii; and *Council Fire*, VII, pp. 3-4 (February issue).

8. The most enlightening of the many letters written by this unusual figure are Beeson to Taylor, Aug. 20, 1867 (*I.O.Misc.* B361); Beeson to E. P. Smith, May 14, 1874 (*I.O.Misc.* B595); Beeson to Hayes, May 1, 1878 (*I.O.Misc.* P329); Beeson to Commissioner, Oct. 27, 1878 (*I.O.Misc.* B1536); Beeson to Congress, Feb. 11, 1879 (*I.O.Misc.* B222); and Beeson to Hayes, June 5, 1879 (*I.O.Misc.* B782).

9. Boyle to Colyer, April 4, 1871 (*B.C.* I 29); and Brunot to Cree, Feb. 7, 1872 (*B.C.* IV 137).

10. Meacham's description of his experience appeared in *Wigwam and Warpath* (Boston, 1875) and *The Tragedy of the Lava Beds* (Washington, 1883).

11. Interesting information regarding Meacham is presented in the biography by his colleague on the *Council Fire* (T. A. Bland, *Life of Alfred B. Meacham*, Washington, 1883).

12. Quoted in *Council Fire*, III, p. 179.

13. Mrs. Jackson's life may be followed in Ruth Odell, *Helen Hunt Jackson* (*H. H.*), New York, 1939.

14. Contemporary reviews of interest appeared in *The Catholic World*, XXXIV, pp. 66-67; *Dial Review*, II, p. 12; and *The Nation*, XXXII, p. 153. For an even more severe but less reliable condemnation of United States Indian policy, see A. Fenelon Methrose, Jr., *Civilization and the Indian*, New York, 1891.

15. Henry E. Alvord to Commissioner, Jan. 15, 1878 (*I.O.Misc.* A33).

16. James Towle to Commissioner, Nov. 12, 1880 (*I.O.Misc.* T1380). Only occasionally did a prospective lecturer request pay (Rev. W. L. Woodruff of the *Western Religious Herald* to Schurz, Dec. 29, 1879 *I.O.Misc.* W88, 1880).

17. Borga to Colyer, Feb. 10, 1870 (*B.C.* I 19).

18. Washington *Daily Chronicle*, Jan. 6, 1873.

Notes

19. Compare James W. M. Newlin, *Proposed Indian Policy* (Philadelphia, 1881) with *Lake Mohonk Proceedings*, 1886, pp. 25-26.
20. *Council Fire*, VI, pp. 137-138, 179-180; VII, p. 13.
21. Manning to "Shurz," received Feb. 10, 1879 (*I.O.Misc.* M296).
22. Wozencraft to Hayes, June 15, 1877 (*I.O. Misc.* P289).
23. S. N. Goodale to E. P. Smith, Jan. 12, 1874 (*I.O.Misc.* G12); and Jan. 18, 1875 (*I.O.Misc.* G30). Goodale rates second only to Father Beeson in the number of private letters sent the government.
24. Ihrie to Schurz, March 26, Sept. 11, and Dec. 7, 1877 (*Schurz Papers*).
25. Meyer to Schurz, Dec. 21, 1878 (*Schurz Papers*).
26. Gunn to "Hays," Sept. 6, 1879 (*I.O.Misc.* G479).
27. W. M. Ryer, *Islands as Indian Reservations*, San Francisco, [1877]; and Sturges to General Sherman, Oct. 24, 1883 (*I.O.Civ.* 19939).
28. Alexander to Schurz, Nov. 11, 1879 (*I.O.Misc.* A831).
29. William T. Butler to Schurz, March 10, 1880 (*I.O.Misc.* B187).

Chapter Six

1. Details of the Modoc outbreak and petitions for leniency may be found in *House Exec. Doc.* 122, 43rd Cong., 1st Sess. Sympathy for the tribe was also expressed in Benjamin Trigge's poem, *The Perplexing Problem*, Brooklyn, 1886; and *Board Report*, 1873, pp. 217-221. The unusual interest of contemporary newspapers is reflected in Brantz Meyer, *Clippings on the Modoc Massacre*, n.p., 1877 (New York Public Library); and *Board Scrap Book*, I, pp. 84ff.
2. See *House Misc. Doc.* 38, 46th Cong., 2nd Sess. for details of the Ute outbreak. Sympathy for the Indians was expressed frequently by Schurz correspondents (A. A. Fisher, Oct. 22, 1879; C. A. White, Oct. 28, 1879; E. J. Hubbard, Jan. 17, 1880; McHenry Green, Nov. 22, 1880). The suppression of details of the uprising by the government and the insistence of Schurz upon acceptance of land allotment by the Indians is revealed by official correspondence (Adams to Schurz, Nov. 11, 1879 *Schurz Papers*; and Schurz to Bell, July 29, 1880 *I.O.Misc.* I440).
3. *House Report* 39, 41st Cong., 3rd Sess., p. II.
4. *House Report* 98, 42nd Cong., 3rd Sess.
5. *Report of Commission . . . to Investigate Certain Charges against Hon. E. P. Smith*, Washington, 1874; and *House Misc. Doc.* 167, 44th Cong., 1st Sess.

6. Report of the Special Committee to Investigate the Affairs of the *Red Cloud Indian Agency*, Washington, 1875; and Charles Schuchert and Clara Mae La Vene, *O. C. Marsh*, New Haven, 1941.
7. For the Belknap scandal, see William B. Hesseltine, *Ulysses S. Grant*, New York, 1935, pp. 395-396.
8. The Indian Office occasionally received complaints regarding indigent neighbors who entered the Indian service and returned with fortunes (R. A. McKee to Secretary, July 7, 1875 *I.O.Misc.* M567½, e.g.).
9. C. A. Works to Inspector Hammond, Aug. 22, 1878 (*Schurz Papers*). Sergeant Stanley had reported in 1869 that contractors avoided scales "as they would the plague" (Stanley to General Clarke, June 20, 1869 *I.O.Misc.* C344).
10. While the Board required all samples to be sent from goods received following 1875 (*Board Report*, 1875, p. 24), there was nothing to prevent submission of an unrepresentative specimen. An interesting instance of weight tampering is described in the confession of John L. Roberts before United States Attorney Hugh J. Campbell, July 24, 1881 (*I.O.Civ.* 9326).
11. Charles Ellison to "Shurtz," May 2, 1877 (*Schurz Papers*).
12. The most important information regarding this dispute may be found in Department of the Interior, *Report of the Board of Inquiry . . . to Investigate Certain Charges against S. A. Galpin* [Washington, 1878]. The personal side of the dispute is prominent in the following letters in the *Schurz Papers*: J. D. Cox to Schurz, July 11, 1877; Seelye to Z. L. White, Aug. 1, 1877; Schurz to J. Q. Smith, Jan. 15, 1878; Seelye to A. M. Howe, Jan. 22, 1878 quoted in Howe to Schurz, Jan. 28, 1878; Charles Francis Adams to Schurz, Feb. 2, 1878.
13. Interesting instances of selfishly-motivated exposures of corruption include J. W. Blair to Commissioner, June 20, 1878 (*I.O.Misc.* B906); W. A. Burleigh to Schurz, Jan. 5, 1879 (*Schurz Papers*); F. M. Foster to Schurz, Dec. 22, 1879 (*I.O.Misc.* F221); and J. H. Rogers to Secretary of Indian Affairs, April 2, 1880 (*I.O.Misc.* R354).
14. Charles E. Jolis to "Shurts," July 23, 1877 (*Schurz Papers*).
15. Welsh to Schurz, Oct. 27, 1877 (*Schurz Papers*).
16. Whittlesey to Roberts, Sept. 24, 1877 (*B.L.S.* II-IV 192).
17. *Council Fire*, III, p. 41, e.g.
18. *Sen. Misc. Doc.* 53, 45th Cong., 3rd Sess., p. 324.

Notes

19. Bell to Commissioner, Aug. 4, 1879 (*Schurz Papers*).
20. *Senate Report 708*, 46th Cong., 2nd Sess., pp. 181, 179.
21. Leeds to Fisk, Dec. 2 and 6, 1879 (*B.C.M.*); and Leeds to Schurz, Jan. 9, 1880 (*Schurz Papers*).
22. Agent Douglas to Governor Howard of Dakota Territory, April 7, 1879; Inspector Carrier to Hayt, April 26, 1879; and Hayt to Schurz, Jan. 31, 1880 (*Schurz Papers*).
23. New York *Times*, Jan. 23, 1880.
24. This transaction is described in detail in *Board Report*, 1879, pp. 68-70.
25. R. F. Hunter to Hayes, Jan. 19, 1880 (*Schurz Papers*).
26. An attack on such critics may be found in M. H. Bright to Schurz, Feb. 12, 1880 (*Schurz Papers*).
27. Edmunds to Schurz, Feb. 17, 1880 (*Schurz Papers*).
28. President Hayes wrote Schurz on Feb. 19, "Please send down Trowbridge's nomination. It is time to end that affair. Let us do it today." (*Schurz Papers*).
29. Fisk to Schurz, Feb. 14, 1880 (*Schurz Papers*), e.g.
30. Schurz to Garfield, Jan. 16 and 28, Feb. 6, 1881; Garfield to Schurz, Jan. 20 and Feb. 2, 1881; and T. M. Nichols to Schurz, Feb. 2, 1881 (*Schurz Papers*).
31. *Com. Rep.*, 1879, p. 104.
32. *Com. Rep.*, 1870, p. 30; and Francis A. Walker, *The Indian Question*, Boston, 1874, p. 76.
33. Postmaster to Representative Morgan, no date (*I.O.Misc.* M370); petition of twelve southerners, April 9, 1883 (*I.O.Civ.* 16758); and two applications for husbands quoted in V. A. Travis, "Life in the Cherokee Nation a Decade after the Civil War," in *Chronicles of Oklahoma*, IV, p. 28.
34. These evidences of congressional sympathy with squatters may be found in *Cong. Globe*, 41st Cong., 1st Sess., pp. 512-513; *Cong. Globe*, 42nd Cong., 2nd Sess., p. 2250; and *U.S.Stat.*, XIX, p. 55. For criticism of official toleration toward trespassers, see Pope to Sawyer, Aug. 1, 1865 in Anon., *Official Communications from General Pope concerning Indian Affairs*, St. Louis, 1865, p. 23; and William Barrows, *The Indian's Side of the Indian Question*, Boston, 1887, p. 189.
35. These events are described in Lucy E. Textor, *Official Relations between the United States and the Sioux Indians*, Palo Alto, 1896, pp. 117-124.

36. Richardson, *Messages and Papers*, VII, p. 401.
37. *Cong. Rec.*, IV, p. 3534.
38. Congressional documents of these years include many petitions against territorial government. A more extended argument was advanced in Isaac N. Morris, *Argument . . . against . . . Territorial Government over the Indian Territory*, Washington, 1870.
39. Charles Lewis Slattery, *Felix Reville Brunot*, New York, 1901, p. 216; and Richardson, *op. cit.*, p. 200.
40. Brunot to Cree, Dec. 3, 1872 (*B.C.* IV 22-24).
41. *Cong. Globe*, 42nd Cong., 3rd Sess. p. 658.
42. *Cong. Rec.*, III, p. 447; and *Board Rep.*, 1875, p. 14.
43. *U.S.Stat.*, XXI, p. 797.
44. *Ibid.*, pp. 797-798.
45. Presidents Arthur and Cleveland both urged modification of laws penalizing invasion of Indian land unsuccessfully (*House Exec. Doc. 145*, 47th Cong., 1st Sess.; *House Exec. Doc. 17*, 48th Cong., 1st Sess.; *Sen. Exec. Doc. 14*, 49th Cong., 1st Sess.; and *Sen. Exec. Doc. 41*, 50th Cong., 1st Sess.). See also *Com. Rep.*, 1880, pp. XIV-XV, XX-XXI; and *Sec. Rep.*, 1885, p. 28.
46. Detailed accounts of the activities of the Boomers are presented in Roy Gittinger, *The Formation of the State of Oklahoma*, Berkeley, 1927, pp. 98ff.; and Solon J. Buck, "The Settlement of Oklahoma," in *Transactions of the Wisconsin Academy of Science, Arts and Letters*, XV, pp. 335-343.
47. W.N.I.A., *An Earnest Petition Needed*, [Philadelphia], 1879; W.N.I.A., *Stand to the Covenant*, [Philadelphia], 1880; and I.R.A., *Annual Reports*, 1883-1885.
48. J. D. Cox, "The Indian Question," in *The International Review*, VI, p. 263; Laban Miles in John Joseph Mathews, *Wah'kon-tah*, Norman, Okla., 1932, p. 89; and M. P. Pierce to Schurz, Dec. 22, 1879 (*Schurz Papers*).
49. Buck, *op. cit.*, p. 334; and Gittinger, *op. cit.*, p. 121.
50. Gittinger, *op. cit.*, p. 111.
51. *Convention to Consider the Opening of the Indian Territory, Proceedings*, Kansas City, 1888, p. 3.
52. This story is told in *Com. Rep.*, 1877, pp. 417-419.
53. The decision may be found in Zylyff, pseud., *The Ponca Chiefs*, Boston, 1880, pp. 106-127; and in XXV *Federal Cases* 695.
54. The ablest of these was Schurz to Atkinson, Nov. 18, 1879 (*Schurz Papers*).

Notes

55. Defense of the administration was most effectively expressed in *Council Fire*, II, pp. 47, 120, 147-148; III, pp. 9-10; Barstow to Marble, Dec. 28, 1880 (*I.O.Misc.* B1330); articles by Barstow in *The Congregationalist*, Sept. 3, 1879 and the *Providence Journal*, Aug. 7, 1879; and General Sherman to Secretary of War, May 20, 1879, in *Senate Report* 670, 46th Cong., 2nd Sess., p. 480.
56. Mrs. Jackson to Dawes, Dec. 30, 1880 (*Dawes Papers*); and Dawes to Allen, Aug. 11, 1881 (*Dawes Papers*).
57. Lincoln to Dawes, Feb. 4, 1881; Frost to Dawes, Feb. 22, 1881; and Mrs. Jackson to Dawes, Dec. 23, 1880 (*Dawes Papers*).
58. Lincoln to Dawes, Dec. 29, 1880 (*Dawes Papers*).
59. Lincoln to Dawes, Dec. 23, 1880 (*Dawes Papers*).
60. Mrs. Jackson to Dawes, Dec. 23, 1883 (*Dawes Papers*).
61. Dawes to Hayes, Nov. 24, 1880 (*Dawes Papers*).
62. *Cong. Rec.*, XI, pp. 1056-1058. Official versions of Big Snake's demise may be found in *Senate Report* 670, 46th Cong., 2nd Sess., pp. 233-235, 245-251, 257-259, 480-483.
63. Hon. Carl Schurz, *An Open Letter in answer to a speech of Hon. H. L. Dawes, U. S. Senate, on the Case of Big Snake*, Washington, 1886, p. 8.
64. Lincoln to Dawes, March 8, 1881 (*Dawes Papers*).
65. Dawes to Allen, Aug. 11, 1881 (*Dawes Papers*).

Chapter Seven

1. Information regarding the Commission may be found in *Board Report*, 1869, pp. 30-31; and New York Indian Peace Commission, *A Thorough Digest of the Indian Question*, New York, [187-   ].
2. Mrs. John Lucas of the Indian Hope Association to President Hayes, received Feb. 5, 1878 (*I.O.Misc.* P84); and Mary C. Morgan to Mrs. Hayes, April 3, 1879 (*I.O.Misc.* P386).
3. The history of the organization may be followed in W.N.I.A., *Annual Reports*.
4. W.N.I.A., *Sketch and Plans of the Indian Treaty-Keeping and Protective Association*, Philadelphia, 1881, p. 12; and W.N.I.A., *Missionary Work of the Women's National Indian Association*, Philadelphia, 1882, p. 1.
5. Mrs. A. S. Quinton, *Indians and Their Helpers*, n.p., n.d., p. 5.
6. The history of this group is recounted in Ellen Terry Johnson,

Historical Sketch of the Connecticut Indian Association from 1881-1888, Hartford, 1888.

7. See *Cong. Rec.*, XIII, pp. 1327-1329 for presentation of a petition by Senator Dawes.

8. W.N.I.A., *Report of Memorials to Government*, Philadelphia, 1886, pp. 7, 15.

9. *Board Report*, 1885, p. 92.

10. W.N.I.A., *Donations to the Women's National Indian Association*, [Philadelphia], Oct. 27, 1883.

11. New York City Indian Association, *Fifth Annual Report*, pp. 7, 9.

12. W.N.I.A., *Fourth Annual Report*, pp. 49-50.

13. See W.N.I.A., *An Open Letter*, Philadelphia, 1888, for Mrs. Quinton's reply to this criticism.

14. W.N.I.A., *Address of the President*, Philadelphia, 1885, p. 9.

15. This visit is reported in Herbert Welsh, *Four Weeks Among Some of the Sioux*, Germantown, 1882.

16. *Ante*, pp. 77-79.

17. Among these were Henry S. Pancoast, *Impressions of the Sioux Tribe in 1882*, Philadelphia, 1883; Herbert Welsh, *Report of a Visit to Navajo, Pueblo and Hualapais Indians*, Philadelphia, 1885; and Charles C. Painter, *A Visit to the Mission Indians*, Philadelphia, 1886.

18. A study of the titles of Association pamphlets at once reveals the division of labor among the three men.

19. New York *Tribune*, Jan. 5, 1885; *Cong. Rec.*, XVI, pp. 483-485, 862, 925-926; Henry S. Pancoast, *Facts Regarding the Recent Opening to Settlement of Crow Creek Reservation in Dakota*, Philadelphia, 1885 (a collection of press extracts); *Cong. Rec.*, XVII, pp. 909-915, 943-948, 967; *Senate Report* 1278, 49th Cong., 2nd Sess., Part I; *Opinions*, XVIII, pp. 141-146; and Richardson, *Messages and Papers*, VIII, pp. 305-307.

20. See Smiley's account of the origin of the conferences in *Lake Mohonk Proceedings*, 1885, p. 1.

21. *Lake Mohonk Proceedings*, 1884, pp. 3-4.

22. See comment of Hartford *Courant* reporter in *ibid.*, p. 23.

23. President Cleveland continued to complain of the impracticality of reformers (*Council Fire*, IX, p. 160; Cleveland to Mrs. Astor, March 21, 1886, in *Lend A Hand*, I, p. 315; and to Mrs. Kinney, Dec. 30, 1887, in Johnson, *op. cit.*, p. 63).

24. I.R.A., *Annual Report*, 1885, pp. 11-12.

Notes

25. *Board Report*, 1884, p. 43, e.g.
26. Price to Armstrong, Sept. 7, 1883 (*I.O.Finance Letter Book*, 90, p. 44).
27. *Board Report*, 1881, p. 61.
28. Senator Dawes in *Lake Mohonk Proceedings*, 1886, p. 38; and S. A. Galpin, "Some Administrative Difficulties of the Indian Problem," in the *New Englander and Yale Review*, XLVI, p. 316.
29. The position of the group is consistently expounded in the *Council Fire*, and its influence on the reform program will be frequently discussed in later chapters. See also T. A. Bland, *The Indian—What Shall We Do with Him?*, Washington, [1887].
30. *Cong. Rec.*, XIII, p. 1327.
31. B. R. Cowen, "Indian Land Titles," in *The Independent*, April 7, 1872, ably presented the need for practicality on the part of Indian friends.
32. This common mistake was commented upon in Francis A. Walker, *The Indian Question*, Boston, 1874, pp. 21-22, and more recently in John Joseph Mathews, *Wah'kon-tah*, Norman, Okla., 1932, p. 79.
33. *Sec. Rep.*, 1880, p. 14.
34. This charge is repeated so frequently in current literature defending the Indians that reference to particular charges is unnecessary.
35. Comment upon the unreliability of the reports of church-nominated agents may be found in J. H. Trask, "Indian Affairs" in *Old and New*, VIII, p. 238, and An Indian Agent, "On the War Path," in *The Cornhill Magazine*, XX, pp. 313-314.
36. J. B. Harrison, *The Latest Studies on Indian Reservations*, Philadelphia, 1887, p. 185.
37. The position of the Indian Rights Association is excellently explained in Herbert Welsh, *The Indian Problem*, Philadelphia, 1886, pp. 6-7. For the stand of Meacham and Bland, see *Council Fire*, II, p. 87; IV, p. 155.
38. Evidences of this desire for co-operation appeared in I.R.A., *Annual Report*, p. 16; and *Cong. Rec.*, X, p. 2152.
39. Criticism of Western claims (Whipple to Taylor, July 8, 1867 *I.O.Misc.* W357; and New York *Herald*, Oct. 28, 1883) should be contrasted with attacks on government hostility to Western demands (Thomas Sturgis, *Common Sense View of the Sioux War*, Waltham, Mass., 1877, p. 8).
40. Mrs. Baker to Hayes, Oct. 30, 1879 (*I.O.Misc.* B1001); John Holmes to Grant, April 20, 1872 (*I.O.Arizona* H1395); J. Miles to

"the Honorable Secratey of the intier," March 14, 1875 (*I.O.Misc.* M280); and Thomas Hindman to Hayes, Oct. 13, 1878 (*I.O.Misc.* P1121).

41. This is the thesis of William Barrows, *The Indian's Side of the Indian Question*, Boston, 1887. See also a letter against nomination of Kansas men to Indian commissions on the ground that it was not possible for them to feel when racial rights were equal that the Indian was entitled to "more than one in five" (Edwin Earle to "Collier", Dec. 31, 1870 *B.C.* I 112).

42. *Council Fire*, I, p. 150; House Bill 178 enclosed in D. W. Wood to "Shurz", Feb. 4, 1881 (*Schurz Papers*); and Mathews, *op. cit.*, p. 175.

43. E. W. Eastman of Eldora, Iowa, to Schurz, Nov. 18, 1880 (*I.O.Misc.* E581).

44. *Lend A Hand*, I, p. 69.

45. A jolly account of this excitement may be found in Cree to Walker, Sept. 13 and 16, 1872 (*B.C.* IV 217, 219-220).

46. *Com. Rep.*, 1877, p. 46.

47. *New York Herald*, April 28, 1883; and Harrison, *op. cit.*, pp. 101-102.

48. *New York Herald*, April 27, 28; May 4, 5; July 1, 2 and 3, 1882; and March 28, 30, 1883.

49. *Com. Rep.*, 1877, pp. 90-91.

Chapter Eight

1. Richard Irving Dodge, *Our Wild Indians*, Hartford, 1882, pp. 643-644.

2. *Cong. Globe*, 39th Cong., 1st Sess., pp. 2010-2013.

3. *Com. Rep.*, 1868, p. 371; and *Board Report*, 1869, pp. 18-19.

4. *U.S.Stat.*, XVI, p. 566.

5. *Cong. Globe*, 40th Cong., 2nd Sess., pp. 3256ff.

6. *Cong. Globe*, 40th Cong., 3rd Sess., pp. 1698, 1813, 1891.

7. *Cong. Globe*, 41st Cong., 1st Sess., p. 21.

8. *Ibid.*, p. 170.

9. *Ibid.*, pp. 417-418, 444, 557, 564.

10. *Ibid.*, p. 58.

11. *Ibid.*, p. 559.

12. *Ibid.*, pp. 563ff.

13. *Cong. Globe*, 41st Cong., 2nd Sess., pp. 1579, 4971.

Notes

14. *Ibid.*, pp. 5607ff.
15. Despite the great power granted to a Republican president by Dawes's plan, but twenty-two of the forty Democrats voting favored surrender to the Senate (*Ibid.*, p. 5643).
16. By a curious oversight this proviso was omitted from the act as first recorded (*Cong. Globe*, 41st Cong., 3rd Sess., p. 763).
17. Brackenridge to Parker, Jan. 7, 1870 (*I.O.Misc.* B518).
18. XI *Wallace* 616.
19. *U.S.Stat.*, XIV, pp. 724, 728, 740, etc.; or Charles J. Kappler, comp., *Indian Affairs: Laws and Treaties*, Washington, 1904, II, pp. 883ff. Interesting comments on these clauses were made in Elwell S. Otis, *The Indian Question*, New York, 1878, pp. 122-124.
20. *Cong. Rec.*, II, pp. 3482-3483.
21. *Cong. Globe*, 41st Cong., 3rd Sess., pp. 1821ff.
22. Tappan to Grant, May 25, 1871 (*I.O.Misc.* T277); Francis A. Walker, *The Indian Question*, Boston, 1874, pp. 12-13; and James B. Thayer, "A People without Law," in *The Atlantic Monthly*, LXVIII, p. 676.
23. *U.S.Stat.*, XIX, pp. 254-264.
24. Bitter comments by Mrs. Jackson on this episode appeared in the New York *Tribune*, Jan. 30, 1880.
25. *Cong. Rec.*, VII, pp. 1822ff.
26. The point of view described in this paragraph was excellently presented by Senator Morgan (*Cong. Rec.*, X, pp. 2121-2128) and J. B. Harrison of the Indian Rights Association (*The Latest Studies on Indian Reservations*, Philadelphia, 1887, pp. 30-31; 165). An account of persistent and ultimately successful efforts of the government to reduce the influence of Chief Sitting Bull was later recorded, with considerable sympathy for the chief, by his agent (James McLaughlin, *My Friend the Indian*, Boston, 1910).
27. Harrison, *op. cit.*, p. 30.
28. Robert Patterson, "Our Indian Policy," in *The Overland Monthly*, XI, pp. 201-214.
29. Bland and Judge Willard presented the Association's position in *Board Report*, 1884, p. 60; and 1886, p. 124.
30. *Cong. Rec.*, XI, p. 908.
31. Bishop Whipple in *Council Fire*, IX, p. 34, *e.g.*
32. *Sec. Rep.*, 1879, p. 6.
33. *Board Report*, 1885, pp. 115-116.
34. For an able discussion of the place of the act abolishing the treaty

system in the history of American Indian policy, see Laurence F. Schmeckebier, *The Office of Indian Affairs*, Baltimore, 1927, pp. 64-66.

Chapter Nine

1. *Ante*, pp. 67-68.
2. Such disputes were reflected in *Cong. Rec.*, X, pp. 2452-2454, 2483, 2861.
3. The contractor's fear of Indian self-sufficiency was commented upon in *House Report* 98, 42nd Cong., 3rd Sess., pp. 14-16.
4. Contrast George E. Ellis, *The Red Man and the White Man in North America*, Boston, 1882, p. 175 and Gibbon to Chandler, June 16, 1876 (*I.O.Misc.* G155) with *Com. Rep.*, 1880, p. 116; 1882, p. XI.
5. *Cong. Globe*, 39th Cong., 2nd Sess., p. 1025.
6. Indian Commissioner Walker offered especially powerful arguments upholding the need of annuity appropriations as a means of war prevention (*The Indian Question*, Boston, 1874, pp. 32-41; and *Com. Rep.*, 1872, pp. 3-10).
7. Annuity statistics were reported annually in the Commissioner's *Report*.
8. Pope to Grant, June 14, 1864, in Anon., *Official Communications from General Pope concerning Indian Affairs*, Saint Louis, 1865, p. 17.
9. The evil consequences of favoring hostile tribes were bitterly condemned in S. C. Armstrong, *The Indian Question*, Hampton, Va., 1883, p. 5; Lawrie Tatum, *Our Red Brothers*, Philadelphia, 1899, p. 30; and *Com. Rep.*, 1882, pp. viii, 11.
10. Francis A. Walker, *The Indian Question*, Boston, 1874, pp. 86-89.
11. Resolution in Stickney to Secretary, April 5, 1878 (*I.O.Misc.* I362).
12. Charles J. Kappler, comp., *Indian Affairs: Laws and Treaties*, Washington, 1904, II, pp. 607-608, 852, 861.
13. *U.S.Stat.*, XVII, p. 461.
14. *Cong. Globe*, 42nd Cong., 3rd Sess., pp. 137ff., 348-350, 369-371, 915.
15. *Ibid.*, pp. 137, 140, 914.
16. *Cong. Rec.*, III, pp. 1525-1527, 1572-1573; IV, p. 3905.
17. *Cong. Rec.*, VII, pp. 3271ff.
18. The advantage of allowing diversion of annuity funds was explained in *Senate Report* 708, 46th Cong., 2nd Sess., pp. 184-185.

Notes

19. The statistics in this paragraph are compiled from United States Interior Department, *Tabular Statements of Disbursements made from Appropriations for the Indian Department*, Washington, 1876-1888.
20. Statistics based on figures included in the annual *Report* of the Indian Commissioner, 1881 and 1885.
21. *Com. Rep.*, 1878, p. 159.
22. *Senate Report* 708, 46th Cong., 2nd Sess., pp. 56-58.
23. *Com. Rep.*, 1882, pp. X-XI.
24. Weekly issues had been required by the 1874 and 1875 Appropriation Bills (*U.S.Stat.*, XVIII, Part 3, pp. 177, 449), but as a means of controlling hostile tribes rather than of preventing improvidence.
25. *Com. Rep.*, 1884, p. 43.
26. *Com. Rep.*, 1885, p. 101.
27. This proposal was defeated by 59-49 after considerable debate (*Cong. Globe*, 41st Cong., 2nd Sess., pp. 1643-1648).
28. *Com. Rep.*, 1873, pp. 3-4. The treaty provision, the first requiring labor in return for annuities, may be found in Kappler, *op cit.*, p. 958.
29. *U.S.Stat.* XVIII, Part 3, p. 176.
30. *Ibid.*, p. 449.
31. E. P. Smith to Whipple, Oct. 2, 1875 (*I.O.Misc.* W1530, 1876).
32. *Cong. Rec.*, IV, pp. 3902-3906; XIII, p. 2372.
33. See varied answers to a questionnaire on the subject in *Board Report*, 1874, pp. 15-47.
34. The latter view was excellently propounded in Stanley Pumphrey, *Indian Civilization*, Philadelphia, 1877, p. 33; *Board Report*, 1879, p. 81; and *Com. Rep.*, 1883, p. 179.
35. The problem of Indian treaties is presented at length in Chapter XVIII.
36. The folly of judging the cost of an Indian policy by its immediate expenditures was frequently condemned (*Sec. Rep.*, 1881, p. IV; . Bishop Seabury Mission, *Missionary Paper No. 30*, Fairbault, Minn., 1864, p. 14; and General Grierson, *Report on Indian Territory, June 1868 to August 1869*, MS. in B.C.M.).
37. While individual items were occasionally reduced (*Cong Rec.*, VII, p. 3234), the total of the Senate bill was invariably higher.
38. *Cong. Rec.*, II, pp. 4424, 5320; III, p. 1533.
39. *Cong. Rec.*, X, pp. 2444-2451, 2861-2867, 3076.
40. Richard Irving Dodge, *A Living Issue*, Washington, 1882, p. 14.

41. *U.S.Stat.*, XVIII, Part 3, p. 449.
42. *U.S.Stat.*, XX, p. 315; XXI, p. 131.
43. See especially *Council Fire*, VII, p. 124; and *Com. Rep.*, 1884, p. 110.
44. *Com. Rep.*, 1882, p. 22.
45. *Cong. Globe*, 42nd Cong., 3rd Sess., p. 138; and *Cong. Rec.*, VIII, pp. 287-289.
46. J. B. Harrison, *The Latest Studies on Indian Reservations*, Philadelphia, 1887, p. 27.
47. Bright Eyes urged the payment of Omaha funds, for example, fully realizing that lazy Indians would soon waste their money (*Board Report*, 1886, p. 120).

Chapter Ten

1. Laurence F. Schmeckebier in *The Office of Indian Affairs*, Baltimore, 1927, p. 43, places the first legislation establishing reservations in 1853.
2. Statistics in the annual *Commissioner's Reports* reveal that the 164,250,339 acres devoted to reservations in 1875 were never exceeded after that date.
3. Francis A. Walker, *The Indian Question*, Boston, 1874, p. 44.
4. The need for isolation was urged with particular emphasis in such books as Rev. W. D. Risher, ed., *The Indian and White Man or the Indian in Self-Defense*, Indianapolis, 1880; George E. Ellis, *The Red Man and the White Man in North America*, Boston, 1882; and William Barrows, *The Indian's Side of the Indian Question*, Boston, 1887.
5. Unusually pessimistic statements regarding the influence of racial contacts may be found in the Providence *Journal*, June 26, 1882 and *Com. Rep.*, 1885, p. 265.
6. Whittlesey to Mahan, et al., Aug. 21, 1874 (*B.L.S.* I-V 913).
7. The replies may be found in *Board Report*, 1874, pp. 15-54. The original letters and a summary of them are preserved in *B.C.M.*
8. Whittlesey to Chute, Nov. 5, 1874 (*B.L.S.* I-V 933).
9. *Board Report*, 1885, p. 115.
10. Anon., *Official Communications from General Pope concerning Indian Affairs*, Saint Louis, 1865, p. 7; and John Pope, *The Indian Question*, n.p., n.d., p. 27.
11. *Cong. Globe*, 40th Cong., 1st Sess., p. 709, e.g.

Notes

12. *Cong. Globe*, 41st Cong., 1st Sess., p. 172; 42nd Cong., 2nd Sess., p. 3417; 42nd Cong., 3rd Sess., pp. 370, 434-435; and *Com. Rep.* 1869, p. 202.
13. Representative Armstrong in *Cong. Globe*, 41st Cong., 3rd Sess., Appendix, pp. 260ff. and material in Chapter XVII provide excellent evidence of Eastern interest in a reduction in the area of Indian holdings.
14. *Com. Rep.*, 1870, pp. 163-164.
15. *Com. Rep.*, 1885, p. 203.
16. *Com. Rep.*, 1886, p. 200.
17. Richard Irving Dodge, *A Living Issue*, Washington, 1882, p. 27.
18. Captain Pratt of the Carlisle Indian School in *Com. Rep.*, 1886, p. 20; and E. L. Huggins, "A Suggestion on the Indian Question," in *The Overland Monthly*, New Series VI, p. 571.
19. Elaine Goodale Eastman, *Pratt: The Red Man's Moses*, Norman, Okla., 1935, p. 259.
20. Dodge, *op cit.*, p. 31; and Francis C. Sparhawk, "The Indian Question," in *Education*, VII, pp. 51-54, e.g.
21. See especially Mrs. G. W. Owen, *The Indian Question*, Ypsilanti, Mich., 1881, p. 20.
22. The attitude of the Association was expressed by Judge Willard in *Board Report*, 1886, pp. 123-124. For a further expression of opposition to destruction of the reservation system, see Gail Hamilton, "The Lion's Side of the Lion Question," in the *North American Review*, CXLVI, pp. 294-309.
23. *Board Report*, 1885, p. 131.
24. Merrill Edwards Gates, *Land and Law as Agents in Educating Indians*, [New York, 1885], pp. 23-25.
25. A further advantage of settling Indians in the East was the presence of more fertile land (Peter Closs to Hayes, Jan. 29, 1878 *I.O.Misc.* P83).
26. "Iowa" to Grant, March 17, 1870 (*I.O.Misc.*, P347); McPherson to Grant, March 10, 1873 (*I.O.Misc.* P393); and Harwood to Schurz, Nov. 21, 1878 (*Schurz Papers*).
27. *Cong. Rec.*, X, p. 2491.
28. *Cong. Globe*, 41st Cong., 2nd Sess., p. 1645; 41st Cong., 3rd Sess., p. 736.
29. John Gilmary Shea, "What Right Has the Federal Government to Mismanage the Indians," in *The American Catholic Quarterly Review*, VI, pp. 538-540.

30. Cong. Rec., III, p. 470.
31. U.S.Stat., XII, p. 1238.
32. B. M. Smith to Schurz, Dec. 21, 1878 (Schurz Papers); "Jacques" to Editor of the Nation, March 7, 1884, in the Nation, XXXVIII, p. 254; and Com. Rep., 1885, pp. 31, 88, 125.
33. Eastman, op. cit., pp. 154-158.
34. Carl Schurz, "Present Aspects of the Indian Problem," in the North American Review, CXXXIII, p. 6.

Chapter Eleven

1. Charles J. Kappler, comp., Indian Affairs: Laws and Treaties, Washington, 1904, II, pp. 700-704. The history of education on these and other reservations may be followed in the annual reports of the agents in the Commissioner's Reports.
2. Ibid., II, pp. 979, 986, 992, 1000, 1010, 1013, 1017.
3. Board Report, 1874, pp. 6-7; and House Report 29, 46th Cong., 1st Sess.
4. Com. Rep., 1870, p. 198; and the Dial, II, p. 12.
5. Dr. J. O. Bronson to Commissioner, March 21, 1874 (I.O.Misc. B409).
6. Edgar McCashey to Commissioner, Feb. 21, 1881 (I.O.Civ. 4276); and Murie to Commissioner, March 12, 1883 (I.O.Civ. 13423).
7. While Pratt claimed that he could have gotten thousands of students for his school during his first visit to Indian Territory (Pratt to Hayt, Dec. 23, 1878 I.O.Misc. P1163), he became less enthusiastic when faced with the opposition of less advanced tribes.
8. Council Fire, IV, p. 9.
9. Stanley Vestal, comp., New Sources of Indian History, 1850-1891, Norman, Okla., 1934, p. 274.
10. Nickerson to Price, Feb. 7, 1882 (I.O.Civ. 3589); and Lightner to Commissioner, Feb. 17, 1882 (I.O.Civ. 3727).
11. Herbert Welsh, Report of a Visit to Navajo, Pueblo and Hualapais Indians, Philadelphia, 1885, p. 6; and S. C. Armstrong, Indian Education at Hampton Institute, New York, 1881, p. 2.
12. U.S.Stat., XVI, p. 359.
13. Cong. Rec., II, p. 446; and Henry L. Dawes, Past and Present Indian Policy, New York, 1892.
14. Cong. Rec., III, pp. 1489, 1491.
15. Sen. Misc. Doc. 53, 45th Cong., 3rd Sess., pp. 91-94.

16. The speech of Representative Donnelly of Minnesota declaring that injustice to Indians would prove injurious to neighboring whites was thus very unusual in tone (*Cong. Globe*, 38th Cong. 3rd Sess., Appendix, p. 62).

17. Senator Plumb of Kansas was the leading opponent of Indian education (*Cong. Rec.*, X, pp. 2256-2257; XIV, pp. 412-415, e.g.) and the political pressure upon agents is described in Mrs. Sawtell to Schurz, Feb. 10, 1878 (*I.O.Misc.* S232); *Council Fire*, VII, pp. 137-138; and Zylyff, pseud., *The Ponca Chiefs*, Boston, 1880, pp. 27-28.

18. This petition was received January 30, 1883 (*I.O.Civ.* 2072) but soon aroused bitter opposition such as that expressed in the Albuquerque *Daily Journal*, April 29, 1886 (*Council Fire*, IX, p. 87).

19. *Cong. Rec.*, VII, Appendix, pp. 224-226; and *Board Scrap Book*, I, p. 56.

20. Sherman to Whipple, Dec. 10, 1888, in Henry Benjamin Whipple, *Lights and Shadows*, New York, 1899, pp. 311-312.

21. Stevens to Arny, Dec. 9, 1871 (*B.C.* V 179); and *Com. Rep.*, 1883, pp. 10-15.

22. *Cong. Rec.*, IV, pp. 1262, 3538.

23. *New York Herald*, April 18, 1882.

24. Quoted in George W. Manypenny, *A Word about Indians*, Columbus, 1867, p. 4.

25. H. Clay Preuss, *Columbus Crockett to General Grant on the Indian Policy*, Washington, 1873, p. 2—for the sake of context "his" is substituted for "my".

26. *Council Fire*, IX, p. 61.

27. Anon., *Sanborn Family in the United States*, St. Paul, 1887, p. 44.

28. White emphasis upon Indian inferiority was frequently used by tribes in resisting changes. Thus negotiators were accustomed to hearing the excuse of tribal representatives who declared, "You can't expect much from us; we are Indians. We have not sense enough to do much." (*Board Report*, 1871, p. 120.)

29. For criticism of the effect of removals in retarding advancement, see Laurence F. Schmeckebier, *The Office of Indian Affairs*, Baltimore, 1927, p. 62. Leading instances of the time were discussed in *Board Report*, 1869, pp. 76-77; *Com. Rep.*, 1886, pp. 167, 189; and Helen Hunt Jackson, *A Century of Dishonor*, New York, 1881, pp. 218-256.

30. Richardson, *Messages and Papers*, VII, p. 475.

31. *Com. Rep.*, 1869, p. 356; 1872, p. 302.
32. *Com. Rep.*, 1873, p. 273.
33. *Com. Rep.*, 1874, pp. 16, 37, 46, 297, 306.
34. *Board Report*, 1875, pp. 64-103.
35. The original appropriation may be found in *U.S.Stat.*, XX, p. 86. Subsequent increases may be followed by studying the annual appropriation bills.
36. *Com. Rep.*, 1875, p. 341; 1880, pp. 2, 46, *e.g.*
37. *Com. Rep.*, 1883, p. 156; 1886, p. 160.
38. The figures and facts regarding Indian freighting may be verified by reference to *Com. Rep.*, 1879, pp. IX-X; *Sec. Rep.*, 1880, pp. 6-7; and *Com. Rep.*, 1880, pp. XII-XIII.
39. The emphasis upon Santee achievements is noticeable in all official reports of the 1870's—see *Com. Rep.*, 1877, p. 147; 1878, p. 99, *e.g.*
40. Woodworth Clum, *Apache Agent*, Boston, 1936, pp. 134-135, 153; *Council Fire*, VII, pp. 143-145; and *Lake Mohonk Proceedings*, 1884, p. 31. The establishment of Indian courts is described in detail on pp. 146-147.
41. See the remarks of fifty-three agents on Indian progress compiled in *Council Fire*, VII, pp. 143-145 and such analyses as those in *Board Report*, 1882, p. 10 and *Com. Rep.*, 1885, p. 395. The most outstanding work on this subject, however, was produced by the able Indian worker, Miss Alice C. Fletcher in her government report, *Indian Education and Civilization*, Washington, 1887.
42. For further details than are given in the following paragraphs, see Elaine Goodale Eastman, *Pratt: the Red Man's Moses*, Norman, Okla., 1935; I.R.A., *Captain Pratt and His Work for Indian Education*, Philadelphia, 1886; and Gen. R. H. Pratt, *American Indians, Chained and Unchained*, Philadelphia, 1912.
43. *House Report 29*, 46th Cong., 1st Sess.
44. This visit is reported in U.S. Office of Education, *The Indian School at Carlisle Barracks*, Washington, 1880.
45. *U.S.Stat.*, XXII, p. 85.
46. Requests for educational appropriations had been made with a definite admission that the possibility of Indian advancement must rest on faith and not assurance (*Com. Rep.*, 1873, p. 10).
47. *New York Herald*, Oct. 6, 1883. Only a few days previously (Sept. 23), a *Herald* writer had remarked of Sitting Bull, "They say that his intelligence is superior to that of his fellows, but that is not saying much."

Notes

48. Captain Pratt's pay was a subject of bitter debate for many years. The vote of nine deserting Democrats enabled the appropriation to pass the Senate in 1881 (*Cong. Rec.*, XI, pp. 817-821); but in 1886 the House succeeded in having the figure omitted (*Cong. Rec.*, XVII, pp. 2675-2684, 2724).
49. Quoted in Pratt to Dawes, March 18, 1882 (*Dawes Papers*).
50. *Board Report*, 1885, pp. 126, 129.
51. *Ibid.*, p. 9.
52. The opinions described in this paragraph were best presented by Senator Sherman (*Cong. Globe*, 40th Cong., 1st Sess., p. 680), Commissioner Price (*Com. Rep.*, 1881, p. IV), Captain Pratt (*American Indians, Chained and Unchained*, Philadelphia, 1912, p. 15), Austin Abbott (*Lake Mohonk Proceedings*, 1886, p. 39), and Secretary Teller (*Sec. Rep.*, 1883, p. III).
53. *Com. Rep.*, 1883, p. 118; 1885, p. 151.
54. See especially J. B. Harrison, *The Latest Studies on Indian Reservations*, Philadelphia, 1887, pp. 168-169; and J. Evarts Greene, "Our Dealings with the Indians," in *Proceedings of the American Antiquarian Society*, New Series XI, p. 41.
55. *Com. Rep.*, 1870, pp. 202-203; 1871, p. 271.
56. U.S.I.O., *Regulations of the Indian Department*, Washington, 1884, pp. 87-90.
57. Testimonials to the success of the plan may be found in *Com. Rep.*, 1884, pp. IX-XI; 1885, pp. XXI-XXIV.
58. *Com. Rep.*, 1886, p. 201.
59. *Ibid.*, p. XXVII.
60. *Com. Rep.*, 1885, p. XXIII; 1886, p. XXVII.
61. *U.S.Stat.*, XXV, p. 233.
62. When Agent Eastman stirred difficulties with the Navajos by forbidding Sunday revelling, the press was extremely critical of his actions (*New York Tribune*, July 25, 1881; *Chicago Tribune*, Aug. 8, 1881; and *New York Herald*, Aug. 15, 1881). Many agents urged the necessity for gradual action in abolishing tribal customs (*Com. Rep.*, 1883, p. 42; 1884, pp. 85, 143, *et al.*).
63. Francis A. Walker, *The Indian Question*, Boston, 1874, p. 94.
64. Most typical of the many letters from half-breeds complaining of their lot was F. B. Harris to Superintendent of Indian Affairs, Jan. 1, 1874 (*I.O.Misc.* H38).
65. Thomas J. Mays, "The Future of the American Indian," in the *Popular Science Monthly*, XXXIII, p. 108.

66. A member of the Board of Indian Commissioners, for example, announced that while he did not recommend intermarriage he did not fear it (*Lake Mohonk Proceedings,* 1886, p. 9).
67. C. F. Fletcher to Seward, May 8, 1876 (*I.O.Misc.* S173).
68. James E. Rhoads in *Lend A Hand,* I, p. 138, e.g.
69. *Council Fire,* IX, p. 32.
70. *Ibid.,* p. 55.
71. The following figures reveal the growing proportion of Indian appropriations spent for education following 1874:

A. *Expenditures for Indian Schools 1874-1887*

Year	Total Appropriation	School Expenditure	%
1874	$6,161,543.14	$ 37,597.31	.8
1875	6,131,869.77	94,320.28	1.8
1876	5,504,931.79	122,920.19	2.5
1877	4,513,119.63	105,172.18	2.8
1878	4,669,861.70	127,649.41	3.2
1879	4,674,857.72	118,928.10	3.0
1880	4,674,573.44	152,411.76	3.6
1881	4,448,320.76	208,996.47	4.9
1882	5,124,648.80	244,209.18	5.0
1883	5,583,185.91	482,336.44	9.3
1884	5,291,985.91	669,974.21	13.4
1885	5,819,104.10	887,690.67	17.1
1886	5,578,656.81	979,716.32	19.9
1887	5,446,015.72	1,146,773.84	22.8

B. *Distribution of Expenditures—1875, 1880, 1885*

1875		1880		1885	
Classification	%	Classification	%	Classification	%
Subsistence	46.8	Subsistence	44.4	Subsistence	38.9
Salaries	20.5	Salaries	16.6	EDUCATION	17.1
Money		Annuities	11.4	Salaries	15.2
Annuities	11.5	Agriculture	9.9	Annuities	6.8
Annuities	9.1	Transportation	7.4	Agriculture	6.6
Transportation	5.3	Money		Money	
Agriculture	5.0	Annuities	6.9	Annuities	6.5
EDUCATION	1.8	EDUCATION	3.6	Transportation	5.9

Note: Minor items are omitted.

Notes

72. Compare *Senate Report 670*, 46th Cong., 2nd Sess., pp. 356-358 with *Senate Report 708*, 46th Cong., 2nd Sess., pp. 212-213.

73. Hampton Institute, *Hampton Institute 1868-1885: Its Work for Two Races*, Hampton, 1885; and *Cong. Rec.*, XVII, pp. 2274ff.

74. Hampton Institute, *Ten Years' Work for Indians*, n.p., n.d., pp. 42-46; and Florence Drake, *Civilization as told by Thomas Wildcat Alford*, Norman, Okla., 1936, *passim*. A complete report of the activities of Hampton graduates to 1892 may be found in *Sen. Exec. Doc. 31*, 52nd Cong., 1st Sess.

75. *Com. Rep.*, 1885, p. 215.

76. Armstrong to Price, Sept. 15, 1881 (*I.O.Civ.* 16742); *Council Fire*, VI, pp. 176-178; VII, pp. 9-10, 12-13, 41-42; and *Com. Rep.*, 1882, pp. 29-30.

77. The need for practical education was forcefully emphasized in Armstrong to Schurz, March 20, 1880 (*Schurz Papers*).

78. *Cong. Rec.*, XVII, pp. 2265-2269, 2273-2278, 2313, 2466-2467, 2512-2516; *House Report 1076*, 49th Cong., 1st Sess.; Edith Armstrong Talbot, *Samuel Chapman Armstrong*, New York, 1904, p. 280; and *Eadle Keatah Toh*, July, 1880.

79. *Com. Rep.*, 1886, p. 117.

80. See complaint of Sitting Bull in Stanley Vestal, comp., *New Sources of Indian History, 1850-1891*, Norman, Okla., 1934, p. 273.

81. Pratt to Schurz, June 24 and July 5, 1880 (*Schurz Papers*); and Spotted Tail *et al.* to President, May 31, 1881, (*I.O.Civ.* 10258).

82. Attacks on day schools may be found in *Cong. Rec.*, XV, p. 2574; XVII, p. 2265; but far more frequent was the support of practical training advanced by Senator Teller of Colorado in *Cong. Rec.*, XI, p. 1031; XIII, pp. 2456-2457.

83. *Lend A Hand*, II, p. 216.

84. These appropriations may be followed in U. S. Interior Department, *Tabular Statements of Disbursements made from the Appropriations for the Indian Department*, Washington, 1882-1887.

85. *Cong. Rec.*, XIV, pp. 92-95, 396-399, 3150-3151; XV, pp. 2574-2575, 4107, 5801-5802.

86. *Com. Rep.*, 1883, p. 166.

87. J. B. Harrison, *Latest Studies on Indian Reservations*, Philadelphia, 1887, p. 139.

88. This development may be followed in the Commissioners' *Reports* and in the description of problems immediately after the Dawes Act which Indian Commissioner Morgan wrote following his retire-

ment in 1891 (Thomas J. Morgan, *The Present Phase of the Indian Question*, Boston, 1891).

89. See the statement of a Ute chief reported in *Board Report*, 1872, p. 111.
90. *Board Scrap Book*, II, p. 79.
91. See the account of Agent Laban Miles's attitude in John Joseph Mathews, *Wah'kon-tah*, Norman, Okla., 1932, p. 257.
92. *Council Fire*, I, p. 113.
93. *Cong. Rec.*, X, p. 2731. Army officers were the chief critics of compulsion (Interview with General Crook in New York *Herald*, July 8, 1883).
94. Romeyn to Commissioner, May 18, 1880 (*I.O.Misc.* R502), *e.g.*
95. *U.S.Stat.*, XXIV, p. 45.
96. Francis A. Walker, *The Indian Question*, Boston, 1874, pp. 62, 120; and Elliott Coues, "The Western Sphynx: an Analysis of Indian Traits and Tendencies," in *The Penn Monthly*, X, pp. 180-193.
97. Garrick Mallery, "The Former and Present Number of American Indians," in *Proceedings of the American Association for the Advancement of Science*, XXVI, pp. 340-366. For use of Mallery's statistics in Congress, see *Cong. Rec.*, XIII, p. 2414, *e.g.*
98. Pratt's position was excellently described in I.R.A., *Captain Pratt and His Work for Indian Education*, Philadelphia, 1886, p. 6. Interesting criticism of his attitude may be found in Scroggs to Garfield, May 9, 1881 (*I.O.Civ.* 8722); Philàdelphia *Times*, July 7, 1883; and *Cong. Rec.*, X, p. 2256; XI, p. 783; XIV, p. 413; XV, p. 4072.
99. Hare to William Welsh, March 19, 1886, quoted in *Cong. Rec.*, XVII, p. 2718.
100. *Sec. Rep.*, 1881, p. VII.

Chapter Twelve

1. An analysis of the groups interested in maintaining the old system may be found in *Council Fire*, VIII, p. 37. A description of the relations of such men with the Indians, as excellent as it is colorful, has recently been presented from the personal experiences of the American anthropologist, Clark Wissler (*Indian Cavalcade or Life on the Old Time Indian Reservations*, New York, 1938).
2. Harlan to Cooley, March 9, 1866 (*I.O.Misc.* I156); and Chandler to Commissioner, March 7, 1876 (*I.O.Misc.* I217).

Notes

3. *Lake Mohonk Proceedings*, 1883, p. 13; and W.N.I.A., *Sketch and Plans of the Indian-Treaty-Keeping and Protective Association*, Philadelphia, 1881, p. 10.

4. Edward Meritt *et al.* to Hayes, May 7, 1883 (*I.O.Civ.* 9451), e.g.

5. For an early discussion of this problem, see *Cong. Globe*, 42nd Cong., 3rd Sess., pp. 347-348, 379-380, 428-429.

6. Sheridan to Adjutant General, Oct. 14, 1872 (*I.O.Misc.* W435).

7. For criticism of Indian trade at Army posts, see Agent Daniels to E. P. Smith, Dec. 4, 1873 (*I.O.Misc.* D865).

8. Price to Hart, Sept. 18, 1882 (*I.O.Letter Book*, 104, p. 515) in reference to report in General Pope to Colonel Williams, Aug. 4, 1882 (*I.O.Civ.* 14993).

9. Thomas C. Battey, *The Life and Adventures of a Quaker among the Indians*, Boston, 1875, pp. 260-261; and Young to Price, Nov. 17, 1882 (*I.O.Civ.* 19520) and April 12, 1883 (*I.O.Civ.* 7947).

10. The high-lights of this dispute may be followed in Price to Secretary, May 16, 1881 (*I.O.Report Book*, XXXIX, p. 273); Teare to Attorney General Brewster, May 24, 1882 (*I.O.Civ.* 11050); and Lawson to Price, June 27, 1882 (*I.O.Civ.* 12044).

11. Stites to Price, Jan. 1, 1883 (*I.O.Civ.* 1695).

12. A. P. Hunt to Hayt, May 11, 1878 (*I.O.Misc.* H995).

13. B. Stebler *et al.* to Attorney General Devens, Nov. 1, 1880 (*I.O.Misc.* S3453), e.g.

14. *Cong. Rec.*, XVI, pp. 893-895, 931-933, 1743-1746.

15. Stanley Vestal, comp., *New Sources of Indian History, 1850-1891*, Norman, Okla., 1934, p. 313.

16. *Com. Rep.*, 1887, p. X. Similar charges were strongly expressed in McGillycuddy to Price, Feb. 3, 1882 (*I.O.Civ.* 2747).

17. *Council Fire*, II, pp. 59-60.

18. *Com. Rep.*, 1875, p. 25; 1884, p. 97.

19. *Board Report*, 1878, p. 82.

20. *Cong. Rec.*, IV, pp. 3568-3570.

21. R. L. Perry to Commissioner, Jan. 3, 1871 (*I.O.Misc.* P10); and such letters as J. W. Lane to Parker, April 28, 1871 (*I.O.Misc.* L153).

22. These problems may be followed in detail in Joseph S. Elkinton, *Indian Scrap Book*, I, 1878-1887, in the New York Public Library. Elkinton was primarily interested in gathering information on the Seneca problem.

23. *Com. Rep.*, 1872, pp. 200-201; and *Board Report*, 1874, p. 73.

24. *Com. Rep.*, 1878, p. 118; 1879, p. 139.
25. Trowbridge to D. W. and C. F. Horner, July 17, 1880, in *Senate Report 1278*, 49th Cong., 1st Sess., p. 318.
26. Teller to Secretary of War, Aug. 5, 1882 (*D.I.L.S.* XXIX, p. 467); and Teller to Fenelon, April 25, 1883, in Edward Everett Dale, "Ranching on the Cheyenne-Arapahoe Reservation," in *Chronicles of Oklahoma*, VI, pp. 47-48.
27. *Council Fire*, VI, p. 108; and *Com. Rep.*, 1885, p. XIX.
28. Devens to Secretary Ramsey, Feb. 25, 1880 in *Opinions* XVI, pp. 470-472.
29. See official statement of 1885 quoted in Muriel H. Wright, "First Oklahoma Oil was Produced in 1859," in *Chronicles of Oklahoma*, IV, p. 326.
30. *Council Fire*, VII, p. 52; and J. B. Harrison, *Latest Studies on Indian Reservations*, Philadelphia, 1887, pp. 105-106.
31. *Com. Rep.*, 1885, p. 90; 1886, p. 177; and provision in *U.S.Stat.*, XXII, p. 590, stating leasing funds should be spent by the Secretary of the Interior for Indian benefit.
32. Of innumerable references to plans for Indian herds, see *Council Fire*, VI, pp. 101-104; *Com. Rep.*, 1882, pp. 66-68; *Lake Mohonk Proceedings*, 1883, p. 9; *New York Herald*, July 20, 1883; and index to *Senate Report 708*, 46th Cong., 2nd Sess.
33. Testimony in *Senate Report 1278*, 49th Cong., 1st Sess., especially page 168; and *Sec. Rep.*, 1883, pp. XV-XVI.
34. *Com. Rep.*, 1879, p. 78; and John H. Seger, *Early Days among the Cheyenne and Arapahoe Indians*, Norman, Okla., 1934, p. 101.
35. A crisis arising from Agent Dyer's efforts to force concentration of Cheyenne Indians is described from varied points of view in Saint Louis *Globe-Democrat* clipping enclosed in E. C. Boudinot to Dawes, July 5, 1885 (*Dawes Papers*); *Com. Rep.*, 1884, pp. 70-77; and *Council Fire*, VIII, pp. 118-119, 140-141.
36. Contrast *Cong. Rec.*, XI, pp. 940-943; XV, p. 4113; XVII, pp. 2276-2278 with *Council Fire*, VI, p. 104; VIII pp. 24-25; IX, p. 100.
37. R. D. Hunter to Major Randall, June 23, 1880 in *Council Fire*, VII, p. 41. An interview in the *New York Herald* of March 9, 1885, reveals the hostility of Captain Payne of the Oklahoma Boomers toward cattlemen.
38. Convention to Consider the Opening of the Indian Territory, *Proceedings*, Kansas City, 1888, p. 67.
39. *U.S.Stat.*, XXIV, p. 1023.

Notes

40. Garland to Secretary, July 21, 1885, in *Opinions* XVIII, pp. 235-238.
41. Edward Everett Dale, *The Range Cattle Industry*, Norman, Okla., 1930, pp. 106-107. Consult the works of Ernest S. Osgood, Louis Pelzer, and Paul I. Wellman for other discussions of the cattle frontier.
42. For the remarks of Rogers and his opponents see *Cong. Rec.*, XVII, pp. 2305-2319, 2467, 2509-2511.
43. Dawes to Editor of the *Tribune*, July 23, 1885, in New York *Tribune*, Aug. 4, 1885. This opinion was shared by Bland (*Council Fire*, VIII, p. 125) and Secretary Whittlesey of the Board (*Board Report*, 1882, pp. 35-36).

Chapter Thirteen

1. Edith Armstrong Talbot, *Samuel Chapman Armstrong*, New York, 1904, pp. 288-289.
2. Quoted in William Barrows, *The Indian's Side of the Indian Question*, Boston, 1887, p. 132.
3. William J. Harsha, "The Indian Question in the United States," in *The Catholic Presbyterian*, V, p. 256.
4. Anon., *Sanborn Family in the United States*, Saint Paul, 1887, pp 41-42.
5. *House Misc. Doc.* 35, 41st Cong., 2nd Sess., *passim*.
6. As early as 1870, Senator Sargent of California urged that the advisability of allotting Indian land was proved by Canadian experience (*Cong. Globe*, 41st Cong., 2nd Sess., p. 1642).
7. M. Eells, *Justice to the Indians*, Portland, Ore., 1883, p. 8; and W. J. Trimble, "The Indian Policy of the Colony of British Columbia," in *The Mississippi Valley Historical Association Proceedings*, VI, pp. 284-285.
8. Report of Superintendent Gilkison of Brant County, Ontario, in Stanley Pumphrey, *Indian Civilization*, Philadelphia, 1877, pp 37-40.
9. Henry Benjamin Whipple, *Lights and Shadows of a Long Episcopate*, New York, 1899, p. 523.
10. For uncomplimentary comparisons of United States Indian policy with that of Canada, see James W. M. Newlin, *Proposed Indian Policy*, Philadelphia, 1881, pp. 26-27; and New York *Herald*, May 21, 1883.

11. *Cong. Rec.*, XI, p. 880. Interesting evidence of the prejudice of Americans against the British may be found in J. B. Harrison, *The Latest Studies on Indian Reservations*, Philadelphia, 1887, p. 122; and in the New York *Herald* of September 28, 1872.
12. W. T. Franklin to Bland, Sept. 3, 1884, in *Council Fire*, VII, p. 158. For a similar attack, see Andrew Dunn to Bland, Feb. 14, 1885 (*Council Fire*, VIII, p. 47).
13. William Trant, "The Treatment of the Canadian Indians," in *The Westminster Review*, CXLIV, p. 527, e.g.
14. *Cong. Rec.*, XI, pp. 1032, 1035, 1066.
15. John Pope, *The Indian Question*, n.p., n.d., pp. 21-22.
16. John Gilmary Shea, "What Right Has the Federal Government to Mismanage the Indian?" in *The American Catholic Quarterly Review*, VI, p. 527.
17. *The Nation*, XXV, p. 147.
18. *House Misc. Doc.* 35, 41st Cong., 2nd Sess., p. 25.
19. Dominion of Canada, *The Revised Statutes of Canada*, Ottawa, 1887, pp. 687-692. See also Dominion of Canada, *Debates of the Senate*, 1887, pp. 656-657.
20. Minister of the Interior Macdonald to Schurz, Jan. 28, 1879 (*I.O.Misc.* B167).
21. See Reverend George Bryce, *Our Indians*, Winnipeg, 1884.
22. Trant, *op. cit.*, pp. 524ff.
23. *House Misc. Doc.* 35, 41st Cong., 2nd Sess., p. 31.
24. Capt. E. Butler, *An Essay on "Our Indian Question,"* New York, 1882, p. 31.
25. J. R. Thompson in Puget Sound *Weekly Courier*, Jan. 30, 1880.
26. Trant, *op. cit.*, p. 520.
27. Duncan Campbell Scott, *Relations of the Government with the Indians, 1867-1912*, p. 36 (MS. in *B.C.M.*).
28. *Ibid.*, p. 4.
29. *Ibid.*, p. 12.
30. Trimble, *op. cit.*, pp. 282ff.
31. Francis A. Walker, *The Indian Question*, Boston, 1874, p. 97.
32. Grindall Reynolds, "Our Bedouins: What Can We Do With Them?" in *The Unitarian Review*, VIII, p. 147.
33. *Board Report*, 1870, p. 83.
34. Isaac N. Morris, *Arguments against Territorial Government over the Indians*, Washington, 1870, p. 17.
35. The problem of citizenship is discussed in detail in Chapter XVI.

Notes

36. Mrs. Goddard to Schurz, Dec. 19, 1879 (*Schurz Papers*).
37. *Wowapi: A Magazine Devoted to the Cause of the Indians*, Boston, Nov. 7, 1883, p. 13.

Chapter Fourteen

1. This report presents an excellent history of allotment proposals as well as a detailed relation of the instances in which it was employed (*House Report 188*, 45th Cong., 3rd Sess.). The statutory history of Indian land policies is exhaustively treated in J. P. Kinney, *A Continent Lost—A Civilization Won*, Baltimore, 1937.
2. *Council Fire*, VIII, p. 156.
3. See especially the defense of the system by Senator Coke in *Cong. Rec.*, XI, p. 779.
4. *Commonwealth of Massachusetts, House Report No. 483*, Boston, 1869.
5. Hiram Martin Chittenden and Alfred Talbot Richardson, *Life, Letters and Travels of Father Pierre-Jean De Smet, S.J.*, New York, 1905, p. 929.
6. *House Report 188*, 45th Cong., 3rd Sess., pp. 37-38, e.g.
7. The results of this carelessness were graphically described by Agent Griest of the Otoes in *Com. Rep.*, 1878, pp. 96-97.
8. Price to Montieth, Sept. 20, 1882 (*I.O.Letter Book*, 102, p. 36).
9. Agent Linn to Price, May 26, 1881 (*I.O.Land* 9153).
10. Price to Fay, July 25, 1881 (*I.O.Land Letter Book*, 184, p. 193). Opposition to this decision was expressed by Inspector Pollock in Pollock to Schurz, Feb. 4, 1881 (*I.O.Civ.* 4641).
11. Price to Eells, Dec. 20, 1882 (*I.O.Land Letter Book*, 105, p. 131); Redpath to Price, Feb. 17, 1883 (*I.O.Civ.* 3666); and Oneida Counsellors to Commissioner, April 6, 1881 (*I.O.Land* 5888).
12. Criticisms of this practice may be found in *Com. Rep.*, 1870, pp. 237-239; and *Board Report*, 1872, pp. 174-175.
13. *U.S.Stat.*, XVIII, Part 3, p. 420.
14. The editor of the *Christian Intelligencer* regarded the measure as "one of the most hopeful acts of legislation that has been yet consummated by Congress in the substantial and permanent interest of the American Indians." (March 11, 1875).
15. *Com. Rep.*, 1875, p. 15; and E. P. Smith to Secretary, July 2, 1875 (*I.O.Report Book*, XXVI, p. 333).

16. Burdett to Delano, July 9, 1875 (*I.O.Misc.* I904).
17. Compare *Com. Rep.*, 1877, pp. 64-65 with *Com. Rep.*, 1887, p. VIII.
18. *Cong. Rec.*, III, p. 2182. Bills on the subject introduced in both House and Senate on the first day of the session were never considered (*Ibid.*, pp. 2, 19).
19. *Ibid.*, p. 2205.
20. Durfee to Price, Aug. 9, 1881 (*I.O.Land* 14213); and Price to Durfee, Aug. 18, 1881 (*I.O.Land Letter Book*, 85, p. 158).
21. *Cong. Rec.*, VIII, p. 1142.
22. Only in 1884 was an appropriation made for aiding Indians in selecting and filing claims for homesteads (*U.S.Stat.*, XXIII, p. 96). This indifference was frequently condemned (Cramsie to Price, May 4, 1882 *I.O.Land* 8788; Bishop Whipple to E. P. Smith, Dec. 5, 1874 *I.O.Misc.* W2257; and General Howard to Commissioner, May 11, 1878 *I.O.Misc.* H962).
23. *Council Fire*, II, p. 62; IV, pp. 19-22.
24. Richard Irving Dodge, *A Living Issue*, Washington, 1882, p. 3.
25. *Com. Rep.*, 1876, pp. X-XI.
26. Elsie Mitchell Rushmore, *The Indian Policy during Grant's Administration*, Jamaica, N. Y., 1914, p. 40; General Howard in Board, *Journal of the Second Annual Conference*, Washington, 1873, p. 42; and David H. Jerome of the Board in *Board Scrap Book*, II, pp. 138-139.
27. *Lake Mohonk Proceedings*, 1885, p. 18.
28. Cleveland's request for establishment of a fixed purpose may be found in his first annual message (Richardson, *Messages and Papers*, VIII, p. 335).
29. *Board Report*, 1872, p. 19.
30. Richardson, *op. cit.*, pp. 357, 521.
31. *Cong. Rec.*, XI, p. 779. Recent studies of the Southwest provide valuable information regarding the development of United States Indian policies in a particular area (Carl Coke Rister, *The Southwestern Frontier, 1865-1881*, Cleveland, 1928; and the articles of Frank D. Reeve and Ralph H. Ogle on New Mexico and the Western Apaches in the *New Mexico Historical Review*, July, 1937 to July, 1938 and October, 1939 to July, 1940 respectively).
32. I.R.A., *Fourth Annual Report*, p. 9.
33. *House Report* 2247, 48th Cong., 2nd Sess.
34. *House Report* 1835, 49th Cong., 1st Sess.

Notes

Chapter Fifteen

1. Whipple to Lincoln, March 6, 1862, in Henry Benjamin Whipple, *Lights and Shadows of a Long Episcopate*, New York, 1899, pp. 510-513.
2. *House Misc. Doc.* 29, 40th Cong., 3rd Sess., p. 3; and *Com. Rep.*, 1869, pp. 119-121.
3. A discussion of one of Stewart's proposals may be found in *Cong. Globe*, 41st Cong., 3rd Sess., pp. 1577-1582. Clarke's bill is enclosed in Van Horn to Secretary (*I.O.Misc.* U92, 1870).
4. *Com. Rep.*, 1876, p. IX.
5. Henry W. Hilliard to Schurz, Jan. 26, 1880 (*Schurz Papers*).
6. *Cong. Rec.*, X, pp. 2027ff.
7. For the climax of this dispute, see *ibid.*, pp. 2158-2164.
8. An analysis of the final vote reveals that, while both Republicans and Democrats favored the agreement, the South was the only section recording a sizeable majority for ratification (*Ibid.*, p. 2320).
9. *Ibid.*, pp. 2257, 2253, 2194.
10. *Ibid.*, pp. 2196, 2224.
11. *Ibid.*, p. 2225.
12. *Ibid.*, pp. 2158-2162, 2226-2228, 2253-2256.
13. *Ibid.*, pp. 2227, 2157; and XI, pp. 785, 905.
14. *Cong. Rec.*, X, pp. 4253-4259, 4261.
15. Contrast the points of view presented in *Ibid.*, *Appendix*, pp. 100-105, 233-236, 236-237, 274-276.
16. Compare *Council Fire*, IX, p. 15 with *Cong. Rec.*, X, p. 4255.
17. Senator Plumb in *Cong. Rec.*, XI, p. 941
18. *Cong. Rec.*, XI, p. 787; and *I.R.A.*, *Fifth Annual Report*, p. 38.
19. *Cong. Rec.*, XI, p. 905; and *Com. Rep.*, 1877, p. 190.
20. Penciled speech in the *Dawes Papers*, pp. 18-19.
21. For this vote on Omaha allotment, see *Cong. Rec.*, XIII, p. 6552.
22. Senator Teller's continued opposition may be found excellently expressed in *Cong. Rec.*, XVII, pp. 811-813, 947-948.
23. *Cong. Globe*, 41st Cong., 3rd Sess., p. 735.
24. *Cong. Rec.*, X, p. 2130; see also pp. 2128-2130, 2199-2200, 2221-2222.
25. *Cong. Rec.*, XI, p. 940.
26. Speech before the Wednesday Evening Club, p. 34 (*Dawes Papers*).
27. Dawes to Teller, Sept. 19, 1882 (*Dawes Papers*).

28. *Lake Mohonk Proceedings,* 1885, p. 42.
29. Lamar to Dawes, Nov. 13, 1885 (*Dawes Papers*).
30. Dodge to Dawes, March 25, 1881 (*Dawes Papers*). The omitted chapters were published the following year as *A Living Issue.*
31. H. W. Lee to Dawes, Feb. 25, 1882 (*Dawes Papers*).
32. Welsh to Dawes, Aug. 31, 1885 (*Dawes Papers*); and *Lake Mohonk Proceedings,* 1886, p. 27.
33. *Council Fire,* VIII, p. 36.
34. Boston *Herald* eulogy on the occasion of Dawes's thirty-sixth year in Congress, March 6, 1883.

Chapter Sixteen

1. *Nation,* V, p. 356.
2. *Board Report,* 1871, pp. 156 et al.
3. Board, *Journal of the Second Annual Conference,* p. 61.
4. *Com. Rep.,* 1874, p. 15.
5. See a petition of Wyoming legislators (*House Misc. Doc.* 123, 44th Cong., 1st Sess), e.g.
6. George E. Ellis, *The Red Man and the White Man in North America,* Boston, 1882, pp. 537-538; and W.N.I.A., *Sketches and Plans,* Philadelphia, 1881, pp. 11-12.
7. *Com. Rep.,* 1877, p. 2; and Carl Schurz, "Present Aspect of the Indian Problem," in *The North American Review,* CXXXIII, pp. 8-9.
8. *Board Report,* 1883, p. 65.
9. *Com. Rep.,* 1873, p. 5.
10. The difficulty of establishing uniform rules was revealed in 1882 by the different methods reported to Commissioner Price by Agents McGillycuddy, Park, Andrews and McLaughlin (*I.O.Civ.* 2747, 2918, 3024, 3886). Price told Agent Riordan early the next year that penalties must be left to an agent's discretion (Price to Riordan, April 4, 1883 *I.O.Letter Book,* 173, p. 196).
11. *Ante,* pp. 141, 146-147.
12. 109 *U.S.Rep.* 556.
13. *Cong. Rec.,* XV, pp. 2577, 4112, 5802-5803.
14. I.R.A., *An Act to provide for the Establishment of Courts of Criminal Jurisdiction,* Philadelphia, 1884. The Association's legal expert wrote Dawes of the group's position in Pancoast to Dawes, Nov. 22, 1884 (*Dawes Papers*).

Notes

15. Whittlesey to Painter, Nov. 26, 1884 (*B.L.S.* II-VII 578). See also *Board Report*, 1884, pp. 6-7.
16. *Cong. Rec.*, XVI, pp. 934-936, 1718, 1748-1749, 2387. The House was encouraged to stand firm by many Indian workers (Noah Porter *et al.* to Representative Ellis, Feb. 26, 1885 enclosed in F. W. Williams to Dawes, Feb. 28, 1885 *Dawes Papers, e.g.*)
17. *Cong. Rec.*, XVI, pp. 2385-2388, 2466; and *U.S.Stat.*, XXIII, p. 385.
18. President Seelye of Amherst quoted in William Justin Harsha, "Law for the Indians," in *The North American Review*, CXXXIV, p. 283.
19. 118 *U.S.Rep.* 375.
20. *U.S.Stat.*, XXIV, p. 390.
21. An account of the discussions regarding Indians which accompanied passage of the Fourteenth Amendment may be found in G. M. Lambertson, "Indian Citizenship," in *The American Law Review*, XX, pp. 183-184.
22. *Senate Report 268*, 41st Cong., 3rd Sess.
23. *Ibid.*, and *Washington Daily Chronicle*, July 6, 1872.
24. Advocacy of citizenship and criticism of treaties were closely connected in Barstow to Schurz, Dec. 24, 1879 (*Schurz Papers*) and by Representative Butler in *Cong. Globe*, 41st Cong., 1st Sess., p. 560.
25. George F. Canfield, "The Legal Position of the Indian," in *The American Law Review*, XV, p. 33.
26. Anon., *The Political Status of the American Indian*, n.p., n.d., p. 8.
27. Bishop Whipple characterized United States *vs.* Cook (XIX *Wallace* 591) as a "crowning act of injustice and robbery" in an indignant letter to Commissioner E. P. Smith on Dec. 5, 1874 (*I.O.Misc.* W225).
28. *Cong. Rec.*, II, p. 3683.
29. *Cong. Rec.*, III, pp. 2182, 2205.
30. *Cong. Rec.*, IV, pp. 1263-1265, 2674.
31. *Cong. Rec.*, VI, pp. 525-527, 549-556; VII, 1130-1131.
32. *Cong. Rec.*, XI, pp. 875-878, 908, 939.
33. 112 *U.S.Rep.* 94.
34. *Board Report*, 1884, pp. 62, 7-10.
35. Francis A. Walker, *The Indian Question*, Boston, 1874, pp. 120-123.
36. The plight of the Pueblo and Mission Indians may best followed by reference to the annual accounts of their agents published in the *Commissioners' Reports*.

37. IV *Otto* 614 (United States *vs.* Joseph).
38. Whipple to Schurz, March 30, 1880 (*Schurz Papers*); and Schurz to Atkinson, Nov. 28, 1879 (*Ibid.*).
39. *Eadle Keatah Toh*, July, 1880.
40. Compare *Wowapi*, Boston, Nov. 7, 1883, p. 94, with *Lake Mohonk Proceedings*, 1885, p. 30.
41. *Lake Mohonk Proceedings*, 1883, p. 8; and 1885, *passim.*
42. *Lake Mohonk Proceedings*, 1886, p. 46.
43. *Ibid.*, p. 42.
44. *Board Report,* 1882, p. 8.
45. *Board Report*, 1885, p. 116.
46. *Council Fire*, IX, p. 29.
47. Lambertson, *op. cit.*, p. 186.
48. Walter Allen, Boston newspaperman, in *Lake Mohonk Proceedings*, 1886, p. 41; and Mrs. G. W. Owen, *The Indian Question*, [Ypsilanti, Mich., 1881], pp. 15, 21.
49. Dr. C. M. Sawtelle in *Council Fire*, IV, pp. 115-116; and Eli Perkins, Chicago *Inter-Ocean* correspondent, in *Board Scrap Book*, II, p. 41.
50. Anna L. Dawes, *The Indian as a Citizen*, Hampton, 1917, p. 4.
51. Miss Lazarus to Dawes, Nov. 11, 1885 (*Dawes Papers*), e.g.
52. *U.S.Stat.*, XXIV, p. 390.
53. Dawes to Whittlesey, April 24, 1887 (*B.C.M.*).
54. Thayer to Dawes, May 27, 1886 (*Dawes Papers*).
55. Tibbles to Dawes, March 16, 1887 (*Ibid.*).
56. Compare Joseph Cook, ed., *Boston Monday Lectures No. 189*, Boston, 1887, p. 61, with James B. Thayer, *Remarks before the Worcester Indian Association*, n.p., n.d., p. 6. Contemporary views of the red man's position were thoroughly analyzed in Robert Weil, *The Legal Status of the Indian*, New York, 1888.
57. James B. Thayer, "A People without Law," in *The Atlantic Monthly*, LXVIII, p. 683.
58. Richard I. Dodge, *Our Wild Indians*, Hartford, 1882, pp. 641-642; *Council Fire*, VII, p. 4 and VIII, p. 176; *Com. Rep.*, 1883, p. 52, and 1885, p. 204; and Merrill Edwards Gates, *Land and Law as Agents in Educating Indians*, [New York, 1885], p. 22; e.g.
59. *Board Report*, 1885, p. 126.
60. Champions of independence occasionally exposed the weakness of their position by requesting such special privileges as tax exemption (Agent Simms in *Com. Rep.*, 1879, p. 140, e.g.).

Notes

61. *Cong. Globe*, 39th Cong., 1st Sess., pp. 2013-2014.
62. *Com. Rep.*, 1875, p. 17; and *Board Report*, 1875, pp. 15-16.
63. *Cong. Rec.*, V, p. 1303.
64. Most decisions in regard to Indian affairs involved the relation between the powers of the state and national governments. Thus federal control of Indian trade was upheld in such cases as U.S. vs. Holliday (III *Wallace* 407) and U.S. vs. Forty-three Gallons of Whiskey (III *Otto* 188; and 108 *U.S.Rep.* 491). In this and other respects, the power of the United States was determined by whether the right of control was specifically reserved in acts of admission. On this point, see such cases as Harkness vs. Hyde (VIII *Otto* 476), Langford vs. Montieth (XII *Otto* 145), U.S. vs. McBratney (XIV *Otto* 621), and Utah and Northern Railway vs. Fisher (116 *U.S.Rep.* 28) upholding the rights of Idaho and Colorado, and such cases as Kansas Indians (V *Wallace* 737) and New York Indians (V *Wallace* 761) restricting the power of Kansas and New York.
65. The arguments of Senators Teller and Plumb in *Cong. Rec.*, XI, pp. 939, 941, reveal this attitude.
66. The services were excellently summed up by Meacham in *Council Fire*, II, p. 116.
67. Blue Horse to Commissioner, March 26, 1883, in New York *Herald*, April 5, 1883.
68. J. B. Harrison, *The Latest Studies on Indian Reservations*, Philadelphia, 1887, pp. 158-159.
69. Lamar to Dawes, Nov. 13, 1885 (*Dawes Papers*). This letter is marked 'Important.'

Chapter Seventeen

1. *Cong. Rec.*, XI, pp. 1032-1033; XV, p. 4991, *e.g.*
2. Anna M. Dobbins to Grant, July 26, 1871 (*I.O.Misc.* P353).
3. *Lake Mohonk Proceedings*, 1887, p. 34.
4. I.R.A., *Provisions of the Sioux Bill*, Philadelphia, 1885, p. 2.
5. Charles C. Painter, *Proposed Removal of Indians to Oklahoma*, Philadelphia, 1887, p. 2.
6. *Lake Mohonk Proceedings*, 1884, p. 17.
7. *Board Report*, 1879, p. 12.
8. *U.S.Stat.*, XIV, pp. 238, 294.

Uncle Sam's Stepchildren

9. For the railroad's case for assistance, see C. J. Hillyer, *The Atlantic and Pacific Railroad and the Indian Territory*, Washington, 1887, p. 61.
10. W. R. Laughlin, *Argument before the Committee for Indian Affairs*, [Washington, 1872], pp. 11-16.
11. Chairman Brunot of the Board backed expansion as early as 1872 (Brunot to Cree, April 11, 1872 *B.C.* IV 179; and *Com. Rep.*, 1872, p. 81).
12. *Cong. Rec.*, XIII, pp. 2857, 6590-6591. Highlights of the debate may be found in *ibid.*, pp. 2526ff., 2565ff., 2579ff., 2848ff., 6589.
13. *Ibid.*, pp. 2576-2577, 2765-2766, 2806-2808.
14. *Cong. Rec.*, XV, pp. 2278, 4727; and *U.S.Stat.*, XXIII, pp. 72, 75.
15. *Cong. Rec.*, XVI, p. 895; XVIII, p. 1594.
16. *Cong. Rec.*, XV, pp. 4721, 5445.
17. *New York Herald*, Jan. 16, 1884.
18. Clerk Stephens to Secretary of the Interior, Nov. 17, 1882 (*I.O.Report Book*, XLIII, p. 571).
19. Contrast I.R.A., *Fifth Annual Report*, p. 38, with *Council Fire*, I, p. 71, and W.N.I.A., *Report of Memorials to Government*, [Philadelphia], 1886, p. 9.
20. *Philadelphia Press*, June 4, 1884.
21. *Cong. Rec.*, XVIII, Index.
22. *Senate Report* 1494, 49th Cong., 1st Sess., p. 5.
23. Richardson, *Messages and Papers*, VIII, p. 473 et al.
24. *Ibid.*, p. 694.
25. *Cong. Globe*, 41st Cong., 2nd Sess., p. 3745; and *Cong. Rec.*, XVII, p. 812.
26. A. L. Riggs to Whittlesey, Dec. 21, 1877 (*B.C.M.*); and Riggs-Hare-Lightner to Hayt, April 20, 1878 (*B.C.M.*).
27. See especially Manypenny to Schurz, Sept. 21, 1880 (*Schurz Papers*).
28. J. R. French to Secretary, Dec. 8, 1880 (*Schurz Papers*).
29. The account of this struggle in *Council Fire*, III, pp. 161-166, 177-181, is confirmed by innumerable letters in the *Schurz Papers* of late 1880.
30. Bishop Hare et al. to Dawes, June 2, 1883 (*Dawes Papers*); *Council Fire*, VI, pp. 83-84, 123; and *Lake Mohonk Proceedings*, 1883, p. 6.
31. The best contemporary information regarding this incident may be found in Henry S. Pancoast, *Facts regarding the Recent Opening to Settlement of Crow Creek Reservation in Dakota*, Philadelphia,

Notes

[1885]; Henry S. Pancoast, ed., *Crow Creek Reservation*, Philadelphia, 1885, a collection of press comments; *Cong. Rec.*, XVII, pp. 909-915, 943-948, 967; and *Senate Report* 1278, 49th Cong., 2nd Sess., Part I. Cleveland's order appears in Richardson, *Messages and Papers*, VIII, pp. 305-307; and Attorney General Garland's decision upholding the Indian's title in *Opinions*, XVIII, pp. 141-146.

32. *House Report* 1576, 46th Cong., 2nd Sess., p. 10.
33. Benjamin Hallowell, *Letter and Memorial of a Convention of Friends*, Washington, 1870, p. 2; and Superintendent Janney to "Collier," July 23, 1870 (*B.C.* I 84).
34. *Cong. Globe*, 41st Cong., 3rd Sess., p. 587; *House Exec. Doc.* 84, 42nd Cong., 2nd Sess., and *Cong. Rec.*, II, pp. 4540-4542.
35. Francis A. Walker, *The Indian Question*, Boston, 1874, p. 90; and Commissioner Hayt in *Board Report*, 1878, pp. 129-131.
36. *Cong. Rec.*, XVII, pp. 968, 1762.
37. While Senator Dawes was interested in mixing the races, he opposed Senator Teller's proposal for alternate settlement because its introduction would seriously delay passage of the measure (*Ibid.*, pp. 969-970, 1762-1763).
38. *Cong. Rec.*, XV, pp. 2241-2242, 2277-2278.
39. Smith *vs.* Stevens (X *Wallace* 321).
40. Elwood *vs.* Flannigan (XIV *Otto* 562).
41. *House Report* 1576, 46th Cong., 2nd Sess., p. 10; and Draper to Riggs, Jan. 2, 1877 (*B.C.M.*).
42. Board, *Journal of the Second Annual Conference*, Washington, 1873, p. 57.
43. The provision was first introduced by Senator Dawes as an amendment to the Coke bill on April 4, 1882, although Senator Coke questioned whether such a specific statement was necessary (*Cong. Rec.*, XIII, p. 3212).
44. For the debate leading to the provision that the period of inalienation might be extended at presidential discretion, see *Cong. Rec.*, XVIII, pp. 224-225.
45. *Cong. Rec.*, XV, pp. 2278-2279.
46. Whittlesey to Secretary, March 20, 1885 (*B.L.S.* II-VII 613).
47. Armstrong to Whittlesey, Dec. 8, 1885 (*B.C.M.*).
48. John Jumper et al., *Objections . . . to the Bill for the Organization of the Territory of Oklahoma*, Washington, 1886, p. 12.
49. Both Armstrong and Pratt, the leading Indian educators, believed

that a reduction of the reservations was essential to racial advancement (*Lake Mohonk Proceedings*, 1885, p. 28; and *Council Fire*, IX, p. 25).

50. S. C. Armstrong, *The Indian Question*, Hampton, 1883, p. 3. For an excellent defense of the position that considerations of white welfare should predominate, see J. B. Harrison, *The Latest Studies on Indian Reservations*, Philadelphia, 1887, p. 138.
51. Mrs. G. W. Owen, *Indian Troubles and Their Cure*, n.p., n.d.
52. *Board Report*, 1883, pp. 66-68; 1884, p. 6.
53. Compare *Council Fire*, VIII, p. 131, with George E. Ellis, *The Red Man and the White Man in North America*, Boston, 1882, p. 577.
54. *Council Fire*, VIII, pp. 137-140, 25. Dawes's fears were ridiculed by the *New York Herald* of Jan. 19, 1884; but evidence justifying his alarm may be found in Harrison, *op. cit.*, pp. 73-74; and J. W. Davis to Fisk, Jan. 12, 1888, in *Board Report*, 1887, p. 132.

Chapter Eighteen

1. *U.S.Stat.*, XXIV, p. 388.
2. *Board Report*, 1879, p. 7.
3. *U.S.Stat.*, XXIV, p. 389.
4. *Board Report*, 1871, p. 179; and *Com. Rep.*, 1881, p. 100, e.g.
5. *Com. Rep.*, 1874, pp. 269-270.
6. Carl Schurz, "Present Aspects of the Indian Problem," in the *North American Review*, CXXXIII, pp. 21-22; and *Lend A Hand*, I, p. 70.
7. *Com. Rep.*, 1886, p. 181.
8. *Lake Mohonk Proceedings*, 1885, p. 53.
9. *Board Report*, 1880, p. 10.
10. Sarah Winnemucca, a Piute who toured the East, backed allotment in hope that her brother would be allowed to make the selections (Miss Peabody to Dawes, Nov. 12, 1883 *Dawes Papers*); Bright Eyes's desire for Omaha severalty was inspired by a longing for increased influence (Wilkinson to Whittlesey, March 11, 1882 *I.O.Land* 6957); and a Dakota petition was declared to come from the laziest man in the tribe as a result of his desire to escape government control (S. R. Riggs to Price, Dec. 17, 1881 *I.O.Land* 22104; and Price to Riggs, Feb. 8, 1882 *I.O.Land Letter Book*, 90, p. 459).
11. For statements concerning the traditional antipathy of Indians toward private ownership, see *Com. Rep.*, 1875, p. 251, and *Cong.*

Notes

Rec., XI, p. 911. Direct statements of Indian opinion are almost impossible to obtain because few red men spoke English; see, however, the interesting effort to construct a red man's view of contemporary policies in Rev. D. W. Risher, ed., *The Indian and White Man or the Indian in Self-Defense*, Indianapolis, 1880.

12. Com. Rep., 1874, p. 254; and 1887 Baltimore speech, pp. 37-38 (*Dawes Papers*).

13. Abelard Guthrie, *The Shawnee Indians*, n.p., 1868, pp. 10-11; and James W. M. Newlin, *Proposed Indian Policy*, Philadelphia, 1881, p. 97.

14. The questionnaire and answers may be found in *B.C.M.*

15. *U.S.Stat.*, XXIV, p. 391; and Cong. Rec., XI, pp. 781-788, 873-875. Both Schurz and Dawes regretted the necessity of surrendering to the opposition of Indian Territory tribes (Carl Schurz, "Present Aspects of the Indian Problem," in the *North American Review*, CXXXIII, pp. 18-19; and Board Report, 1887, pp. 134-135).

16. Anon., *The Case of the Seneca Indians*, Philadelphia, 1840, p. 1; and Joseph S. Elkinton, *Indian Scrap Book*, I, passim, New York Public Library.

17. See such publications of the tribes as *An Appeal to the United States for Justice*, n.p., n.d.; and *Statement of the Principal Chief and Cherokee Delegation* . . . , January 24, 1879, n.p., n.d., passim. The significant contributions of the tribes to United States Indian legislation and American Indian civilization may be understood by reading Angie Debo, *And Still the Water Run*, Princeton, 1940.

18. Council Fire, VIII, pp. 157-158; IX, pp. 32-33, 136.

19. Cong. Rec., XI, pp. 934-935, e.g.

20. Board Report, 1885, p. 114.

21. Sec. Rep., 1885, p. 26.

22. Meacham excellently presented their point of view when he wrote, "We started out with the idea of brute force in governing the Indians, and two hundred years have not taught us to own the mistakes. We have never civilized an Indian yet by forcing civilization upon him; we never can. True, we have civilized them by the thousand, but only when they were ready for civilization and demanded it." Council Fire, III, p. 66.

23. Richardson, *Messages and Papers*, VIII, pp. 357-358.

24. House Report 1076, 49th Cong., 1st Sess.

25. Sec. Rep., 1886, p. 5; Council Fire, IX, pp. 121-122; and Cong. Rec., XVII, pp. 3197-3201, 3642, 4550-4561.

26. W.N.I.A., Report of Memorials to Government, Philadelphia, 1886, pp. 12-13.
27. Council Fire, VII, p. 7; IX, p. 110.
28. Unfavorable comments upon this amendment may be found in [Herbert Welsh], The Indian Problem, Philadelphia, 1886, p. 2.
29. Elkinton, op. cit., p. 93.
30. Bland's account of this episode appeared in T. A. Bland, The Indian —What Shall We Do with Him?, Washington, [1887].
31. Board Report, 1886, pp. 134-136.
32. Lake Mohonk Proceedings, 1885, p. 39; and penciled speech, p. 4 (Dawes Papers).
33. Henry Benjamin Whipple, Lights and Shadows of a Long Episcopate, New York, 1899, pp. 516-517.
34. Francis A. Walker, The Indian Question, Boston, 1874, pp. 124-136; Elwell S. Otis, The Indian Question, New York, 1878, pp. 178-181, 256; J. H. Hibbetts, The Indian Problem: Peace, Civilization and Citizenship, Topeka, 1877, p. 16; etc.
35. George E. Ellis, The Red Man and the White Man in North America, Boston, 1882, p. 572.
36. Montieth to Whittlesey, Dec. 9, 1885 (B.C.M.).
37. Com. Rep., 1882, p. 35; 1883, p. 151, e.g.
38. Com. Rep., 1884, p. 111.
39. Cong. Rec., IV, p. 3953.
40. Cong. Rec., XI, pp. 785-787, 910-911, 1000-1003, 1031-1032, 1060-1064; and Council Fire, IX, p. 64.
41. Abbott to Dawes, July 20, 1885 (Dawes Papers).
42. Lake Mohonk Proceedings, 1884, pp. 25ff.
43. Elaine Goodale Eastman, Pratt: The Red Man's Moses, Norman, Okla., 1935, p. 93.
44. J. R. Brown in William Welsh, comp., Taopi and His Friends, Philadelphia, 1869, p. 65, e.g.
45. Com. Rep., 1874, p. 6; 1876, p. XI.
46. General Davidson to General Pope, May 19, 1879 (I.O.Misc. W3) bitterly condemned this action.
47. See especially Cong. Rec., XVII, p. 2471; Gardiner G. Hubbard, The Indian Problem, n.p., [1876], p. 29; and Ellis, op. cit., pp. 581-582.
48. Charles C. Painter in Board Report, 1883, p. 66.
49. House Report 1076, 49th Cong., 1st Sess., p. LX.
50. Lake Mohonk Proceedings, 1885, pp. 50-51, e.g.

Notes

51. Welsh to Dawes, July 25, 1885 (*Dawes Papers*).
52. *Board Report*, 1886, p. 132.
53. *Ibid.*, pp. 129-130.
54. Charles C. Painter, *The Dawes Land in Severalty Bill and Indian Emancipation*, Philadelphia, 1887.
55. For emphasis upon the importance of dealing with individual Indians, see Henry S. Pancoast, *Indian Land in Severalty, as provided for by the Coke Bill*, Philadelphia, 1884; and James B. Thayer, *Remarks made at a Meeting in Cambridge, Mass. . . . May 3, 1886*, n.p., n.d., p. 2.
56. Elaine Goodale, "How to Americanize the Indian," in the *New Englander and Yale Review*, LII, p. 454.
57. *Sec. Rep.*, 1887, p. 29. This statement did not apply directly to the Severalty Act, it is true, but it immediately followed a passage stating that Indians must learn not to oppose severalty.

Chapter Nineteen

1. Interesting comments on the Dawes Act may be found in S. A. Galpin, "Some Administrative Difficulties of the Indian Problem," in the *New Englander and Yale Review*, XLVI, p. 315; and Fisk to Dawes, Dec. 21, 1886 (*Dawes Papers*).
2. Pratt to Dawes, Dec. 20, 1886 (*Dawes Papers*).
3. Robert McElroy, *Grover Cleveland*, I, New York, 1923, p. 232.
4. In his final speech before passage of the Act, Dawes announced that much must be left to future Congresses and that plans for keeping money from the sale of surplus land out of Indian hands, along with other proposals introduced too late, must be postponed. (*Cong. Rec.*, XVIII, p. 974).
5. *Washington Critic*, Jan. 7, 1887.
6. *Board Report*, 1886, p. 131.
7. I.R.A., *Fourth Annual Report*, pp. 9-10. Similar appeals by the Women's National Indian Association may be found in Mrs. A. S. Quinton, *A Retrospect and Its Lessons*, n.p., n.d., p. 13; and Ellen Terry Johnson, *Historical Sketch of the Connecticut Indian Association*, Hartford, 1888, pp. 20-21.
8. See especially the statement of the Boston Indian Citizenship Association on the back cover of the 1887 edition of T. H. Tibbles, *The Ponca Chiefs* with Edward Everett Hale, Louis D. Brandeis

and Miss Alice Longfellow among its signers. Individual declarations of the need for continuing effort may be found in *Com. Rep.*, 1886, pp. 117-119; *Board Report*, 1886, p. 130; and *Lake Mohonk Proceedings*, 1886, p. 33.

9. Dawes to Gates, Dec. 29, 1891 (*B.C.M.*); and Board to Congress, March 29, 1892 (*B.C.M.*).

10. Penciled speech, p. 24 (*Dawes Papers*).

11. Anna L. Dawes, *The Indian as a Citizen*, Hampton, 1917, p. 4.

12. *Board Report*, 1887, p. 133; and Richardson, *Messages and Papers*, VIII, p. 796.

13. McElroy, *op. cit.*, I, p. 234.

14. Penciled speech, p. 30 (*Dawes Papers*).

15. *U.S.Stat.*, XXXIV, Part 1, pp. 182, 326. Contemporary criticism of administration of the Severalty Act was best expressed in Fayette Avery McKenzie, *The Indian in Relation to the White Population of the United States*, Columbus, Ohio, 1908, passim.

16. Charles C. Painter, *The Dawes Land in Severalty Bill and Indian Emancipation*, Philadelphia, 1887, p. 1.

17. Mrs. Eastman emphasizes the completeness of the break with the past by writing of Commissioner Collier's policy, "In historical perspective, this program appears not only to reject most of the conclusions reached by Generals Pratt and Armstrong, Bishops Whipple and Hare, Senator Dawes and Commissioner Morgan, but to run counter to the government's main line of policy, which was endorsed by Mohonk Conferences of Indian workers, by mission boards of various denominations, and by every President of the United States from Grant to Hoover inclusive." (Elaine Goodale Eastman, *Pratt: The Red Man's Moses*, Norman, Okla., 1935, pp. 8-9).

INDEX

A Century of Dishonor, 61-62
Abbott, Lyman, 235, 244, 245-246
Abel, Annie H., 13
Administrative problems of the Dawes Act, 248-249
Agency courts, 200-201
Agency employees, limitation of, 119
Albuquerque Indian School, 135
Allison, William B., 185
Allotment (see Severalty)
Alternate sections, white settlement of, 130, 228
American Missionary Association, 224
Annuity issues, reformation of, 110-116
Annuity system, 106-116, 180-181, 206
Apache Indians, 117-118, 141
Apache removal, prohibition of, 10-11
Arizona, Indian difficulties in, 26, 90-91
Arms trade, 156
Armstrong, Henry J., 242-243
Armstrong, Samuel Chapman, 141-142, 150-151, 165, 197, 232
Army and the Indians, the, 15-17, 24-25, 26-27, 29
Arny, W. F. M., 139
Arthur, Chester A., 84, 226
Assimilation as a solution of the Indian problem, 145-148
Astor, Mrs. John Jacob, 82
Atkins, John D. C., 13, 146
Atkinson, Edward, 78
Atlantic and Pacific Railroad, the, 237
Augur, Christopher C., 18
Axtell, Samuel B., 128-129

Baker, E. M., 19
Bannock Indians, 91
Baptist Church, 29, 230
Barstow, A. C., 78
Beck, James B., 27, 112
Beeson, John, 59-60, 66
Belknap, William W., 68
Black Hills invasion, 19, 73
Blackfeet Indians, 157
Blake, F. N., 168, 171
Blanchet, Archbishop, 35

Bland, Theodore A., 25, 63, 86, 133, 137, 148, 158, 161-162, 197, 210-211, 222, 232, 239-240
Board of Indian Commissioners, the, 12, 37, 42-53, 66, 74, 96, 103, 110, 123, 132, 145, 159, 184, 187, 219-220, 234, 235, 236
Bonney, Mary, 81
Boone, Andrew R., 22
Boston Indian Citizenship Association, 78, 83, 213
Boudinot, Elias C., 74
Bowman, John B., 225
Bright Eyes, 78
British Columbia, the Indian policy of, 173-174
Brouillet, J. B. A., 35
Brunot, Felix R., 25, 45, 47-48, 51, 52, 199
Buck, Solon J., 75
Burke acts of 1906, 251
Burleigh, Walter A., 7
Burnside, Ambrose E., 27
Butler, Edward, 24-25, 172

Caldwell (Kans.) arms traffic, 156
Calhoun, John C., 177
California Indians, 124, 128-129
Call, Wilkinson, 103-104, 206
Camp Grant massacre, 26
Canadian Indian legislation, 170-172
Canadian Indian policy, 167-174
Canadian Indian policy, explanations for the success of, 168-169, 172-174
Canadian Indian policy, inter-relationship between American Indian policy and, 170-172
Canadian Indian superintendents, 168, 173
Canadian Indian treaties, 172-173
Canfield, George F., 204-205
Cannon, Joseph G., 21, 150
Carlisle Indian School, 141-144, 150-151, 195, 209
Carpenter, C. C., 74
Cash annuities, 120

Index

Catholic Bureau of Indian Missions, 35
Catholic Church and the Indians, 24, 31, 34-36, 52, 129
Cattlemen and the Indian problem, 160-164
Chandler, Zachariah, 155
Cherokee Indians, 5, 72
Cherokee Tobacco Case, 99
Cheyenne and Arapahoe Indians, 40, 140
Cheyenne Indians, 40, 118, 140, 142-143, 153
Cheyenne leasing crisis, 162-163
Chicago *Times*, 74
Chickasaw Indians, 221
Chief Joseph, 12
Child, Lydia Maria, 58
Chilocco Indian School, 149
Choctaw Indians, 221
Christian Disciples, 32
Christian Union, the, 235, 244, 245, 246
Churches and the Indians, the, 12, 24, 28-41, 87-88
Citizenship (see Indian Citizenship)
Clarke, Sidney, 99, 188
Cleveland, Grover, 13, 35, 75, 84, 162-163, 183, 184, 186, 196, 223-224, 226, 239-240, 247, 250
Clum, John P., 141
Coke, Richard, 27, 185-186, 206
Coke severalty bill, 185-186, 190, 206, 222, 226, 240, 244
Colfax, Schuyler, 108
Colorado House of Representatives, 89
Colyer, Vincent, 27, 45-46, 52
Compromise nature of the Dawes Act, 192-193, 198-199, 212-213, 217, 227-231, 233, 252
Compulsory education, 152-153
Concentration, 6-14
Confederacy and the Indians, 15, 96
Congregational Church, 32-34
Congress: and concentration, 6-11; and transfer, 17-23; and church nominations, 36-37; and the Board, 42-44, 46, 47-50; and Indian frauds, 67-68; and the invasion of Indian Territory, 74; and the treaty system, 96-102; and annuity issues, 108-117; and Indian appropriations, 111-112, 117-120; and Indian education, 134-135, 148-149, 151-152, 250; and the liquor traffic, 157; and squaw men, 159; and

cattlemen, 163; and early severalty legislation, 179-180; and the extension of homestead privileges, 180-182; and severalty legislation, 185-193; and Indian amenability to law, 201-203; and Indian citizenship, 204-207; and railroad entry into reservations, 220-224; and the sale of surplus land, 228; and inalienability, 229; and the selection of land allotments, 233-234; and the use of force, 243-244
Connecticut Indian Association, 82
Council Fire, the, 25, 60, 88, 89, 141, 160-162, 169, 197, 239-240
Courts of Indian affairs, 202
Courts of Indian offenses, 141, 146-147, 201
Cox, Jacob D., 44, 69
Cox, Samuel S., 22
Crawford, William H., 177
Cree, Thomas K., 47, 74
Criminal law, declaration of Indian amenability to, 202
Crook, George, 27
Crounse, Lorenzo, 9, 24
Crow Creek reservation, opening of, 84, 226
Crow Dog, ex parte, 201-203, 206
Crow Indians, 230-231

Danforth, E. H., 90
Dawes, Henry Laurens: opposition to Schurz, 78-80; praise of Indian organizations, 85; work for abolition of treaties, 97-98; opposition to discretionary Indian appropriations, 112; comment on leasing, 164; comment on lack of precedents, 167; sponsorship of severalty, 186; belief in inevitability of severalty, 192; changing attitude toward severalty, 193-195; work as an Indian reformer, 195-196; co-operation with Democrats, 196; criticism of Elk-Wilkins decision, 207; opinions regarding Indian citizenship, 211-212; statement on the inevitability of white expansion, 219; support of railroad entry into reservations, 223; interest in speeding racial contact, 228; views on the expenditure of surplus funds, 228; fears regarding severalty, 232, 248-249; opposition to a consent amendment, 241; opposition

Index

to force, 241, 245; denial of treaty violation, 246-247; comments on destruction of tribal authority, 246-247; disappointment over the results of the severalty act, 250-251
Dawes Severalty Act of 1887, 164, 181, 185-187, 188, 191-193, 198-199, 203, 211-213, 216, 217-218, 223, 224, 227-241, 243-244, 246-252
Dawes Severalty Act of 1887, failure of, 250-251
Debates regarding severalty, 185-187, 189-192
Delano, Columbus, 6, 45-46
Democrats, the: and transfer, 19-22; and the Board, 48-50; and Indian appropriations, 117-119; and severalty, 189-190
Denominational appointments, 28-41
Department of Indian Affairs, plans for a, 25-26
de Smet, Pierre-Jean, 25, 179
Devens, Charles, 160
Dodge, Richard Irving, 39, 119, 196
Dolores (Col.) News, 61
Downey, Stephen W., 128
Dundy, Elmer S., 77
Dutch Reformed Church, 30
Dyer, David P., 47-48

Eastern educational institutions, 149-152
Eastern Indians, 125, 136
Eastern land fever, 219-220
Eastern opinion: regarding concentration, 8-12, regarding transfer, 24; of the Board, 49; of Indians, 86-88; of Indian appropriations, 117-118; of the reservation system, 122; of removals to the East, 128; regarding severalty, 191-193; of railroad entry into reservations, 221-223
Edmunds, George F., 71, 102
Education, Indian opposition to, 133-135, 143, 151
Education, neglect of Indian, 132-137
Education, problems of Indian, 148-154
Educational appropriations, increase of, 148-149
Eells, Edwin, 212
Elk, John, 206-207
Elk vs. Wilkins, 206-208, 210
Ellis, George E., 242

English instruction, absence of, 132, 195, 224
Ewing, Charles, 35

Fessenden, William P., 43
Fisk, Clinton B., 51, 52, 70
Fitch, Thomas, 129
Five Civilized Tribes, opposition to severalty by the, 237-238
Five Civilized Tribes, the, 67, 237-238
Force, the decision to use, 186, 233-247
Force, the opposition to, 238-241, 245-246
Foreign criticism of American Indian policy, 16, 169
Forest Grove Indian School, 144, 149, 151
Foulk County, Dakota Territory, 91
Fourteenth Amendment, 174-175, 204, 207, 208
Freighting of supplies by Indians, 139-140
Friends, Society of (see Quaker Church)

Galpin, Samuel A., 68-69
Garfield, James A., 19, 32, 38
Gates, Merrill E., 127
Genoa Indian School, 149
Gittinger, Roy, 75
Governmental indifference to Indian rights, 72-73, 100, 125, 132, 182, 230-231, 244-245
Grant, Ulysses S., 19, 29, 36, 44, 45-46, 67-68, 73, 74, 183

Hale, Edward Everett, 23
Half-breeds, 147, 179
Hampton Institute, 141-142, 150-152, 195
Hare, William H., 33, 39, 154
Harlan, James, 46, 97, 155
Harper's Monthly, 57
Harrison, Benjamin, 35
Harrison, Jonathan B., 40, 103, 151, 160
Haskell Institute (see Lawrence Indian School)
Hawley, Joseph R., 50
Hayes, Mrs. Rutherford B., 81
Hayes, Rutherford B., 32, 37, 38, 67, 71, 74, 78-79, 81, 138
Hays City, Kansas, 63
Hayt, Edward A., 37-38, 69-70
Hayt scandal, 69-70

Index

Hazen, William B., 136-137
Hebrews and the Indians, 32
Henderson, John B., 8
Hill, Nathaniel P., 189
Hinman, Samuel D., 33
Hoar, George F., 206
Holman, William S., 239-240
Homestead Act of 1862, 180
Homestead privileges, extension to Indians of, 180-182, 205
Hooker, Charles E., 21
House Appropriation Committee, 45, 50, 67, 111
House Indian Committee, 11, 50, 67, 132, 186, 202
Howard, Oliver O., 27, 52, 139
Hudson's Bay Company, 168

Ihrie, George P., 64
Inalienation provisions, 178-179, 180, 217-218, 227, 229-231, 251
Indian advancement, evidences of, 138-141, 143
Indian agents: opposition to transfer, 17; nomination by churches, 28-41; participation in fraud, 68, 70-71; oversentimentality, 87-88; opinion of the reservation system, 123; selfishness, 125; opinion of Indian abilities, 135; opposition to liquor trade, 157; as judges, 200-201; attitude toward severalty, 236; recommendation of force, 242-243; importance in enforcing severalty, 249
Indian annuities, 106-116, 159, 180-181, 206
Indian annuities, requirement of labor for, 115-116
Indian appropriations, 108-109, 111-112, 117-119, 134-135, 146-147, 148-149, 250
Indian attorneys, 67, 106
Indian Bureau and church nominations, 36-39
Indian characteristics, comments on, 87, 123, 135 141, 143, 148, 153-154, 194-195
Indian chiefs, 102-105, 114, 236
Indian citizenship, 174-176, 181, 185, 199, 203-213, 251
Indian citizenship, campaign for immediate, 208-213

Indian citizenship, dangers of, 208-209, 211, 213
Indian citizenship, opposition to immediate, 207-211
Indian citizenship, theories of, 204-206
Indian claims, 67, 106, 227-228
Indian consent, amendment to require, 240-241
Indian contracts, 46-47, 49, 68, 107, 112-113
Indian depredations, 88-89, 139
Indian education, 36, 64, 113, 132-154, 170-171, 224, 250
Indian farming, 113, 119, 171
Indian frauds, 67-72, 107, 213-214, 224-226
Indian improvidence, 107-108, 114-115
Indian land policies, 217-218, 227-232
Indian legislation, general requirements for, 183-185
Indian legislation, purposelessness of post-Civil War, 183
Indian legislation, selfishness of post-Civil War, 224-226, 232
Indian neighbors, 88-92, 126, 157, 214-215
Indian offenses, punishment of, 134, 141, 199, 201
Indian opposition to education, 133-135, 143, 151
Indian opposition to severalty, 235-238
Indian organizations, 81-86, 187, 234, 249-250 (see also names of individual organizations)
Indian organizations, contributions to, 82, 250
Indian Peace Commission of 1867, 18, 29, 58, 96, 97
Indian police, 138-139, 146-147
Indian policy of 1942, 251-252
Indian problem before 1865, 3-5
Indian problem of 1865, 5-6
Indian problem, public indifference toward the, 57
Indian Rights Association, 75, 82-84, 85, 88, 185, 197, 202, 209-210, 213, 219, 222, 226, 249-250
Indian self-government, examples of, 140-141, 146-147, 168
Indian Territory: removals to, 6-11, 76; opposition to removals to, 9-11; invasion of, 73-75, 81, 219; moves for a territorial government over, 74;

Index

opening of the Oklahoma district of, 75; creation of, 121; Indians of, 125; cattle leases in, 162; expulsion of cattlemen from, 162-163; railroad entry into, 220-222; exemption from Dawes Act of, 220, 236-237

Indian traders, 68, 155-158

Indian treaties, 95-102, 111-112, 116, 122, 125, 132, 221-222, 244-246

Indian wardship, advantages of, 200, 213-216

Indian wardship, efforts to end, 213-216

Individuals, annuity issues to, 114

Ingalls, John J., 11, 169-170, 206, 222, 243

Inter-marriage problems, 147

Inter-racial contact, debate regarding advisability of, 123-131, 194-195

Interior, Department of the: and transfer, 15-17, 27; and the Board, 43-47, 49-50

Investigating commission, rejection of an, 239-240

Iowa Indians, 139

Islands as reservations, 64-65

Jackson, Helen Hunt, 61-62, 78-79, 208

Joint Transfer Committee, 20

Jones, Charles W., 222

Kansas: and concentration, 6-7, 10-11; and transfer, 23-24; and desire for trade, 91-92

Kansas City Convention against invasion of the Indian Territory, 75

Kansas Indians, 231

Kautz, August V., 26

Kaw Indians, 6

Keifer, Joseph W., 21

Kickapoo Indians, 178

Kiowa Indians, 142-143, 156

Kirkwood, Samuel J., 79, 154

Klamath Indians, 160

Labor requirement for annuity payments, 115-116

Lake Mohonk conferences, 84-85, 88, 156, 187, 209-210, 219, 244

Lamar, Lucius Q. C., 104, 124, 196, 210, 216, 239-240, 247, 250

Land hunger, 72-75, 124-125, 189, 218-220

Land policies, Indian, 217-218, 227-232

Lane, La Fayette, 22

Lang, John D., 52

Lawrence Indian School, 149, 151 (also Haskell Institute)

Lawson, S. S., 157

Leasing problem, 159-164

Leeds, William M., 70

Legal status, debate over changing the Indian's, 199-203

Lightfoot, Thomas, 139

Lincoln Institute, 151-152

Lincoln, William H., 78-79

Liquor trade, 139, 156-157, 168

Llewellyn, William H. H., 146

Long, John D., 78

Lower California, 65

Ludlow, Helen, 150

Lutheran Church, 30, 32

McCook, Edward M., 125

McCrary, George W., 142

McGillycuddy, V. T., 242

Maginnis, Martin, 17

Mallery, Garrick, 153

Manning, William, 63

Manypenny, George W., 25, 86, 177, 178, 225

Marble, E. M., 215

Marsh, O. C., 67-68

Massachusetts and Seneca land, 237

Massachusetts Indians, 179

Matthews, Justice Stanley, 201

Meacham, Alfred B., 25, 60-61, 78, 153, 225, 239

Mears, Otto, 225

Mescalero Indians, 146

Methodist Church, 30, 33, 34, 52

Mexican treaty of 1848, 208

Michigan Indians, 123, 178, 215

Miles, John D., 40

Miles, Nelson A., 12, 27

Miller, John F., 230

Mills, Roger Q., 9

Milroy, R. H., 141, 242

Minnesota Indians, 123

Mission Indians, 208

Modoc massacre, 60, 66

Montana, Indian difficulties in, 84, 89, 90, 91

Morgan, John T., 190, 243

Morgan, Lewis H., 25

Mormon Church, 32

Morrill, Lot M., 73

Index

Nation, the, 23, 170, 199
National Indian Defense Association, 86, 103, 127, 147-148, 161-162, 214, 240-241
Navajo Indians, 139
Nebraska: and concentration, 6-7, 9; and transfer, 24
Negro and the Indian, 58, 64, 82, 142, 174-176
Nevada Indians, 124, 128-129
New England, 10, 87, 118, 222
New York City Indian Association, 82
New York Herald, the, 51, 91, 143, 222, 240
New York Indians, 136, 159, 215, 237
New York Times, the, 66
New York Tribune, the, 84, 164
Nez Percé Indians, 132, 146-147
Nez Percé removal, 10, 12
Noble, John W., 251
Non-treaty appropriations, 118
North Carolina Indians, 215
Northern Cheyenne removal, 12
Northern Pacific, the, 230

Oberly, John H., 86
Ogden Land Company, 237
Oklahoma Boomers, 74-75
Omaha Indians, 120
Oregon Indians, 59-60, 90-91, 182
Osage Indians, 6, 72, 91-92, 224
Otis, Edward S., 102, 241-242
Otoe Indians, 6
Ottawa allotment, 130
Our Indian Wards, 25

Paddock, Algernon S., 9, 73
Painter, Charles C., 84, 183, 202
Pancoast, Henry S., 84, 209-210
Parker, E. S., 44-45, 67
Patterson, Robert, 103
Pawnee Indians, 6, 143
Pawnee leases, 160
Paxson, Frederic L., 26
Payne, David L., 74-75
Peace policy, the, 19, 183, 189
Peru, Kansas, 157
Phillips, Wendell, 59
Piegan massacre, 19, 26
Plans for Indian advancement, 62-65
Plumb, Preston B., 87, 144
Pomeroy, Samuel C., 7, 23-24
Ponca dispute, 76-80, 83, 193

Ponca removal, 11-12, 76-77
Pope, John, 39, 72, 109, 124
Popular Science Monthly, the, 147
Pottawatomie severalty experiment, 177-178, 179
Practical education, need for, 150-151
Pratt, Richard Henry, 130, 133, 141-144, 150-151, 154, 176, 244, 248
Precedents for reform, 167-180
Price, Hiram, 85, 114, 146, 156
Private Indian instruction, 151-152, 171
Protestant Episcopal Church, 29, 33, 42
Pueblo Indians, 141, 208
Puget Sound Weekly Courier, 172
Puyallup Indians, 230

Quaker Church, 29, 31, 33-34, 36-37, 38, 40, 188, 227
Quinton, Amelia, 81

Racial equality, demand for, 126-127, 199-200, 213-214, 229-230
Railroads and the Indians, 6, 7-8, 220-224
Ramona, 61
Range cattle industry, collapse of the, 162-163
Red Cloud scandal, 67-68, 107
Red Cloud Sioux, 139, 140
Reed, Thomas B., 21
Reformation of the Indian Bureau, 22, 68-72
Removal Policy, 4-14, 128
Removal to the East, 124, 128
Republic, the, 57
Republicans, the: and transfer, 19-22; and the Board, 48-50; and Indian appropriations, 117-119; and severalty, 189-190
Reservation day schools, 149-152
Reservation system, abolition of the, 121, 123-131, 198
Reservation system, the, 64-65, 121-131, 192
Reservations, entry of railroads upon, 220-224
Reservations, reduction of, 124, 129-130
Resignation of the Board of Indian Commissioners, 47, 51
Returning students, difficulties of, 150-151
Rhoads, James E., 246
Riggs, Alfred L., 51

Index

Riley, John B., 151
Roanoke College, 143
Rogers, John H., 163
Roosevelt, Franklin D., 42, 251
Roosevelt, Theodore, 90, 235
Rushmore, Elsie M., 13

Saint Augustine educational experiment, 142
Saint Ignatius Mission School, 152
Saint Louis and San Francisco Railroad, 221-222
Salamanca, New York, 159
Sale of surplus land, 179, 185, 186, 217-218, 227-228, 232, 234
Sanborn, John B., 137, 168
Santee Sioux accomplishments, 139-140
Santee Sioux severalty bill, 51, 224
Sargent, Aaron A., 45
Scales, Alfred M., 12, 185, 233
Schurz, Carl: attiude toward concentration, 13; battle against transfer, 22; opposition to church nominations, 37-38; defense of the Board, 49-50; criticism by Mrs. Jackson, 62; reformation of the Indian Bureau, 67-72; defense of Ponca removal, 76-79; complaint against critics of the government, 87; recommendation of consultation of chiefs, 104; opposition to discretionary Indian appropriations, 112; changing attitude toward the reservation system, 130; support of Indian education, 142; championship of severalty, 188-189; opposition to immediate citizenship, 209; support of the Ute Commission, 225; advocacy of the Ute bill, 234-235
Seelye, Julius H., 68-69, 153
Segregation as an Indian policy, 121-131, 198
Selection of severalty holdings, 179, 186, 218, 228, 233-234
Senate Appropriation Committee, 97
Senate Committee on Military Affairs, 18
Senate Indian Committee, 18, 79, 193, 204, 205, 222
Seneca Indians, exemption from Dawes Act of, 236-237
Seneca leases, 159-160
Seneca treaty of 1794, 237

Sentimentality of Eastern reformers, 86-88
Severalty: and transfer, 27; and the leasing problem, 164; Canadian experiment with, 171; early plans for, 177-182; government discouragement of, 182; debates regarding, 185-187, 189-192; sectional reaction toward, 191-193; attitude of Senator Dawes toward, 194; and railroad entry into reservations, 223-224; executive discretion in application of, 233, 247; Indian opposition to, 235-238; advisability of, 236; decision to use force in administration of, 238-247; recent criticism of, 251
Severalty Act (see Dawes Severalty Act)
Severalty proposals, early, 188
Shawnee Indians, 178
Sheridan, Philip H., 22, 156, 162
Sherman, John, 214
Sherman, William T., 16, 17, 26, 136, 142
Sioux agreement of 1877, 101, 109
Sioux bill debate, 219, 225-226
Sioux Indians, 19, 73, 76, 83, 114, 143, 219, 225-226
Sioux removal, prohibition of, 7, 9
Sioux reservation, 6, 73, 159, 219, 225-226
Sioux war, 7, 19-20, 73
Sisseton and Wahpeton Sioux, 115
Sitting Bull, 133-134
Smiley, Albert K., 84
Smith, Edward P., 67, 70, 115, 139, 181, 199, 200-201, 245
Smith, John Q., 67, 68-69, 70, 183, 188
Snake Indians, 91
Spotted Tail, 143, 151, 201
Spotted Tail Sioux, 140
Squaw men, 158-159
Standing Bear, case of, 77
State control of tribes, 124, 128-129, 214-215
Stewart, William M., 188
Stockbridge Indians, 178
Stowe, Harriet Beecher, 58-59
Suffrage movement, 82
Sully, Alfred, 26
Superintendent of Indian schools, 152
Supreme Court and the Indian, United States, 99, 201, 203, 206-207, 215, 229

Index

Tappan, Samuel F., 86
Teller, Henry M., 85, 160, 169, 189-190, 194-195, 224, 226, 228, 243
Terry, Alfred H., 18, 91
Thayer, James B., 213
Thayer, John M., 7
Thompson, J. R., 172
Throckmorton, James W., 21
Tibbles, T. H., 77-78
Tiff City, Missouri, 72
Tomazin, Father, 35-36
Transfer problem, 15-27, 48, 189, 239
Transportation of Indian supplies, 106, 139-140
Treaty system, action of 1871 abandoning the, 96-102, 244
Treaty system before 1871, 95-96, 106
Treaty violation, recommendation of, 244-246
Trespassing on Indian reservations, 72-75, 139
Tribal autonomy, 95-96, 102-105, 198, 236, 243-247
Tribal herds, 161
Tribal separation, citizenship as the result of, 171-172, 180-182, 204-205

Umatilla Indians, 91
Unitarian Church, 37-38
United States Indian Commission of New York, 81
United States vs. Kagama, 203
Utah Indians, 32
Ute bill, 187, 189-190, 194, 225, 234-235
Ute Commission, 61, 225
Ute incident, 66
Ute Indians, 101

Vestal, Stanley, 133-134, 158

Walker, Francis A., 67, 68, 147, 174, 208, 241-242
War guilt, 87

Washington Daily Chronicle, 63
Welles, Gideon, 16
Welsh, Herbert, 23, 83-84, 245-246
Welsh, William, 23, 44-45, 62, 69, 83
Western Indian schools, 135, 149
Western opinion: regarding concentration, 8-11; regarding transfer, 23-24; of the Board, 49; of the invasion of Indian Territory, 75; of Indians, 86-92; of Indian appropriations, 117-118; of the reservation system, 122; of Indian education, 135; of cattlemen, 162, 164; regarding severalty, 191-193; regarding grant of legal privileges to Indians, 199; of citizenship, 206; of federal control of the Indians, 214; of railroads, 220-222; of severalty, 227-228
Wheeler-Howard Act of 1934, 121, 251-252
Whipple, Henry Benjamin, 8, 62, 136, 188, 205, 209, 241
White Earth reservation, 35
Whitman, Royal E., 26
Whittier, John Greenleaf, 59
Whittlesey, E., 70, 123-124, 202
Wilkins, Charles, 206
Wilkinson, Mrs. M. C., 144
Willard, Judge S. A., 148, 214
Williston Seminary, 62
Wilshire, William W., 22
Windom, William, 136
Winnebago Indians, 139, 196-197
Winnebago removal, 8-9
Wisconsin Indians, 123
Women reformers, 58-59, 61-62, 81-83
Women's Christian Temperance Union, 82
Women's National Indian Association, 75, 81-83, 156, 222, 240
Wozencraft, O. N., 63-64
Wyandott severalty experiment, 177

Yakima Indians, 132, 141